you know who you are, especially Anne Douglas, Kathe Lieber, Paul Lima, Pippa Rispin, Bruce Wilson, and many more. Extra-special thanks to Steve Slaunwhite for years of encouragement, wise counsel, and helpful coaching.

Last but certainly not least, thank you to all my clients from Australia to Finland, who saw the potential of marketing with the unique form of content called white papers and who weren't content to publish "just okay" efforts but urged everyone involved to do our very best. Special thanks to Ben White and everyone at MJ Impulse for your understanding as I delayed your white papers to get this book completed. This book contains the many lessons I learned from working with all of you. And I trust our learning isn't over yet.

Publisher's Acknowledgments

We're proud of this book; please send us your comments at http://dummies.custhelp.com. For other comments, please contact our Customer Care Department within the U.S. at 877-762-2974, outside the U.S. at 317-572-3993, or fax 317-572-4002.

Some of the people who helped bring this book to market include the following:

Acquisitions, Editorial, and Vertical Websites

Senior Project Editor: Victoria M. Adang

Acquisitions Editor: Stacy Kennedy

Copy Editor: Jennette ElNaggar

Assistant Editor: David Lutton

Editorial Program Coordinator: Joe Niesen

Technical Editor: Russell Willerton, PhD

Editorial Manager: Michelle Hacker

Editorial Assistants: Rachelle S. Amick, Alexa Koschier

Cover Photo: © John Wiley & Sons

Composition Services

Project Coordinator: Sheree Montgomery

Layout and Graphics: Carrie A. Cesavicek Jennifer Creasey, Joyce Haughey

Proofreaders: Melissa Cossell, Bonnie Mikkelson

Indexer: BIM Indexing & Proofreading Services

Publishing and Editorial for Consumer Dummies

    Kathleen Nebenhaus, Vice President and Executive Publisher

    David Palmer, Associate Publisher

    Kristin Ferguson-Wagstaffe, Product Development Director

Publishing for Technology Dummies

    Andy Cummings, Vice President and Publisher

Composition Services

    Debbie Stailey, Director of Composition Services

Contents at a Glance

Table of Contents

Part II: The Three Flavors of White Papers..................... 85

Introduction

*W*hen I tell people I write white papers for a living, most look at me with a blank expression. The bravest manage to ask, "Um, what are those again?" I usually give a short answer like, "White papers are fact-based marketing pieces for companies — a lot like the essays we wrote in college." Then we get back to talking about more-interesting topics, like who's the greatest rock-and-roll band, why anyone would ever drink light beer, and our favorite oxymorons (mine is currently "jumbo shrimp").

But in my mind, I'm thinking, "White papers are a time-tested format for long-form copy that combine expository and persuasive writing, whose roots go back more than 100 years and whose future stretches ahead for as long as companies sell anything relatively new, complex, and expensive that needs explaining to a B2B prospect." But I don't actually say all of that.

When I first commissioned a white paper, I was the marketing manager in a fast-growing technology company. Before that, I'd spent many years as a computer journalist and technical writer. I'd seen many white papers from other companies, so I figured we needed one, too. I looked around for advice, a book, or some helpful material on the web. Back in 1997, the web was just getting started, and Google wasn't available yet. I didn't find much guidance, so in two weeks, my team and I put together something partway between a slide show and a specification. Amazing to all, it turned out well enough that it helped close sales and won an award for technical communication.

I rang in the new millennium with my first-ever assignment to write a white paper. By then, I was working as an independent copywriter. (No, I wasn't fired for wasting money on white papers! The company did so well that a competitor bought it out.) Once again, I scoured bookstores and the web. By 2000, a little more material existed, including a few articles called "How to Write a White Paper" and a couple of e-books for $99 each. I read them all and learned a little, but clearly not quite enough. My first freelance white paper project went around in circles and dragged on for months.

That experience spurred me on to do better. Ever since, I've been devouring everything I can find about white papers. In 2005, I set up my website at ThatWhitePaperGuy.com and started posting articles there; today, it features almost 100 how-to articles plus a white paper FAQ. And by now, I've written close to 200 of these documents for companies all the way from one-person startups to Google.

Not many people have studied, pondered, debated, and worked on so many of these challenging documents. In this book, I share tips, advice, and anecdotes about the wonderful world of white papers. When I first started writing white papers, I would have loved a book like this one, packed full of real-world tips and advice. Without it, I've spent 15 years learning on my own, reading everything I could get my hands on, making every possible mistake, and comparing notes with the handful of other writers struggling to develop high-quality white papers for the 21st century. This books sums up my knowledge so you can plan, produce, and promote your own white papers effectively without going through all of that.

About This Book

White Papers For Dummies strives to clearly explain the theory and practice of using white papers in B2B content marketing. This book is organized to make everything easy to find and simple to apply. It starts with an overview of the power of white papers and the huge opportunity they present to marketers and copywriters. Then it drills down into the details, including the main flavors of these documents; a proven step-by-step process for creating them; and a wealth of practical, tactical advice on how to research and build an argument, express your points in clear and accessible language, and promote your finished white paper to the four corners of your market.

You won't find this kind of detailed treatment of white papers in any other book. I know, I've read them all. And whether you're just getting started with white papers or you've already created and published many of them, *White Papers For Dummies* has something for you. If you're a marketing manager, this book reveals the benefits that white papers can deliver to your company and shows you how to choose and develop the best format to meet any marketing challenge. If you're a writer, this book is packed with tips on how to plan, research, write, and even design a compelling document that stands head and shoulders above most other white papers being circulated today.

Conventions Used in This Book

This book uses the following conventions to make things consistent and easy to understand:

- ✔ **Bold** highlights key words in bulleted lists and the action parts of numbered steps.
- ✔ New terms appear in *italic,* followed by an easy-to-understand definition. And speaking of terms, here are a few I use consistently throughout the book:
  - *B2B* means "business-to-business" or selling to other businesses, the total opposite of . . .

- *B2C,* which means "business-to-consumer" or selling to individual consumers.

- *FUD* means "fear, uncertainty, and doubt," a classic marketing tactic used to undermine the competition.

- *Offering* means any B2B product, service, technology, or methodology being sold by a company.

- *SME* means "subject matter expert" or someone who serves as a source for a white paper, usually from the sponsoring company.

✔ **Web addresses** appear in `monofont`.

White papers are an extremely versatile form. You can write one about any product, service, technology, methodology, regulation, policy, or ethical or philosophical position on any issue. And beyond B2B vendors, almost any type of organization can publish white papers.

So if you work for an agency, association, foundation, government ministry or department, hospital, institute, military command, municipality, nongovernmental organization (NGO), nonprofit, political party, school, college, university, or yourself, substitute whatever term works best for you whenever you see the words *business, company, enterprise,* or *vendor* in this book. Don't worry: You can apply virtually all the tips and ideas in this book to your white paper projects, no matter what type of organization you work for.

What You're Not to Read

I know you're busy, so I don't expect you to read every word of this book. To save you time, feel free to skip over the following elements:

✔ If you're a B2B marketing person whose management team is already completely sold on using white papers, you can skip Chapters 1 and 2.

✔ If you're a writer who's already convinced of the vast opportunity in writing effective white papers, you can skip Chapter 2.

✔ You can also skip any sidebars, the shaded text boxes that go into more detail than you may need on certain topics.

Foolish Assumptions

You know what they say about assumptions, right? But I have to start somewhere, so here goes. My main foolish assumption about you, dear reader, is that you're either a B2B marketing person or a B2B copywriter (or someone who aspires to become one).

✔ **If you're a B2B marketing person, I assume the following about you:**

- You want to use white papers to build recognition, generate leads, nurture prospects, and help close sales for your company.

- You're quite interested in how to plan or promote white papers effectively.

- You're less interested in how to research and create a white paper, although this knowledge will help you be a better client when you hire a white paper writer or designer.

- You have a basic understanding of marketing with content.

✔ **If you're a B2B copywriter, I assume the following:**

- You're keen to understand how to create white papers and offer that service to your clients.

- You work as an independent freelancer — although if you work as an in-house writer, 95 percent of this book applies to you, too.

- You're quite interested in how to research and write effective white papers because these marketable skills are in high demand.

- You're less interested in how to plan or promote a white paper, although this knowledge can help you be a better supplier when a client engages you.

- You're a seasoned writer, who has no need for me to point out one end of a sentence from the other.

- You're willing to go back to school and rediscover how to dig for solid research to help prove the points of your arguments. If you need a refresher on research techniques, check out Geraldine Wood's excellent book *Research Papers For Dummies* (Wiley).

How This Book Is Organized

This book has five parts, which you can read in any order. The five parts start from a high-level overview and zoom down into more detail. For example, the first chapter sketches in how B2B marketing uses white papers, while the last shows ten ways to pump up a white paper title.

Part I: Getting Started with White Papers

White papers have been called "the king of content" because of their profound ability to engage B2B prospects through a complex sales cycle. This part describes how white papers have become a standard marketing tool for B2B vendors in a growing number of sectors and shows the untapped demand for writers who have mastered this format. It also looks at where white papers emerged more than 100 years ago, where they are now, and the most likely possibilities for their future. And this part is where you find the answers to the most common questions about white papers, organized by the five *w*'s (and one *h*): who, what, why, where, when, and how.

Part II: The Three Flavors of White Papers

This part simplifies the vast possibilities of white papers down to a simple choice of three flavors of ice cream:

- ✔ Vanilla is a plain and predictable backgrounder, a detailed description focused on the technical or business benefits of a specific offering.
- ✔ Strawberry is a light and lively numbered list, framed around a set of tips, questions, concerns, or points about some issue.
- ✔ Chocolate is a rich and satisfying persuasive essay that delves into a nagging business problem and a new, improved way to solve it.

These three flavors cover 90 percent of all B2B white papers in the world today. This part explains how to pick the perfect flavor for your next white paper, depending on your purpose and audience. And for each flavor, I recommend what to include, what to leave out, when to use it for best results, and how to repurpose that content into further marketing pieces. This part also describes what happens when you mash up different flavors of white papers: Two possibilities turn out well, while two make a mess that's tough to stomach.

Part III: From Foggy Idea to Finished Document

This part describes a step-by-step process for transforming a vague idea into a polished, effective white paper — even if you've never done one before. This process grew out of my hands-on experience with close to 200 white papers over the past 15 years. Some steps will be familiar to anyone with writing or publishing experience; others are new and unique, designed to help you avoid the most common pitfalls in any white paper project.

Part IV: Succeeding with White Papers

This part shows how to succeed in writing white papers by following three simple maxims: Think like a lawyer, write like a journalist, and promote like a madman. This part explains how to research a white paper and build an open-and-shut case with a mountain of irrefutable evidence and ironclad logic. Then it describes how to write clear, crisp, and compelling text as fast as any reporter — and with more accuracy. Then it describes how to get the word out about your white paper, using your choice of 40 promotional tactics with tips and insights on each one.

Part V: The Part of Tens

This part provides a summary of key pointers to follow to make sure your white papers succeed. Topics include problems that can strike when you're writing, designing, or naming a white paper and what to do about them; how to design a white paper effectively; and how to give it a title that gets noticed.

Icons Used in This Book

To make this book easier to read and simpler to use, the following icons mark off different sections of the text.

This icon points to advice you can use to help make your next white paper more persuasive, more readable, or better designed, or to help the whole process run smoother.

Any time you see this icon, remember: What follows is so important that it's worth reading more than once. Think of these as the key take-away messages from the book.

This icon appears next to any personal anecdote from my years as a marketing manager and white paper writer. These stories often show me bumbling my way through some project and seeing the real solution only in hindsight.

This icon flags any serious danger to the health of your next white paper. Pay attention: The white paper you save may be your own.

Where to Go from Here

This book is organized so you can dip in anywhere and find useful tips and advice. For more guidance, use the table of contents to find broad categories and the index to look up specific topics.

If you're not sure where to begin, start with Part I for an introduction to white papers and answers to the most common questions about them. If you're just starting a new white paper, you may want to begin with Chapter 5 for help picking the perfect flavor. Then review the specific chapter for that flavor in Part II to see what to put in and what to leave out. After that, Part III lays out a step-by-step plan for developing your white paper. If you have a white paper drafted and ready for design, check out Part V to make sure you've avoided all the common problems with content and titles and to find some useful design tips to pass on to your designer. And if you have a finished white paper that you need to start promoting, Chapter 16 is your best bet.

Part I

Getting Started
with White Papers

getting started with

white papers

In this part . . .

- ✔ See how white papers are revolutionizing B2B marketing.
- ✔ Find out how the demand for white paper writers outweighs the supply and how much you can earn writing them.
- ✔ Take a look at how white papers are shaping decision making today and how they're likely to influence business practices in the future.
- ✔ Discover who writes and reads white papers, when it makes sense to use these persuasive essays, and how to figure out if you need one.

Chapter 1

Unleashing the Power of White Papers

....

....

Have you ever had to look into buying something big for your company? I'm not talking about an espresso machine for the lunchroom; I mean something really big. Something like when your boss calls you into his office and says, "We've got a problem. We've got to find a way to get our team out from under all this paper. We're drowning in it." And he wants you to dig into the problem and report back with some suggestions by Friday. Gulp.

What do you do? If you're like most people, you head to your desk and start madly searching the web for phrases like "buried in paper" or "paper burden." You skim down the search results until you see something promising. You click on the link and go to a web page — and what do you find? Ideally, you find a thoughtful examination of your problem with some useful tips on how to overcome it, most often in a document called a *white paper*. Armed with a few good white papers, you can prepare to make your report.

The same scenario happens every day in companies all over the world. Businesses buy loads of things, and business people need help deciding what to buy. An effective white paper is the best source for this kind of help.

In this chapter, I introduce you to white papers and show how business people use these documents to help select products and services worth many billions of dollars a year. I describe how any business that sells to other businesses can benefit by using white papers in its marketing. Whether you're a marketing person or a copywriter, this chapter shows how you can benefit from the amazing power and reach of white papers, which are truly the "king of content."

Seeing a White Paper for What It Is

Maybe you're already familiar with white papers because you've read them or even written one or two yourself. Or maybe you have a fuzzy idea about white papers but aren't sure how to describe them. Here's the definition I use:

> A white paper is a persuasive essay that uses facts and logic to promote a certain product, service, or solution to a problem.

Notice the key elements in this definition. A white paper is *persuasive* but somewhat formal like an *essay* because it uses *facts and logic* to make its points and to promote some *product, service, or solution.*

And here's what a white paper *isn't.* A white paper isn't a sales pitch. A white paper isn't an advertisement, brochure, case study, direct mail piece, or flier. It doesn't have a "Buy Now" button. It doesn't say how good you'll feel to see your new purchase sitting in your office.

Instead of a sales pitch, an effective white paper provides useful, practical, and educational content. Companies use white papers to generate leads, nurture prospects, and build mindshare (as I describe in more detail later in this chapter).

Of course, every white paper must be tailored to a specific audience and a desired outcome. To make that easier for you, this book identifies three basic types of white papers and shows how to use each one in different situations. And to make the writing experience as smooth as possible, I outline my 12-step process that takes you through a white paper's creation from start to finish.

Getting the scoop on the three flavors of white papers

You may think there are many types of white papers with subtle variations that make them hard to tell apart. In fact, there are only three main flavors of white papers, plus the mixtures between them. And they're as simple to tell apart as vanilla, strawberry, and chocolate ice cream.

- ✔ A **backgrounder** is an old-fashioned type of white paper that focuses on the features, functions, benefits, and payback of a product or service from one vendor. You can say this flavor "zooms in" on one offering to describe it in depth. A backgrounder is so simple, classic, and predictable that I think of it as vanilla ice cream (more on that in Chapter 6).

- ✔ A **numbered list** is a lively set of questions, points, issues, or tips about a certain topic. This format is extremely popular and easy to skim. And you can combine it with either of the other two types of white papers. Because a numbered list is so light and easy to digest, I like to compare it to strawberry ice cream (to see what I mean, skip to Chapter 7).

✔ A **problem/solution** is a factual discussion of a major problem that has never been solved. It considers the scope of the problem, describes the existing solutions and their drawbacks, and recommends a new, improved solution for best results. You can say this flavor "zooms out" to give a high-level overview of an entire industry. The problem/solution is the hardest-working and longest-lasting white paper of all. And a problem/solution white paper is so rich and long lasting that I compare it to chocolate ice cream (see Chapter 8 for details).

Following a proven system for creating white papers

Doing a white paper is a big, challenging project, far tougher than writing a blog or a sales letter. A white paper must be packed with research and useful information and run at least five pages with an attractive design. Many people are involved, and many things can go wrong. To help you keep all your white paper projects on track and avoid making common mistakes, I provide a 12-step process for planning and producing a white paper — the very same process I use with my own clients. Here's how it goes:

1. **Assemble the team.** Pull together all the people you need to complete the white paper, such as a writer, a designer, an illustrator, subject matter experts, and reviewers.

2. **Hold the initial conference call.** Discuss the project and get everyone on the same page. If any differences arise, sort them out now to avoid surprises later.

3. **Prepare the plan.** Write up a brief plan for the white paper. Circulate and tweak it until all reviewers approve.

4. **Gather your research.** Take a deep dive into the subject through company background, web research, and interviews with experts.

5. **Prepare an executive summary.** Write a one-page summary of the white paper's proposed direction. Circulate it until all reviewers approve.

6. **Create the first draft of the paper and graphics.** Write the first full-length draft of the white paper and create graphics to go with it.

7. **Get the first round of feedback.** Gather comments from all reviewers on the text and graphics. Clarify any unclear or contradictory comments.

8. **Revise to create the second draft.** Rework the first-draft text and graphics to incorporate comments.

9. **Solicit a second round of feedback.** Gather comments from all reviewers on the second-draft text and graphics.

10. **Collect and check sources.** Prepare a bundle of sources to spot-check and file away for later reference, if needed.

11. **Prepare the final document.** Finalize the text, graphics, and page design for the finished white paper. Generate the final PDF.

12. **Wrap up the project.** Take care of any payments, permissions, and post-mortem to tie up any loose ends.

I explain each of these steps in detail in Chapters 12 and 13, including who does what and any common pitfalls to watch out for along the way. And in Chapter 16, I describe 40 tactics you can use to promote a finished white paper to your target audience and note which ones are must-do's.

Declaring White Papers the "King of Content"

My personal experiences plus a stream of survey results for many years have convinced me that white papers are the top of the pops, the cap of the pyramid, the acme, the pinnacle, the absolute king of content. In fact, I believe white papers are the single most powerful piece of content any business-to-business (B2B) vendor can create. Why do I say so? Because no other piece of content can generate so many business benefits for so long — when it's done right.

But sadly, most white papers aren't nearly as engaging or persuasive as they could be. Three serious drawbacks afflict many white papers: too much selling, too much hype, and too much focus on the vendor.

The following sections show how B2B buyers appreciate effective white papers, discuss how to avoid the three worst flaws, and provide a "white paper mantra" to help you stay focused on creating the best possible documents.

When I was a marketing executive, my team tried everything in the playbook: advertising, case studies, channel promotions, direct mail, microsites, placed articles, press releases, sales calls, slide decks, trade shows, and white papers. You name it, we tried it. The two tactics that topped everything for generating leads and building mindshare were case studies and white papers. We had to keep producing more case studies every quarter, but we needed only one or two white papers a year. Nothing could touch a white paper for generating a strong return on the effort we invested in it.

Separating B2C from B2B

You see one side of the economy every time you go to a corner store or the mall. Think about a grocery store that sells everything from soup to nuts. Any company that makes any product you can find in that store, from A1 Steak Sauce to Ziploc containers, is called *business-to-consumer* or B2C. Most of these companies advertise on TV, radio, and on the web, trying to burn their logos into people's brains. Making a B2C purchase in a store is simple: You just pick out what you want and pay for it.

The other side of the economy is harder to spot, but it's there. Every company needs things to run the business, and they have to get them somewhere. This type of shopping, where business people buy something for their company, is called *business-to-business* or B2B. Making a B2B purchase is more complicated: It involves more people, time, paperwork, and money.

When a businessperson buys a major item like accounting software, factory equipment, or lab services, the process is much more deliberate than running to the store to pick up a can of beans. The decision can involve a group of people — as many as 25! — who talk about it for weeks, months, or even years. The ticket price can be huge, up to tens of millions of dollars. The buying committee always looks at the cost/benefit of the purchase and figures out how long it will take to see a payback on that money, also known as the return on investment (ROI).

This kind of B2B transaction is called a *complex sale*. The B2B economy involves millions of complex sales every year, adding up to many billions of dollars. Today's B2B buyers need information to help them make their decisions, and they find a lot of it in white papers.

Seeing the growing trend to white papers

In 2002, I ran a Google search for "white papers" that yielded 2.8 million hits. A decade later, in 2012, the same search got 39.5 million hits — 14 times as many. Clearly, during those ten years, a lot more people started talking about white papers, and a lot more companies started using them. But you don't have to take my word for it.

The effectiveness of white papers at generating leads, nurturing prospects, and building mindshare has been recognized in survey after survey and study after study. Here are some specifics that confirm the power of these documents in B2B marketing:

- ✔ "Probably the most important tool in the B2B marketer's kit is the white paper." — MarketingSherpa, June 15, 2011
- ✔ "When done right, nothing pulls in qualified sales leads like a well-targeted offer for a juicy white paper." — marketing guru Larry Chase, March 7, 2011

✔ White papers "continue to be the 'must-have' asset in the technology marketer's toolkit." Two out of three B2B buyers surveyed find white papers "very" or "extremely influential" in buying decisions. — Eccolo Media 2011 B2B Technology Collateral Survey Report, October 2011

✔ White papers are the favorite sources for 64 percent of B2B buyers during the early stages of decision making, higher than any other type of marketing collateral. — Sirius Decision, 2010

✔ Sixty-one percent of all B2B marketers surveyed use white papers. — Content Marketing Institute, 2012

✔ White papers are the most popular form of content for B2B technology buyers in Australia, France, Italy, New Zealand, South Africa, the United Kingdom, and the United States (and the second-most popular in Germany and India). — TechTarget, 2010

Spotting three flaws in many white papers

So all you have to do is type up a few white papers, promote the heck out of them so they show up in Google, and wait for the sales to roll in, right? Well, not exactly. Not all white papers are created equal.

I've followed this field for close to 20 years as a journalist, marketing executive, and copywriter, looking at fresh white papers every week. And I'm sad to say that the vast majority of the documents I've seen have been much less engaging and persuasive than they should have been. Far too many white papers suffer from the critical flaws outlined in the following three sections.

Too much selling, too little useful information

Far from providing helpful information, too many white papers are just a sales pitch in disguise. They may have a promising title and a good-looking cover, but the guts amount to little more than a brochure. Surveys show that business people want useful information, not a sales pitch.

If your white paper is little more than a sales pitch, the business people who see it will be irritated and deeply disappointed. Why wouldn't they be? You committed two of the worst infractions in business: You lied to them, and you wasted their time. Unless your company is the only game in town, they'll probably knock you off their list of possible suppliers. They may even start saying nasty things about you to other B2B buyers and in forums across the web. Rather than help your company's cause, a poor white paper can actually set you back by generating negative word of mouth and turning off prospective buyers.

Too much hype, too little proof

If your white paper avoids becoming a sales pitch and you honestly try to fill it with useful information, a second pitfall awaits: Making claims with no proof to support them. I'm surprised how many people have forgotten everything they learned about writing essays in college. To build an argument, you don't just state your views as though they're self-evident. You need to go out and find evidence to support what you're saying. If you can't find any proof to support your argument, your white paper is nothing but hot air. For tips on how to research a white paper and build a strong argument, see Chapter 14.

Too much focus on the seller, not the buyer

No B2B buyer cares a fig about your company's history, awards, state-of-the-art research labs, or total commitment to quality. Buyers care only about their problem and whether you can help them with it. If you can, they may take a few moments to check out all your company's achievements. But if you lead with those in your white paper, you'll lose them for sure.

You can't afford to look at a white paper as just another piece of marketing collateral. You can't get away with trotting out the same marketing speak and indulging in the same chest-beating. White papers are different. Your readers look at everything from their perspective as B2B buyers with a problem. Unless you put yourself in their shoes, answer their questions, and provide information with real value, they won't even bother to finish your paper.

Those are the three biggest problems, but there's more. You can see the top ten white paper problems to avoid in Chapter 17.

Using a mantra to avoid problems

A simple way to avoid all the problems in the previous sections is to use a mantra every time you think about a white paper. Repeat it as often as you need. Post it on a sticky note to your screen. E-mail it around to your whole team and to any writer working on a white paper for you. The following mantra provides an excellent summary of what the best white papers do:

An effective white paper helps prospective B2B buyers understand an issue, solve a problem, or make a decision.

An effective white paper doesn't fall all over itself to make a sales pitch. It doesn't make silly promises or unsupported claims. Instead, it gives a B2B buyer well-researched facts and logical arguments. If your white paper can do that, your company is seen as a trusted advisor, elevated far above any run-of-the-mill vendors that are just trying to peddle their wares.

From this heavenly position, all the usual objections about price or delivery often melt away in the warm glow of the sun. Your white paper has impressed your B2B prospects so much that they want to do business with you, and only you. Congratulations! If you do all of that, you reach white paper nirvana.

Understanding Today's Complex Sale

Companies sell to business buyers differently from how they sell to consumers. The challenge of reaching business buyers is called *B2B marketing*. For many years, the only way to do B2B marketing was through *outbound marketing,* where a company goes out and beats the bushes to find customers with advertising, direct mail, telemarketing, or even door-to-door salespeople.

The Internet forced B2B marketing to develop several new approaches: first, permission marketing, then SEO/SEM/social media marketing, and finally content marketing. These last two methods fit within *inbound marketing,* where a vendor encourages B2B buyers to come to it online. Inbound marketing is really in tune with the times because most B2B buyers now do their own research without relying on salespeople. Google plays a huge role in content marketing; if your company isn't on the first page of Google's search results, it doesn't exist.

These are all huge changes from just a few years ago. And these changes help explain the meteoric rise in the number and influence of B2B white papers over the past 15 years.

B2B marketing has evolved quickly

For many years, B2B marketing consisted of buying ads, sending out mailings, handing out trinkets at trade shows, and cold calling, in the hope that 1 or 2 percent of the people who heard your message were ready to buy whatever you were selling.

But in the past 20 years, this whole field has turned upside down. Today, marketers have better-targeted and less-expensive ways to reach B2B buyers and keep them engaged throughout a complex sale. Table 1-1 shows four approaches to B2B marketing, two each for outbound and inbound marketing. The bottom line is pretty convincing: Inbound marketing with content is up to 62 percent less expensive per lead than outbound.

Table 1-1	Four Approaches to B2B Marketing		
Approach	*Definition*	*Pros*	*Cons*
Interruption marketing (outbound)	Interrupt people when they're reading, listening, watching, or working on something else	Works on some of the people some of the time	Irritating; wasteful; low success rate; highest cost per lead
Permission marketing (outbound)	Get permission before sending promotions to B2B buyers	Less irritating; more effective; better targeted; lower cost per lead	Still "pushing" promotions at buyers; not complete without good content
Search engine marketing, social media marketing (inbound)	Attract B2B buyers with SEO, SEM, and social media	Customers come to you; works 24/7; even lower cost per lead	Not complete without good content
Content marketing (inbound)	Attract B2B buyers with online content like blogs, case studies, infographics, videos, and white papers	Customers come to you; works 24/7; lowest cost per lead	Difficult to create good content; hard to stand out now that almost everyone uses it

Interruption marketing is out

Advertising on radio and TV, direct mail, and cold calling all interrupt whatever you're doing to give you a sales pitch. YouTube also interrupts you when you have to watch a commercial before you can see the cute kitten playing the piano. You tell me whether that works: Do you remember whose ad ran before the kitten? These techniques afflict B2B marketing, too. For example, legions of B2B telemarketers still hit the phones every morning, dialing for dollars. Although it can work on some of the people some of the time, it's irritating, wasteful, and expensive.

Permission marketing is so 1999

In the late 1990s, an amazing new concept emerged: What if a company actually got your permission before it interrupted you? Getting your permission can take many forms: You sign up for a newsletter, subscribe to an RSS feed, or drop your card into a fishbowl at a booth. Marketers call this *raising your hand* to show that you're interested. Permission marketing does save a lot of time, trouble, and annoyance. With it, a B2B vendor knows everyone on its list has some interest in what the company sells. But it still relies on "pushing" promotions at possible buyers, interrupting all those people.

Marketing with SEO, SEM, and social media is in (sort of)

More recently, another approach came to the fore: Why not use the web and Google to attract customers to you? The first wave of inbound marketing used search engine optimization (SEO) and search engine marketing (SEM) to match a company's website to what B2B buyers were searching for.

Then came social media, which is still creating a huge buzz. Social media is fine for B2C buyers who can "like" a fast-food company and get a coupon for $1 off their next meal. But it's much harder to use in B2B marketing, where buyers take a more systematic approach to making a much bigger purchase. Most business people never "like" any supplier on Facebook or follow one on Twitter; they're too busy doing their real jobs.

Marketing with content is growing fast

Content marketing builds on SEO, SEM, and social media by providing the missing ingredient that all these approaches depend on: engaging content that B2B buyers actually want to access. Social media can be an ideal channel for promoting the great content that a B2B vendor has to offer. Posted online, that content works 24/7 and tends to snowball over time as people pass around materials, retweet links, and discuss the company.

Marketing with content enables you to focus like a laser on the B2B buyers who are most likely to buy next. And this approach is getting bigger every year. The 2013 benchmark report from the Content Marketing Institute surveyed 1,416 marketers who said they now spend, on average, one-third of their budgets on content marketing. And a lot of this funding has been taken away from the outbound side of the budget. Because white papers are a "must-have" tool in the content marketer's toolkit, they're being swept along with this fast-moving trend.

Today's B2B buyers do their own research

Before the Internet, the B2B salesperson was a powerful gatekeeper. Now, B2B buyers find their own information and call up a salesperson at the very last moment, maybe never. That means the life of a B2B salesperson isn't a happy one. Many salespeople have been effectively replaced by content placed online and indexed by Google. And when a B2B vendor gets noticed and blessed by Google, content marketing works like a dream, generating leads and helping to cement sales for far less cost than any salesperson.

Closing the door on salespeople

Every B2B buyer used to have to talk to a salesperson to get the smallest scrap of information, even a brochure or data sheet sent by snail mail. B2B salespeople were the gatekeepers holding all the information about their company's offerings. Today, that's gone out the window. Surveys show that 80 to 90 percent of all B2B buyers now do their own product research, thank you very much.

B2B buyers can use the web to find all the information they need to evaluate a purchase, along with reviews and recommendations from other business people who bought the same thing. Calling a salesperson is now one of the last steps in any purchase. In other words, salespeople have been cut out of the action.

Getting noticed by Google

Google has become the great god of inbound marketing, serving the vast majority of all searches done around the world and leading B2B buyers to the companies they do business with. How many people ever look past the first page of their search results? No one outside Google knows exactly how it evaluates websites. But one thing's for sure: If your company has fresh, helpful content on its website, Google will move your company up in the search results, past other companies that lack this kind of content.

Many companies still use their websites as an electronic brochure with nothing beyond the expected information about their location, product line, and undying commitment to customer service. Ho hum. That won't get you noticed by Google. Having effective content can mean the difference between being noticed in Google or ignored. These days, not many B2B vendors can afford to be ignored by Google.

Checking out content marketing in action

When your boss asks you to look for a solution to your company's paper burden, what do you do? Well, the marketing team at Acme Scanners anticipated your searches and put together a white paper designed to help B2B buyers like you understand the issue of paper burden. That white paper offers practical tips on solving the problem and urges you to take the next step: using an online calculator to see how much your company can save by buying a few Acme ScanOMatic 3000s.

And because Acme's content is good, and its SEO, SEM, and social media promotions are solid, Google noticed Acme and put it on the first page of the search results for the keywords "paper burden," which you type in when you do your Googling, which brings you to Acme's white paper, which you click to download. This is content marketing in action, exactly the way it's supposed to work.

Profiting from White Papers

As I touch on in "Getting the scoop on the three flavors of white papers," earlier in this chapter, white papers come in three main flavors. A *backgrounder* focuses on the technical details and business benefits of a certain offering. A *numbered list* rounds up a set of questions, points, or tips about a certain issue. And a *problem/solution* describes a new, improved solution to an industry-wide problem. Each flavor has unique strengths that make it most effective for B2B buyers at the top, middle, or bottom of the sales funnel. When you understand the key differences between these three flavors of white papers, you can select the best flavor to meet whatever marketing challenge you're facing.

The funnel as a numbers game

Throughout this book, I refer to *the funnel* as shorthand for a classic theory about B2B sales. In case you never studied marketing, here's how the theory goes: A complex sale is like a funnel, and each buyer a drop of water. As shown in the figure, the funnel is wide at the top and narrow at the bottom, but it leaks all the way down.

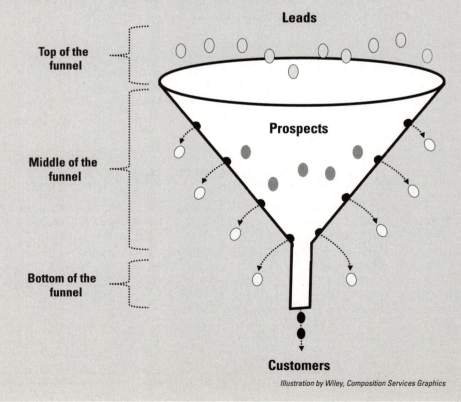

Leads

Top of the funnel

Prospects

Middle of the funnel

Bottom of the funnel

Customers

Illustration by Wiley, Composition Services Graphics

Here's how the funnel works. Say a company, such as Acme Scanners, seeks to attract B2B buyers into the top of the funnel. This step is called *generating leads* or *filling the funnel.* Acme uses a great white paper to attract potential buyers looking for help with a certain problem, such as paper burden, even if they've never heard of Acme.

Next, the Acme marketing team determines which leads seem most promising. Some may match the profile of an ideal customer. Some may have an urgent problem, so they're on a fast track to buy. Others may not fit, have no urgent need, or lose interest in Acme; all those leak away. But some stay in the funnel, where they're now called *prospects.* Acme nurtures prospects by providing more value, often in the form of useful content (hint, hint). Naturally enough, this process corresponds to the middle part of the funnel, where it begins to narrow.

Sooner or later, each serious prospect that remains in the funnel creates a shortlist of possible vendors, and Acme wants to be on that list. Of course, the narrowest part of the funnel is the tube at the bottom. That's where more prospects lose interest or buy from someone else. Only a few prospects buy from Acme and drip out the bottom of the funnel as paying customers.

The funnel is a simple image, but it conveys a profound truth: Every B2B vendor must attract far more leads than it needs to close, because some leak away at every stage. In other words, B2B selling is a numbers game.

If someone at Acme keeps track, he can develop metrics around its funnel. For example, say that a two-year pattern shows that for every ten leads, five become prospects, and two end up buying. The marketing team can then calculate how many leads it must generate to reach certain sales targets.

The following table shows some sample revenue goals, where the typical deal size is $100,000. You can see that to reach $10 million in sales, Acme needs to generate 500 leads. It takes a lot of phone calls and expensive mailings to generate that many leads with outbound marketing alone.

Here's the beauty of marketing with content. An effective white paper posted on Acme's website can generate leads 24/7 for a year or two with no further effort. No other marketing tactic can do that. Of course, one white paper alone may not bring in all 500 leads that generate $10 million in sales. But it might. The performance of each white paper is another metric Acme can track. Then the company can start to predict how many white papers it needs to generate X number of leads and Y dollars of sales. Marketing with content is a numbers game, too.

Leads, Prospects, Customers, and Revenues

	Track Record	Sales Goal: $1 Million	Sales Goal: $10 Million	Sales Goal: $100 Million
Number of leads	10	50	500	5,000
Number of prospects (50% of leads)	5	25	250	2,500
Number of customers (40% of prospects, or 20% of leads)	2	10	100	1,000
Total sales reached at $100,000 each	$200,000	$1 million	$10 million	$100 million

Assumption: The ratio of leads to prospects to customers remains constant.

At the top of the funnel

White papers are especially useful at the top of the sales funnel for generating leads and educating your own sales force (if any); channel partners like distributors or resellers (if any); and opinion leaders, like analysts, bloggers, and journalists who cover your market. You can also use white papers for the more ambitious project of redefining a market space and the all-around goal of building mindshare.

The best flavors of white papers to use at the top of the funnel are a problem/solution, a numbered list, or a mash-up of the two.

Generating leads

The simplest way to generate leads is to provide content that follows the white paper mantra to help a B2B buyer understand an issue, solve a problem, or make a decision. Because most business people Google their issues, problems, or upcoming decisions, a well-targeted problem/solution white paper that discusses an industry-wide problem — backed up with a good promotional campaign — should appear in all the appropriate search results.

For example, a problem/solution white paper from Acme Scanners could be called "How to Get Out from Under a Mountain of Paper with Unattended Scanning." (For tips on how to create and use a problem/solution white paper, see Chapter 8.)

Another way to get attention and attract leads is to be provocative. That certainly works for Lady Gaga. In B2B marketing, you can't exactly drape your product in a meat dress, but you can still be outspoken. A white paper formatted as a numbered list can challenge perceived wisdom, knock down sacred cows, and generate heat and light that attracts attention and draws in onlookers. For example, a provocative numbered list from Acme could be called "7 Gotchas in Automated Scanning and How to Avoid Falling for Them." (For tips on how to create and use a numbered list, see Chapter 7.)

Educating salespeople and partners

A vendor's own sales force can benefit from hearing all the powerful arguments and detailed information in a white paper. They can use these same proof points and arguments when they interact with prospects, or they can pass the white paper along directly to possible buyers.

Channel partners can include any distributors, resellers, retailers, and consultants that work with your company plus add-on marketers that create products, such as books, newsletters, or training for your product. Any flavor of white paper can be useful to these groups. Because they're involved with

B2B buyers from top to bottom of the funnel, channel partners or add-on marketers can give your white paper directly to a lead or prospective buyer. Just remember: Many vendors compete for the limited time and attention of partners. If you have better white papers than your competition, you can win more mindshare with channel partners, which can pay off in more sales.

Redefining a market space

Sometimes a new company wants to shake up an existing market space. Sometimes an established company wants to expand into neighboring markets. Sometimes a company wants to shrink and refocus all its efforts on one promising niche. All these strategies call for redefining a market space, which is extremely challenging. A white paper can spell out the company's best thinking on the limitations or opportunities facing it and why the management team wants to set out in a new direction.

Of all the goals you can have for a white paper, redefining a market space is the most ambitious. It can take a couple of years and more than a million dollars' worth of publicity to create a new technology buzzword and lodge it into people's minds. One white paper alone won't do it; it could take 10 or 20.

Building mindshare

You can think of mindshare as the answer to a couple of questions: "How many people in your target market have heard of your company?" and "How many of those people think your company has something useful to offer?" The more, the better. You want to send your white papers to all the analysts, bloggers, and journalists who cover your market. You want your white paper to spread through word of mouth and social media and be passed around the company and to peers in other companies. To find out many possible tactics about how to promote a white paper, see Chapter 16.

In general, the easier it is to access a white paper, the more mindshare it generates. An obnoxious registration form with too many pesky questions can kill the interest in even the best white paper. If you don't use any registration gate, a white paper tends to spread much farther and faster. So if you're aiming more for mindshare than for leads, stay away from registration.

Throughout the funnel

White papers can also be useful at the middle of the sales funnel, during the long period when a complex sale is deliberated. During this period, white papers can engage and nurture B2B prospects and cast fear, uncertainty, and doubt (FUD) on competitors to try to knock them off the prospect's shortlist.

The best flavors of white papers to use at the middle of the funnel are a numbered list or a mash-up of a numbered list and problem/solution. The numbered list format is always easy to scan and entertaining to read.

Nurturing B2B prospects

By the middle of the funnel, you can assume that a prospect has heard of your company and engaged somewhat with you. But you must keep your prospects interested through the long decision-making process ahead. Publishing a new white paper as a numbered list gives you a good reason to contact them without making a sales pitch. At this point in the funnel, prospects are more likely to notice and skim through a lively numbered list than a more detailed technical white paper that requires a lot more focus and thought.

Casting FUD on competitors

By the middle of the funnel, the B2B buyer has most likely drawn up a shortlist of possible vendors with two or three companies on it. You can use a white paper to throw mud at those competitors, darken their name in the buyer's eyes, and ideally knock them off the shortlist. This classic marketing technique is called FUD (fear, uncertainty, and doubt). For example, Acme could use a numbered list called "8 Things You Should Know Before You Buy an Automated Scanner." By appealing to a buyer's fear of failure or embarrassment, uncertainty about a lesser-known vendor or product, or doubt about the claims made by competitors, this kind of white paper can effectively block an opponent. For more tips on FUD and how to use it, see Chapter 7.

At the bottom of the funnel

Even at the bottom of the funnel, white papers have a role to play. It's too late now to impress buyers with the scope of your company's vision in a problem/solution or to titillate them with provocative comments in a numbered list. At the bottom of the funnel, it's time for facts and figures.

The best flavor to use at the bottom of the funnel is a backgrounder. A backgrounder provides the technical details and payback numbers an evaluator needs to make a recommendation to the B2B buying committee.

When prospects finally reach the bottom of the funnel, they want to do their due diligence on each vendor on their shortlist. A knowledgeable person from the prospect's company often gets the job of evaluating all the choices, figuring out the strengths and weaknesses of each one, and reporting back with some recommendations. At this point, a backgrounder packed with technical details and benefits can really help that person complete his evaluation. For example, this kind of backgrounder from Acme could be called "Fifth-Generation Technology Innovations in the Acme ScanOMatic 3000." (For tips on how to create and use a backgrounder, see Chapter 6.)

Can white papers help close sales?

You can debate whether a white paper can help close a deal. Just before B2B buyers make a decision, they're more likely looking at data sheets, configurations, and delivery dates and checking references from existing customers.

Most marketers believe white papers are more powerful at the top and middle of the funnel to help generate leads and nurture prospects, and not so useful at the bottom to help close sales. I tend to agree, but there's a little more to the story. The latest surveys show that B2B buyers still look at white papers even in the last stage of making a purchase.

And when B2B buyers get right down to making a decision, the cumulative effect of the white papers they've seen (or not seen) plays a part in their decision. If one vendor consistently provided useful, helpful, and professional white papers that stood head and shoulders above the competition, that certainly gives that vendor an edge.

Late in the buying process, each vendor puts in a last-ditch effort to impress a prospect with the unmatched strengths of its offering. And if one of the companies on the shortlist has no technical white papers to contribute at this point, can you imagine what that does to its chances?

Discovering Who Uses White Papers and Who Should

B2B marketers in many sectors routinely use white papers as a standard tool in their marketing toolkit. In other sectors, white papers are just starting to be known. And in some, these documents are seldom or never seen. The sectors that most often use white papers today include

- Business services: Finance, HR, insurance, marketing, and outsourcing
- Electrical manufacturers: Audio-video gear, components, lighting, and heavy power equipment
- Electronic manufacturers: Chipmakers, computers, peripherals, and printers
- Government: Policy positions, research reports, and trial balloons
- Healthcare: Device makers, pharmaceuticals, and medical product and service providers
- Manufacturers of B2B equipment: Aerospace, heavy equipment, factory systems, processing equipment, ships, transit systems, and trains
- NGOs and nonprofits: Policy and position papers and research reports

✔ Processors of B2B materials: Glass, metals, plastic, rare earths, and silicon

✔ Software: Any B2B software except apps selling for $1

✔ Technical services: Engineers, laboratories, quality control, and testing

The following sectors could certainly benefit from using white papers:

✔ Construction: New materials, methods, and technologies

✔ Consultants: New methodologies or data, such as using social media for marketing, research, and customer engagement

✔ Delivery and transport: Energy efficiency, fleet management, and new RFID or tracking systems

✔ Education: New methods and technologies, online and distance learning, and reports to attract donors, students, and funding

✔ Energy, oil and gas: New approaches like fracking, pipeline, or cleanup technologies

✔ Environmental or "green tech": New technologies and methods for everything from light bulbs to monitoring the oceans

✔ Real estate: New B2B business models, construction materials and methods, energy efficiency, and renovations

✔ Utilities: Energy efficiency, smart meters, and smart grid

In fact, you can ask three simple questions to determine whether any B2B company could benefit from white papers:

✔ Does the company sell something relatively new?

✔ Does it sell something relatively complex?

✔ Does it sell something relatively expensive?

If you answer "yes" to one of these questions, that company could probably use white papers. If you answer "yes" to two or three questions, that company can definitely use white papers. For more on these questions, see Chapter 4.

As more companies discover the wonders of content marketing, more are adopting white papers every day. I get frequent queries from people asking, "Can we use white papers in my business or my sector?" More often than not, I answer, "Sure!"

Chapter 2

An Exciting Opportunity for Writers

*D*o you want to live an independent lifestyle as a freelancer? Make good money as a writer? Work on interesting projects about leading-edge topics? Constantly be learning, so you never get bored? Party with supermodels on your own private island? Oh, whoops, got a little carried away there. But if you answered "yes!" to the first four questions, you've come to the right place. (You're on your own with the supermodels.)

As part of the huge trend of marketing with content, white papers provide one of the best opportunities to make money as a writer today. If you master how to create compelling and persuasive white papers, you can pretty much write your own ticket to fame and fortune. That's going to take time and effort, but you're on the right track by reading this book. If you apply yourself, you can build an independent copywriting business with a steady stream of well-paying work in white papers. How can I say that? Because I've done it.

In this chapter, I describe the ample opportunities for any writer who can create white papers that get results. It comes down to a simple formula:

High demand + Low supply = A great market for your efforts

This chapter also describes the three most likely paths into white papers. If you're an experienced copywriter, journalist, or technical writer, you have a tremendous background to build on. But no matter what walk of life you hail from, this chapter lists all the skills you need — plus a few limiting beliefs and attitudes you may need to forget — to succeed at writing white papers. Good luck!

Sizing Up the Possibilities

White papers are on the right side of several strong trends in B2B marketing. Buyers want them, and many competitors have them, so they've become a standard part of the B2B toolkit. White papers have been called "the king of content" for good reason: They're the most substantial, most powerful, most respected form of content in the market today. They're riding the immense wave known as *content marketing*. And the rise of social media is another huge trend carrying white papers along, because this form of content can be promoted quite effectively with social media.

The white paper market is subject to a classic imbalance: a high demand for white papers but a low supply of writers who know how to create them. This imbalance has pushed up the rates for writing white papers and created a tremendous opportunity in this area. If you're already a nonfiction writer, redirecting your skills into this area is a smart move. If you're not yet a writer but are looking for a good opportunity to live a more independent lifestyle, there's a lot of room for you, too.

In the following sections, I explore the major trends in white papers, explain why good white paper writers are in short supply, show how much a white paper writer can earn and how vast this market really is, and discuss whether white papers are really here to stay.

Looking at three trends pushing white papers to the top

White papers have been booming ever since the web took off in the late 1990s. Today, white papers are an accepted part of B2B marketing, well funded as a form of inbound marketing, and well suited to promote through social media. Here, I review three rising trends that have brought white papers to the very top of the list for how to make money as a writer today:

✔ **Trend #1: White papers are expected by B2B buyers.** White papers are highly valued by B2B buyers, especially for technology products. And these days, a vast range of products have some sort of technology component, like software, embedded chips, a link to the web, and so on. Before B2B buyers make a purchase, they want to size up all their options. Where do they turn for help when making a decision? To the white papers from each company whose offering is in the running. Any company that doesn't have a white paper to promote its product or service could well be out of the running for that buyer's business.

Because so many buyers request white papers, B2B sellers have to produce them to keep up with competitors. In other words, white papers are becoming a standard piece in the marketing toolkit for more and more B2B vendors.

✔ **Trend #2: White papers are a key part of content marketing.** Content marketing is already booming, and it still has a long way to grow. Also known as *inbound marketing,* for years, this side of the budget has been steadily siphoning dollars away from traditional *outbound* activities, like direct mail, telemarketing, trade shows, and print advertising. And that's bound to continue for the foreseeable future. Why? Mainly because inbound marketing can generate a qualified B2B lead for far less money than outbound marketing. And content marketing is on the right side of history as the business world moves away from interruption marketing and toward permission marketing.

✔ **Trend #3: White papers are rocket fuel for social media.** Social media is most powerful when you have something important to say. A white paper is the ideal kind of content to promote through social media because it's free and easy to access. All you have to do is publicize the URL to the white paper's landing page. And if that content proves useful to those who download it, they can easily "like" it, retweet it, blog about it, or otherwise share it with their own social media networks. That's when your white paper can really catch fire, blast off, and travel far beyond where any B2B marketing team can send it.

Understanding why marketers can't find qualified writers

Many marketing managers want to create white papers to promote their company's offerings, but they can't find anyone to write them. It happens. A few years ago, I got a call from a marketing manager in New York City who found me on the web. She was from a little company you may have heard of: Google. "We have such a hard time finding writers," she confided. "I wanted to call and see whether you could help us." I just about fell off my chair. I mean, you can't swing a cat in New York City without hitting a writer! What she meant, I've come to realize, is that it's difficult to find writers who can research and produce good B2B copy about challenging topics, hit their deadlines, and not be prima donnas who are impossible to work with. By now, I've written half a dozen white papers and close to 20 case studies for Google.

Even the largest, hippest companies are always looking for good writers. Thousands of marketing managers in B2B companies are searching for writers who can understand their business and tell their story in a compelling way — and they're having trouble finding them. It's not really a matter of money; there's simply a big shortage of skills and knowledge in this area.

A quarter million dollars for ten pages: Considering a white paper's payoff

Imagine that you're a salesperson for Acme Scanners, sitting in the office of an executive who's thinking about spending a quarter of a million bucks on your products. "I like what you're telling me," he says. "But I'll have to run this by my technical team. What kind of white papers can you send them?"

Gulp. Acme doesn't have any. "Well, we haven't...um...seen the need to do any white papers," you start. "Our system is...ah...so easy to use that I could offer your IT people a personal demo in...um...60 minutes." Gulp. You really hope that tiny bead of sweat doesn't drip right off your nose and land on his desk.

"No, they hate those," says your prospect, with a fierce look. "They really prefer some kind of document they can look at, you know, to size up every vendor. Don't you have anything you could send them?"

Gulp. "I'm sure we do," you manage to croak, watching your fat commission on the deal fly out the window. "I'll shake a few trees back at the office and see what I can come up with for you." And as soon as you get out of there, you call up your marketing manager, yelping that you really need a white paper to close a deal for a quarter million smackers.

A similar scenario gets played out often. Many B2B buyers demand white papers to help them decide about making a large purchase. Many competing companies have them. And that leaves any vendor without them feeling pressured to keep up. If everyone but Acme sends those IT guys a white paper or two, what chance does Acme have to make the sale? Acme could be out of the running. A quarter million dollars lost, all for the sake of a ten-page document that nobody bothered to write. And if this happens every month of the year, that's $3 million a year in sales lost by a single salesperson for a single company. Multiply that across the entire B2B marketplace, and you can see the huge payoff for effective white papers.

Calculating the earning potential for a white paper writer

Here's a question from Economics 101: In a market economy, what happens when you have high demand for an item but low supply? The answer is, the price goes up, sometimes way up. That's why an average white paper writer can earn $500 a page for creating these documents, and a proven writer with a good track record can earn considerably more. That's right: You can earn up to $1,000 a page writing a white paper if you're really good. And if you work efficiently, that translates into hundreds of dollars an hour.

Why would companies fork over that much money? Because they know that a white paper, done correctly, pays for itself many times over. They know they can likely use a good white paper for a year or two and spread that fee across many hundreds or thousands of downloads and many dozens or hundreds of leads generated. That makes $1,000 a page a sensible investment.

But don't take my word for it. Consider the informed sources shown in Table 2-1: executives from the content networks KnowledgeStorm and TechTarget, the latest survey of white paper writers from 2007, the leading training center for copywriters, AWAI, and the leading market directory for freelance writers, *Writer's Market*. According to all these sources, the average fees for writing an average-sized white paper range from just over $3,000 to almost $5,000.

Table 2-1	Fees for Writing a 7- to 10-Page White Paper		
Source	*Low*	*High*	*Average*
Interviews with content networks	$3,000	$5,000	$4,000
WhitePaperSource survey of about 600 white paper writers	$2,000	$10,000+	$3,300
American Writers and Artists, Inc.	$2,500	$6,500	$4,500
Writer's Market	$2,500	$10,000	$4,927
Average of averages			**$4,180**

Beyond what you see in Table 2-1, the white paper writers' survey showed that one in four white paper writers charges between $5,000 and $10,000 for a single paper. My conclusion: A typical white paper for a reasonably big company, done by a reasonably experienced writer, costs about $5,000 today. And the more experienced the writer, the more he can charge.

Using these numbers, I created three earning scenarios for white paper writers: A beginner who works slowly but diligently can likely do 12 to 15 white papers for $3,000 each to gross around $40,000 a year. At the other end of the scale, a proven white paper expert who charges $6,000 a project and works quickly can probably complete 30 projects to gross about $180,000 a year. And an intermediate writer can come in somewhere in the middle, probably topping $100,000 a year. Of course, these are back-of-the-envelope calculations, and your mileage may vary. For details, see Chapter 4.

How many white papers are published?

Sometimes an earnest writer thinking about going out on his own or a marketing person working on a business plan asks me, "How many white papers get published every year?" Honestly, I don't know, and I don't think anyone else knows, either. No one tracks this number; that would be like tracking how many press releases or B2B case studies are published every year. What's the point?

With some digging, you could come up with a few data points, like how many white papers are syndicated every year with the main services like KnowledgeStorm and TechTarget.

But then what — multiply that number by 10, 20, 50, or 100 to cover all the white papers that aren't syndicated?

If I had to guess, I would venture that scores of thousands of white papers are published every year. And that number is growing. But instead of trying to put a precise figure on it, here's a better way to look at this: More B2B companies are looking for good writers than you and I and all the other readers of this book will ever be able to uncover if we spend the rest of our lives trying. And you can put that in your business plan, and tell them I said so.

Discovering who uses white papers

A common market-sizing question that often pops up is, "How many companies need white papers anyway?" I did some market research into this a few years ago, and then updated that just before this book went to press. Table 2-2 shows what I found, based on the latest available data.

Table 2-2	The Size of the White Paper Market	
Domain	*NAISC Codes*	*Number of Companies*
Equipment Manufacturers	333, 334, 335, 335122, 3363, 3364, 3365, 336611, 3372, 3391 (excludes 333112, 3351, 3352, 336612)	62,369 (U.S.)
Scientific and Technical Service Providers	541 (excludes 5411, 5412, 54132, 54141, 5418, 5419)	365,867 (U.S.)
Software and Information Providers	5112, 517, 518, 51911	26,008 (U.S.)
Potential white paper clients in U.S. only		**454,244**
Add 35% for similar companies in Australia, Canada, Finland, Ireland, Israel, New Zealand, Norway, and U.K. that do business in English.		158,986
Total potential clients for white papers in English		**613,230**

Sources: U.S. Census 2008, OECD 2011

In the column labeled *Domain, Equipment Manufacturers* includes any company making computers, peripherals, medical devices — you know, hardware — but not household appliances, cars or trucks, smaller boats, lawn equipment, or lighting. *Scientific and Technical Service Providers* includes any company doing technical consulting, measuring, or testing (but not accounting, advertising, interior design, landscaping, or law firms). *Software and Information Providers* includes anyone publishing apps, databases, or syndicated media. I've done white papers for companies in all three domains from all over the world.

The column labeled *NAISC Codes* lists the North American Industry Classification System codes I counted or excluded under each domain. Only firms with employees are included; I didn't count a self-employed person or couple, because these tiny businesses don't often hire a white paper writer.

The column labeled *Number of Companies* shows how many companies existed in each domain in the United States at the time of the 2008 census. I took the comparative GDP for several other countries that do business in English to bump up the American numbers by about one-third for a global total.

As you can see from the table, well more than half a million companies in the English-speaking world could use white papers. And that's counting only the science- or technology-driven sectors where white papers are an established tradition. Many other sectors could benefit from white papers, too.

Wondering whether the white paper opportunity will last

Some people accept that a lot of companies use white papers today, but they worry about the future. Won't something else come along to replace them? What about video? How long will this wonderful market opportunity last? Don't worry. If you can help a B2B company describe some relatively new, complex, and expensive offering in compelling terms, you'll never be short of work. If you polish your skills so you can dig up and present useful information to help a B2B buyer understand an issue, solve a problem, or make a decision, you'll never be short of work. To see why, consider these points:

- ✔ **White papers have already stood the test of time.** The white paper has existed as a useful format for more than 100 years now. Originally, white papers were short, factual reports and policy papers from the U.K. government. Many of these reports covered industries, and as business people began to see them, their popularity grew. Executives liked the authoritative voice and vast sweep of research in these documents, so businesses began to imitate the same format and issue white papers of their own.

Since then, white papers have become a standard tool in the B2B marketer's toolkit. These documents are incredibly useful for building recognition for a company or product, generating leads at the top of the sales funnel, nurturing prospects through the middle of the funnel, and supporting technical evaluations at the bottom of the funnel. Do you imagine that any companies will still need to do those things in the future? I do.

✔ **White papers provide the latest and greatest information.** Today's white papers are ideal for describing any B2B offering that's relatively new, complex, or expensive. Do you suppose any B2B offerings of tomorrow will involve new breakthroughs that take some explaining? Certainly. Do you think next year's B2B products and services will be remarkably simpler and cheaper than what's on the market today? Perhaps, but only if they involve some sort of breakthrough that takes some explaining. So any way you look at this, vendors will need a persuasive and thoughtful way to publish their latest information for B2B buyers.

✔ **White papers contain information that business people seek.** An effective white paper can help a B2B buyer understand an issue, solve a problem, or make a decision. Do you suppose business people will still have issues, problems, or decisions to make in the future? I do. And do you suppose that watching a video will ever be as effective as reading and thinking? Some people believe that. But here's the kicker: Who do you think writes the script and often directs the entire production for a video? That would be the writer who understands the content, probably because he already wrote the white paper about it.

Any way I look at this issue, I come to the same conclusion: The white paper market is going to be healthy for a long time. And even if some new media forms eventually come along to replace it, the skills you develop writing white papers will be transferable to these new media. See Chapter 3 for a longer discussion on the past, present, and likely future of white papers.

Coming into White Papers from Three Common Paths

Most of the white paper writers I've met entered the field by accident. No one goes off to college thinking, "I'm going to graduate and become a white paper writer!" No degree exists for white papers anyway. The most useful courses you can study are all over the map, perhaps a smattering of computer science, English, history, marketing, philosophy, rhetoric, sociology, and any of the sciences that you're curious about.

But the white papers writers I know do have a few things in common. For one, they're all accomplished communicators who enjoy building an argument with facts and logic. For another, many have worked in a few similar roles. In fact, the three most common careers people work in before they start writing white papers are copywriters, journalists, and technical writers.

Depending on the path you've traveled so far, you've likely developed some great skills that can help you succeed in this field. You may have some areas where you need to pick up some new skills. And you may have to get rid of some unhealthy attitudes that won't serve you well as a white paper writer. If you come from one of these paths, flip through the rest of this chapter to find the section that fits you best.

How do I know so much about these fields? Well, I spent many years working in each one. As a freelance journalist, I wrote close to 1,000 magazine articles for everyone from accountants to woodworkers. I worked full time and then on contract as a technical writer for more years than I care to remember, producing software manuals and online help. Most recently, I've worked as an independent B2B copywriter since the late 1990s. And I've won awards for writing in all three domains. So if you come from any of these domains, I've walked a mile in your shoes.

If you don't have experience as a copywriter, journalist, or technical writer, don't worry. No matter what other jobs you've held, if you can present a compelling argument backed up by solid evidence, you can figure out everything else you need to know to succeed in writing white papers. For tips on researching and writing white papers, see Chapters 14 and 15, and use the index to find specific notes on these skills. Also see the many free articles available on my website at www.thatwhitepaperguy.com/articles.html.

Copywriters and white papers

If you've worked as a copywriter, you probably understand more about marketing than people from any other career path. You may have seen content marketing in action. You already know how to do research, interview experts, write smoothly, and meet short deadlines. You can follow a house style guide and handle reviews and comments. So you already have some wonderful skills you can apply to this field.

But you'll need to develop some new skills, and you'll need to erase a few attitudes that could hurt your white paper writing. Above all, you'll have to master writing to persuade by using facts and logic rather than appeals to emotion as in business-to-consumer (B2C) copywriting. And you must master how to write to explain an issue or prove useful information, without selling anything. These challenges aren't insurmountable. But whenever you sit down to write, your habits from the past may tempt you to gloss over any holes in your evidence with glib statements and fluffy promises rather than solid facts and arguments. If you can get past that, you can have a wonderful future as a white paper writer.

Table 2-3 shows the skills you likely have as a copywriter and those you may need to work on.

Table 2-3	Copywriting Skills and White Papers
Skills You Already Have	*Skills You May Need to Develop*
Analyzing an audience	Writing to explain
Doing in-depth research	Handling quotes and sources
Understanding why B2B buyers buy	Proving all your claims with evidence
Interviewing experts	Formatting documents for quick scanning
Writing to persuade	Telling an engaging story
Following house style	
Meeting short deadlines	
Handling reviews and comments	

Most copywriters have a few things drummed into their heads at college, on the job, and in bull sessions with colleagues. Here are some habits you may need to rethink to succeed in white papers.

Appeal to logic, not emotions

The best copywriting calls to the consumers' emotions, making them ache for the product you're describing. This kind of writing paints a detailed vision of all the wonderful benefits people will enjoy after they buy. Great copy holds out the promise of things like stunning beauty, radiant health, untold wealth, and a lifetime of leisure.

White papers are different. They're not directed at consumers buying shampoo, vitamins, or chewing gum. They're directed at people making a serious business decision worth a lot of money. In a white paper, you write mainly to explain. And when you do persuade, you use facts and logical arguments, not appeals to emotion. White papers are in the same league as press releases and annual reports. These business documents are expected to deliver facts and arguments, not fluff and pipe dreams. So copywriters need to tone down the adjectives, superlatives, promises, and emotional appeals. If you can't do that, you won't last long as a white paper writer.

I'm not saying business buyers are heartless automatons with no feelings. But few business people can afford to spend millions of dollars on impulse or because they heard a cute jingle on the radio. They buy because they're convinced that a vendor has something that will help their company make money, save money, beat the competition, or serve their customers better. Nothing else really matters. So drop the calls to emotion, stick to the facts, and everyone will be happier.

Sell the steak, not the sizzle

A copywriter must give his work pizzazz. Any successful ad, brochure, jingle, or sales letter needs to be snappy to make an impression. But white papers are different. They're serious business documents that should be dignified and helpful, not packed with zest and zing. To write an effective white paper, tone down the hype, delete all the fluffy adjectives, and abandon the worn-out gambit of "selling the sizzle." In fact, you could say that a white paper needs to work much harder than that. It needs to set the table, present the menu, suggest a good wine, deliver a fabulous meal, bring coffee and dessert, and then give the reader a coupon to bring them back for another visit. That's more than just a little sizzle.

Talk features, not benefits

When writing copy, you're supposed to link every feature to the benefits it delivers. You don't often have to describe how anything works, just how much better people's lives will be after they buy it. You can sketch in a few highlights or cherry-pick the most appealing features to touch on as you build to your stirring conclusion — buy now!

In a white paper, you may need to spend most of your text describing how some feature is implemented. Maybe the product uses a completely new approach to solve an age-old problem. Maybe its materials are more durable, or its algorithms more precise. Many readers download a white paper specifically to discover the technical details about a company's offerings. They want to understand the nitty-gritty about each key feature. So skimming over the features and focusing on the benefits often isn't enough.

Don't ask for the order

Copywriting is often defined as "salesmanship in print." But this definition is dangerous for a white paper writer. You never "ask for the order" in a white paper. These documents are used for complex B2B sales, where numerous people come together to make a weighty decision. This decision can take weeks or months to complete. Your goal in a white paper is to provide useful content that positions your company as a trusted advisor and engages prospects for the long haul. At the end of the document, you encourage readers to take the next step in the sales cycle, something like visiting a website to use an online ROI calculator. You seldom ask readers to pick up the phone and call customer service to place an order.

In fact, the number-one mistake too many writers make in too many white papers is too much selling. White paper readers aren't looking for a sales pitch. They're looking for useful information to help them understand an issue, solve a problem, or make a decision. If you make your white paper a thinly veiled sales pitch, you'll distort its purpose, confound your readers' expectations, and perhaps turn off your prospect permanently. By pushing for the sale too hard in a white paper, you can lose the sale.

Journalists and white papers

If you've worked as a journalist, you likely have the makings of a great white paper writer. You already know how to write fast, write well, and tell a compelling story to a specific audience. You're used to interviewing and making a quick study of new material. You can sift through a 50-page report and come up with a few choice nuggets and quotable quotes.

Here's how U.K. brand journalist Ashley Curtis explains the value of a journalism background:

> Delivering engaging, interesting, and relevant content is the beating heart of content marketing, a focus that journalists can identify with. . . . Journalism by nature involves tracking the latest events happening in a particular industry, so firms hiring a professional journalist know they're going to get a return on their investment in the form of highly developed writing skills, engaging written content, and an eye for a story.

So you certainly do have some fabulous skills to apply to this field. You'll probably have to pick up a few new things and drop negative attitudes that could hurt your white paper writing. But all in all, as a trained journalist, you have better-than-average chances of success in white papers. Table 2-4 outlines the skills you likely have as a journalist and those you may need to work on.

Table 2-4	Journalism Skills and White Papers
Skills You Already Have	*Skills You May Need to Develop*
Understanding an audience	Analyzing an audience
Doing quick research	Understanding why B2B buyers buy
Interviewing experts	Doing in-depth research
Telling a story	Writing to persuade
Handling quotes and sources	Formatting documents for quick scanning
Meeting deadlines	Handling reviews and comments
Writing in a concise and lively style	Parking your ego (you'll never get a byline for a white paper)
Following house style	
Working with an editor	

Most journalists have a few things drummed into their heads at college, on the job, and in bull sessions with colleagues. Here are some self-limiting beliefs you may need to rethink to succeed in white papers.

Marketing isn't evil; it's essential

Saying "marketing is evil" makes about as much sense as saying "breathing is evil." When a company makes something, how is the rest of the world supposed to know it exists? That's marketing. Journalism has been supported by marketing, in the form of advertising, for the past 175 years. The recent bloodbath — in which close to 50,000 newspaper people have been laid off in the United States alone — happened for one simple reason: Advertising dollars moved from newspapers to the web. If you ever worked as a journalist, your job was propped up by marketing. Sure, some marketers are dishonest, and some ads are misleading. But some journalists make up their sources and some fabricate their stories. The failings of a few don't make both fields entirely corrupt. So get over yourself. Get rid of this attitude, or you can forget about writing white papers.

Forget both sides of the story; tell your client's story

Journalists are supposed to get both sides of the story, which results in a lot of phrases like "on the other hand . . ." or "but critics say . . ." that are designed to inject the opposite point of view. It doesn't matter whether that view is that dinosaur bones are only 6,000 years old or that global warming is a myth. No matter what you think about objectivity in journalism, it doesn't exist when you're writing to persuade. In a white paper, there's only one side of the story: your client's. In a problem/solution flavor of white paper (see Chapter 8), the other side of the story sums up every other attempt to solve a problem and the failings of each attempt. You never write "on the other hand . . ." in a white paper, so get out of that habit.

You're not in a race; get it right the first time

Journalism is a constant race to see who breaks the story first, which can lead to shoddy work, where fraudulent tweets or media hoaxes are picked up without being checked out. But you don't have a second edition of a white paper. You have to get it right the first time. Speed isn't the most important thing; explaining and persuading with facts and logic is your top priority. Don't rush out a white paper like it's front-page news. Take your time, check and recheck your sources and build a thoughtful piece that gets results. Yes, you can always upload a corrected version of a white paper, but any B2B buyers who saw your first edition with mistakes in it have already formed a poor impression of your company that you can't easily repair.

Technical writers and white papers

If you worked as a technical writer, you've probably seen a few white papers in your time. You may have reviewed or even written some yourself. You've interviewed technical experts and business executives and handled their comments and reviews tactfully. You already know how to write precisely and explain how things work. You know how to work smoothly in a team. You've mastered the software you use for publishing, so you can design pages, insert graphics, and use text enhancements like tables and headings. And to top off everything else, you have experience in the kind of technology-driven firms that make up the ideal market for white papers.

Although you can apply all these fabulous skills to this field, you'll probably have to figure out a few new things and lose a few negative attitudes that could hurt your white paper writing. In particular, you must let go of the fierce restraints imposed on every tech writer. Don't be afraid to be more passionate, opinionated, and forceful in your writing. Writing to persuade demands all of that. If you can break free from these constraints, your background gives you a good chance of success.

Table 2-5 lists the skills you likely have as a technical writer and those you may need to work on.

Table 2-5	Technical Writing Skills and White Papers
Skill You Already Have	*Skills You May Need to Develop*
Analyzing an audience	Understanding why B2B buyers buy
Interviewing subject matter experts	Doing in-depth research
Writing to explain	Handling quotes and sources
Following house style	Telling a story
Mastering software for publishing	Writing to persuade
Formatting documents for quick reference	Meeting shorter deadlines
Handling reviews and comments	

Most tech writers have a few things drummed into their heads at college, on the job, and in bull sessions with colleagues. Here are some things you may need to rethink to succeed in white papers.

Sales and marketing aren't "the dark side"

Tech writers often encounter mistrust of sales, marketing, and business in general from the engineers and scientists they rub shoulders with. Moving from R&D or engineering into marketing is called "going over to the dark side." Marketing people are called *suits* or even *weasels*. What the name-callers forget is that without sales, no company would have the money to pay their salaries. Without marketing, no one would know about the wonderful products they're building. So if you ever worked as a technical writer, your job depended on sales and marketing to bring in the customers.

And another thing: When you write a white paper, no one is going to ask you to lie, cheat, or steal. You won't be writing breathless infomercials ("How much would you expect to pay?") or ditzy sales letters ("Act now: This limited-time offer is available only to the first 250 buyers!") In fact, part of your job as a white paper writer is to resist plunking the same old sales pitch or marketing speak into your document. Does that sound like "selling out"? Banish this attitude from your mind, or there's no point trying to write white papers.

You must let your voice be heard

Did you ever try to use a striking turn of phrase or a lighter tone in a technical manual? Or point out that one feature was superior to another? I bet you were slapped down like a misbehaving child. Then you got a lecture on how a tech writer must be invisible, neutral, detached, and unemotional; a veritable Spock of the writing world.

But white papers are different. You may need to write about an industry challenge or tell a story about people in a place with a problem. To write in a compelling way, you must take a reasoned but passionate stand. You must express your position forcefully and eloquently. You must take off the tech-writing muzzle and find your voice. If you can't, your white papers may sound too cold and unpersuasive and may not get the results you need.

White papers require both content and style

As a technical writer, your success depends on writing effectively about "things." This involves explaining how to use a product to perform a task or accomplish a goal. Conveying that content accurately is your top priority. How well you express it is much less important. As you know, most documentation follows a house style that determines everything, from your headings to nomenclature to your choice of tenses and pronouns.

But white papers are different. Yes, you need to keep your facts straight, but no style guide can tell you how to express those facts. And because you're writing to persuade, an effective white paper must get the argument exactly right. That means backing up all your assertions with proof. I bet you never had to do that in any technical manual. And you must rewrite and polish like never before. One draft or two for technical accuracy won't be enough. You must labor over your words to craft a message that explains and persuades. You must control your material and build a convincing case. You must ignore many of the confines you're used to from writing documentation. In short, you must let your style take flight in a way you never could in any technical manual. If you're up for that, you can do very well writing white papers.

Finding White Paper Clients

Suppose by now you're convinced that the opportunity is there, you're excited about the earning potential, you've studied up on white papers, and you're all set to take on your first project. The only question is: Where do you find a white paper client?

Whole books have been written on how to start up and develop a freelance writing business, so I'm not going to try to repeat all that advice here. Some especially good books are *The Wealthy Freelancer* (Alpha), *The Six-Figure Freelancer* (Paul Lima Presents), and *The Well-Fed Writer* (Fanove Publishing). All three have fantastic advice about analyzing your knowledge, approaching clients, and making money. Three excellent online resources aimed specifically at individual freelancers who may not enjoy selling are Get Clients Now! (www.getclientsnow.com), Action Plan Marketing (www.actionplan.com), and the International Freelancers Academy (www.international freelancersacademy.com). All three online resources have e-newsletters, online courses and webinars, and pages with lots of helpful advice.

In the following sections, I give you a couple of pointers on what to do and what not to do to get a potential client's attention, and then I offer some insights on how to keep your business healthy and thriving.

Avoid most of what you hear

A lot of the marketing advice you hear isn't useful to you. Most "small business" marketing advisors think "small" means 50 employees. They tell you to set up a website and grow your online presence. Join groups on LinkedIn and extend your network. Tweet useful items and gain followers with Twitter. Put up a company page on Facebook and get people to like you. Publish an e-newsletter and get subscribers. Go to your local Chamber of Commerce meeting, network, and pass out business cards. Don't forget to send out hundreds of direct mail letters. And e-mail — you've got to be doing warm prospecting with e-mail.

Use the web. Use social media. Use networking. Use direct mail. Use e-mail. Will everyone *puleeeze* give it a rest! Don't buy into the hype from all these hair-on-fire, running-off-in-all-directions-at-once marketing-ninja types who think they're advising some sort of corporate enterprise. An independent writer is a one-person microbusiness, not Acme Scanners. You can only do so much, so anything you do to market yourself has to be completely strategic, as described in the next section.

Getting started with the basics

Of course, you need a basic website and LinkedIn presence so a potential client takes you seriously. It helps to have a few sample white papers that you've already completed. Just as no one wants to be the first person a surgeon ever operates on, no one wants to be the first person you ever write a white paper for. Aside from that, finding white paper clients is no different than finding clients who need any copywriter, social media expert, designer, photographer, or other creative supplier.

To find prospective clients, focus on the three factors that help you determine whether a company can use your services: Does the company sell anything relatively new, complex, or expensive? You know your own background, and where you have domain knowledge you can draw on, what you find interesting, and what industries leave you completely cold. And you likely have some companies you'd love to write for. So make a list, and get busy.

One great place to find leads is Jigsaw (`www.jigsaw.com`), a huge online Rolodex of contacts. If you know a company name, odds are you can find the name, phone number, and direct e-mail of any marketing manager there through a quick search. You can pay a few dollars a month to get contacts throughout the year, or upload your own contacts, or correct existing listings to earn points you can redeem for contacts.

no longer exists

The absolute fastest way to check out a potential white paper client is to simply call the company, and ask "Who's responsible for doing your white papers?" In a call or two, you'll be routed to, most likely, a hardworking marketing manager who will be busy but probably delighted to speak to you. After all, he can't find good writers, remember? Just start off the call by saying you're a white paper writer who knows the industry. That will get his attention.

If you want to make it as a writer, don't get sucked into time sinks like Facebook, YouTube, or forums for sad-sack writers who never land any clients. That may feel like work; after all, you're sitting at your computer doing "research" and building your network, but you're not accomplishing much. At least, hang out on LinkedIn and look for marketing managers who may hire you, or read websites and blogs about white papers to build your knowledge.

The secret of freelance success

Here's the secret I've learned from more than 25 years of self-employment: Find a good client that you enjoy working with, get paid fairly, and do such a good job that he hires you to do it again — and he tell his colleagues about you. Then do it all over again. You'll soon have more work than you can handle. You'll have loyal clients who will stick with you for years and even put their projects on hold until you're free to work with them. That's freelance success, regardless of whether you ever send out a single tweet.

Consider this: A recent survey of close to 1,500 freelancers revealed that their top three ways of getting clients were referrals, word of mouth, and tapping their network. All three tactics go back to the basic principles of freelancing: Do a great job every time, and you'll get repeat business from the same clients, word-of-mouth referrals when happy clients tell their colleagues and peers about you, and an expanding network that brings you more opportunities all the time.

Chapter 3

The Past, Present, and Future of White Papers

"If you would understand anything, observe its beginning and its development," said Aristotle. In other words, to help understand the present, study the past. This statement certainly applies to white papers. Tracing the past history and evolution of these documents gives us a better understanding of their current formats and likely futures.

In this chapter, I give you a brief overview of the past, present, and likely future of white papers. I look at where white papers originated more than 100 years ago, where they are today, and the most likely four paths they could take in the future. This chapter defines three distinct generations of white papers: Generation 1.0 for the past, 2.0 for the present, and 3.0 for the future. Table 3-1 shows the key features of each generation, and the rest of this chapter discusses each generation in detail.

Table 3-1 Three Generations of White Papers			
	Generation 1.0	*Generation 2.0*	*Generation 3.0*
Era	1910s to 1990s	1990s to today	Coming soon
Tag	Your grandfather's white paper	Your father's white paper	New kid on the block
Media used	Text only	Text plus good typography, graphics, design, and color	All from Gen 2.0 plus multimedia, such as animation, audio, and video, plus web links interactivity
Designed for	Reading on paper	Reading on paper or on-screen	Reading and interacting on-screen
Models	Business report	Annual report, science magazine	Multimedia PDF, microsite
Pros	Inexpensive, easy to produce	Engaging for today's decision makers	Engaging for both older and younger audiences
Cons	Bland, no graphics, not compelling	Hard to produce, may be too much reading for younger audiences	Very hard to produce, multimedia can distract from key message

Where It All Began: Generation 1.0 (1910s to 1990s)

The white paper first began in the United Kingdom early in the 20th century. Printed by Her Majesty's Stationery Office, these white papers were shorter reports or position papers named for the color of their white covers, distinguishing them from the much longer reports and policy books bound with blue covers. All these early white papers were formatted with basic typesetting, including bold headings, italic for subheads, and occasional tables.

This format spread from government to business, remaining virtually unchanged for most of the 20th century. In the following sections, I break down the characteristics of the Generation 1.0 white paper and explore a comparable model.

Characteristics of Gen 1.0 white papers

Completely dry and factual, Generation 1.0 white papers set the standard for decades to come. Gradually moving beyond politics, white papers explained advances in science and technology during the decades leading up to World War II and then the 1950s and '60s. With the rise of the personal computer in the 1970s and '80s, white papers became especially popular in information technology, a sector that creates a steady stream of developments that must be explained to potential buyers.

These text-only Generation 1.0 documents were intended to be read on paper. Although fairly inexpensive to produce, they looked bland, with limited typography, no graphics, and no color. Such unexciting formatting helped confine these documents to a narrow range of technical subjects aimed at B2B engineering-type readers. You can consider the text-only, Generation 1.0 white paper as your grandfather's white paper, now retired and over the hill. But for many years, these documents provided information that helped countless decision makers understand an issue, solve a problem, or make a decision.

Because integrating graphics into documents was so difficult and costly, most white papers looked more or less the same for many years: one column of unadorned text set in a single typeface. Every page was a wall of gray, occasionally relieved by a table.

Any marketing piece that needed better production — such as a glossy brochure — was done by outside suppliers who used typesetting, silver-based photography, manual design and page makeup, and offset printing. All of this was too costly and time-consuming to justify for most white papers.

The closest model: Business reports

The closest model for a Generation 1.0 white paper is an internal business report. With a bland cover, a wide line of typewritten text in a single typeface, and a complete lack of graphics or photos, the classic business report of the 1920s didn't change for decades. Even though word processing had been on the scene since the 1970s, it was still a text-only world. No stand-alone word-processing systems or the PC software that replaced them could incorporate graphics until the 1980s.

If you find this hard to believe, remember that many of the technologies everyone takes for granted today — PC-compatible laser and inkjet printers, desktop scanners, and digital cameras — weren't available until the mid-1980s or 1990s. Earlier versions of some of these devices existed, but they didn't fit on a desktop or work with a PC. By now, all these technologies offer powerful specs at a fraction of the original cost and are must-have tools for producing a white paper.

Forcing White Papers to Evolve

Late in the 20th century, several advances in technology combined to raise expectations for B2B communication and forced white papers to evolve. The first was desktop publishing, ushered in with the arrival of the Apple Macintosh in 1984. Desktop publishing put powerful editorial and design tools into the hands of regular business people, enabling anyone with a little training to accomplish these three things more easily and at a lower cost than ever:

- ✔ Use different typefaces of different sizes in a document.
- ✔ Mix text and graphics on the same page.
- ✔ Design pages on-screen that print out more or less the same on paper.

Over the next few years, the impact of desktop publishing was profound, sweeping through the business world and turning traditional print production upside down. Within ten years, by the mid-1990s, the expected standards for written communication in every organization were elevated dramatically. Your grandfather's business report was a thing of the past, along with your grandfather's white paper. Even inexpensive marketing materials like fliers gained far higher production values.

But that was only the beginning. Some other key technologies followed:

- ✔ Starting in 1991 with HTML and in 1993 with the Mosaic browser, the **World Wide Web** became an instant, global distribution channel.
- ✔ In 1993, **Adobe's Portable Document Format (PDF)** was released. This universal file format saved the design and typography of a document in a format that anyone could view with a free reader.
- ✔ Starting in 1998, **Google's search engine** became the best way to find relevant content on the web.

All these technologies together caused an incredible shift. B2B marketers could now publish attractive documents in-house for low cost, freeing vendors from the expense and delay of printing and shipping their content. B2B prospects could search for white papers and download them by themselves, freeing them from the delay of getting content through the mail or the hassle of dealing with a salesperson. These innovations created fertile ground where a whole new generation of white papers could spring up: Generation 2.0.

Where White Papers Are Now: Generation 2.0 (1990s to Today)

The white paper really came into its own as a B2B marketing piece in the 1990s. But a bland, text-only, Generation 1.0 document was no longer enough to engage decision makers. Driven both by technology and the changing marketplace, these documents evolved into Generation 2.0. In the following sections, I discuss this generation's characteristics, two close models, and its ongoing relevancy in today's market.

Characteristics of Gen 2.0 white papers

Generation 2.0 white papers are marked by good typography, frequent graphics, and more attractive page design. Color often appears on every page, used in company branding, graphics, or text enhancements like shaded text boxes. These documents are designed to be read either on paper or on-screen.

Having higher production values than Generation 1.0 white papers helped Generation 2.0 emerge as the ultimate expression of many companies' content marketing. This new, improved format suits the ongoing information overload of most executives, who have too much to do, too much to remember, and too much to think about to tolerate a text-only document.

The only downside? Generation 2.0 white papers are harder to produce, and they often require a separate pass through the hands of a professional designer. And although the white paper as a six- to eight-page document is tolerable for today's B2B decision makers, this length may present too much reading for younger audiences, who tend to prefer video and interacting with peers. You should consider the Generation 2.0 document your father's white paper, still in service today, but already with an eye on retirement.

Two close models: Annual reports and science magazines

For all its advances, a Generation 2.0 white paper is still a text-based document. Although the text is adorned with good typography, graphics, and color, all assembled into highly readable pages, this generation is still firmly rooted in printed documents. To help you understand Generation 2.0 white papers, I present two of the closest parallels in the following sections: annual reports and science magazines.

Annual reports

For many years, the front part of any public company's annual report showcased that organization's products, services, management, and employees. With a lot of pictures, exquisite design, and carefully crafted text, these documents aim to inform and persuade — to inform readers about the company and its most recent results, and to persuade shareholders to hold onto their shares and even buy more. In this sense, an annual report has the same purpose as a white paper: to inform and persuade, using facts and logical arguments. These annual reports make a natural model for writers and designers who want to study how a Generation 2.0 white paper should look and sound.

Science magazines

Any well-designed magazine for popular science, computers, or photography — or any serious hobby like amateur astronomy — can be a good model for a Generation 2.0 white paper. In this case, the intent is most often to inform, not to persuade. But even this type of magazine may run editorials, columns, or product reviews that get pretty opinionated. Look at how the text and graphics are integrated and how they support one another. Study how the captions are written and how the articles refer to the supporting graphics. A magazine like *Popular Science* or *Scientific American* can be an excellent model for blending text and graphics in a highly readable format.

But aren't white papers old-fashioned?

The rise of social media, like Facebook and Twitter, gives many marketers pause as they struggle to integrate these new channels into their marketing mix. Fans of social media are nothing if not noisy. Every week another thousand blogs shout out that every company must use every social media channel or else risk going under. "Maybe white papers are too old-fashioned," some marketers wonder. "Maybe we should forget about those and focus on getting 'likes' and followers."

This barrage of noise about social media can drown out the fact that these new channels align perfectly with marketing with content. To be engaging, social media needs compelling content, not just mindless chitchat. What are you going to tweet about anyway — the weather? What your CEO had for lunch? Or the useful ideas in your latest white paper?

It's true that white papers are built around narrative text, and not everyone likes to read. For example, a lot of young people would rather use their smartphones or watch videos than do something that reminds them of school. Sorry to tell you, but work isn't always "fun." Often people on the job have to do things that aren't their top choice for having fun. And when your company is making a major decision to buy something that's relatively new, complicated, and expensive, you'd better believe your executives want something to read — something more substantial than 140 characters.

Yes, white papers are old-fashioned. So is designing a good product and selling it for a fair price. So is telling the truth and taking responsibility for your own life. A vast difference exists between being old-fashioned and being over the hill. White papers have tremendous staying power. After all, they've proven effective at informing and persuading for more than a century. Where will Twitter and Facebook be in 100 years?

Still evolving, not dying

Like everything else, white papers will continue to evolve along with our culture, demographics, and technology. One thing I'm sure about: Narrative text that helps business people solve a problem, understand an issue, or make a decision will continue to be valued for many years to come. And if this narrative is packaged in a slightly different way, so what?

The evolution from Generation 1.0 to 2.0 white papers — although it called for new skills that weren't needed before — helped deliver B2B messages in a more effective way that appealed to the audience of the day. By the same token, the evolution from Generation 2.0 to Generation 3.0 white papers, which is now underway, will call for new skills that weren't needed in the past. But with the right content, the right skills, and the right media, this evolution should help create B2B content that's even more engaging, more compelling, and more persuasive to the audiences of the future.

Where White Papers Are Going: Generation 3.0 (Coming Soon)

Remember that idea about studying history to help understand the present and predict the future? History teaches a significant lesson about white papers. As technology makes using media like animation, audio, and video faster, easier, and more affordable, readers expect to see these new media in B2B marketing.

To stay engaging and relevant for tomorrow's audiences, white papers must encompass these new elements and evolve to Generation 3.0. Paper will fade away, and newer materials will be designed for reading and interacting on-screen. Retaining text but adding multimedia and interaction should help engage audiences of all ages. You can consider Generation 3.0 white papers as the new kid on the block: He's full of promise but still has to prove his reputation.

In the following sections, I discuss how white papers continue to evolve and four likely paths they may follow in the future.

Some trends to watch

Business people now have simple, inexpensive tools for creating audio and video content, posting it for distribution, and promoting it quickly. For example, inexpensive MP3 recorders can pick up conversations anywhere inside or out. Software like Audacity (downloadable from www.audacity.sourceforge.net) provides powerful audio-editing tools for no cost. Both Apple and Microsoft offer free video editors, iMovie and Windows Movie Maker. Individuals who know how to use these new tools can now record video with a smartphone, edit it on a laptop, post it to YouTube, and promote it around the world through social media, all within a few hours.

Of course, the web is all about linking to other information, sometimes drilling through numerous layers to arrive at a more complete understanding, as well as interacting with peers, colleagues, and experts. Marketers need to consider these interactive elements for future white papers.

Another huge trend is the use of mobile devices that are always on and always connected to the web. Many of the so-called Millennial Generation, born after 1985, have grown up with "the web in their pocket," constantly accessing new media through their ever-present devices. As members of this cohort become more influential and ultimately become decision makers, B2B marketing must provide this audience with the content they need in the format they prefer.

One likely downside of Generation 3.0 white papers is how difficult and costly they'll be to produce. And unless multimedia elements are used with taste and restraint, they could end up distracting viewers from the key messages of the entire piece.

Four possible paths to the future

Gazing into my crystal ball, I glimpse a spindly black tree with four spindly branches sticking out in different directions. Each branch points to a hazy pathway through the dark and dangerous woods. Ah, these must indicate the four possible paths that Generation 3.0 white papers can take in the future:

- ✔ Multimedia PDFs
- ✔ Microsites built around a white paper
- ✔ Infographics with layered content
- ✔ Mobile apps

In the rest of this section, I share notes on each possibility. For more discussion and examples of Generation 3.0 white papers, visit www.thatwhitepaperguy.com/the-future-of-white-papers.html.

Multimedia PDFs

The first and most likely path to Generation 3.0 is a multimedia PDF. This builds on the current model of the white paper as a document, adding further media, such as animation, audio, video, and interactivity. All this content is contained in a multimedia PDF driven by narrative text. The current version of the free Adobe Reader supports a multimedia PDF, and some B2B vendors are now creating this type of document.

For example, check out the white paper from Eccolo Media called "Five Cost-Effective Ways to Create More Interactive Content" available at `www. eccolomedia.com/publications.htm`. This two-page PDF is short, but it contains an intriguing video chat with the company founder, Lorie Loe. By the way, this paper recommends embedding audio and video into B2B content to help engage your audience and then goes on to take its own advice. In coming years, I expect to see many similar examples of text-driven white papers with multimedia content added to the same PDF "container."

Microsites built around a white paper

The second possible path to a Generation 3.0 white paper is a microsite on the web with multimedia that visitors can access anywhere, anytime. A white paper can form the heart of this format, with its content repurposed as various forms of media on the associated web pages, including audio, video, and interactivity.

You can see an example of this approach from EMC/IDC at `www.emc.com/ collateral/demos/microsites/emc-digital-universe-2011/ index.htm`. This microsite explores a single topic — the vast scope of the world's information — in just a few web pages. When you arrive, the welcome page automatically runs a video executive summary, where a company VP delivers a scripted excerpt from the core white paper. Viewers can click links to jump to different sections of the text, graphics, and each sponsor's website. IDC describes this approach as "a market overview in a quick-reference, mixed-content, and mixed-media format."

This kind of microsite can provide all the expected Generation 3.0 elements of text, graphics, audio, video, web links, and interactivity. This model certainly sets out an interesting path to explore; a key challenge may be finding the additional budget to do the required HTML coding, video, and digital production.

Infographics with layered content

An infographic conveys data or knowledge by using visual metaphors in a scientific or playful way; in other words, they include text and graphics on the same page. In recent years, the use of infographics has exploded in B2B marketing. Naturally enough, a well-done infographic can help business people visualize and understand a numbered list, trend, or market space.

As a third possible path to Generation 3.0, an infographic could visually present the executive summary of a white paper, with various areas a viewer can click or zoom to see more details on any particular point. Although the viewer could choose his own path through the infographic, the presentation would be driven by a compressed set of points boiled down from a longer discussion in the white paper and packaged as a document.

I haven't seen a white paper repurposed this way yet, perhaps because most infographics are developed as stand-alone graphics. But there's no reason this couldn't be done on the web or with software like Prezi (`www.prezi.com`) that enables you to pan and zoom around a presentation to incorporate different media and layers of information.

Mobile apps

The fourth possible future, and the furthest off, is a mobile app running on a smartphone or tablet, presenting a cluster of information with no need for the old-fashioned concept of a document. Freed from the restrictions of a defined document — just as individual songs are now freed from packaging into CDs or albums — this content could be accessed, updated, or personalized on the fly. In fact, the information in a white paper could be tailored and distributed according to the psychographics, demographics, or preferences of each individual viewer.

You can see the start of this trend in the digital versions of some magazines created for the iPad. For example, the digital versions of *The Economist, Vanity Fair, Wired,* and other forward-thinking magazines feature embedded video, links to other stories by the same authors or on the same topic, outtakes from photo sessions, animations, product demos and reviews, and so on. These digital magazines go partway along this fourth path. They're even purchased and downloaded to mobile devices just like apps.

Charts and graphs updated "automagically" — like a live report on the up-to-the-minute value of pork bellies, various world currencies, or your team's pennant chances — aren't hard to visualize on the always-on mobile device. Nor is content that's personalized according to the demographics or psychographics of an individual viewer. For example, a mining executive may see a front cover of a white paper showing a mining operation, while a prospect working for an airline sees an airport lounge. You could swap whole chunks of multimedia in and out as likely viewing to different prospects. All these ideas can sound like idle speculation, but as technology enables these sorts of publishing approaches, B2B marketers will try them. And some form of the venerable white paper will live on in all its glory.

Chapter 4

Just the FAQs on White Papers

You may be wondering, "What the heck is a white paper, anyway?" That's an excellent question. I asked the same thing myself when I first started writing white papers more than 15 years ago and looked all over for a list of frequently asked questions. I couldn't find one. Eventually, after I found or worked out the answers for myself, I decided to create an FAQ and put it online. My White Paper FAQ page at `www.thatwhitepaperguy.com/ white-paper-faq.html` has now been visited more than 85,000 times. This chapter presents many of these questions and answers in print form for the first time.

In this chapter, I answer more than 20 questions that most often occur to business people and writers about white papers. These answers are grouped by the five *w*'s (and one *h*): who, what, why, where, when, and how — everything from "What is a white paper anyway?" to "How many white papers are 'enough' for a company?"

And if you ever have a question about white papers that isn't covered in this chapter, I invite you to post it to my LinkedIn Group called "Get More From Your White Papers." You'll get an answer from me and perhaps spark some discussion from other group members.

Working Out the Whats of White Papers

White papers are a mainstay in B2B marketing, but not everyone understands what they're all about. This section answers all the frequently asked questions starting with *what*. Here, you find what a white paper is, what industry standards or conventions define a white paper, what other names white papers go by, and what makes them different from other marketing pieces, like blogs, brochures, case studies, or e-books.

What is a white paper anyway?

Ask ten people this question, and you'll likely get 12 different answers. People call anything and everything a white paper. When I've asked that question over the years to marketing executives and seasoned copywriters, I've heard the following responses:

- A bait-piece
- A buzz piece
- The glue that holds any marketing campaign together
- A manifesto
- Any information widget used to promote a company
- A way to freeze-dry your ideas
- That rare document that can be all things to all people

For me, none of these exotic definitions quite do the trick. The best definition I've found, after many years of looking, says it this way:

> A white paper is a persuasive essay that uses facts and logic to promote a B2B product, service, technology, or methodology.

You can identify a white paper by its content and format:

- **The content of a white paper** ideally provides useful information for readers seeking to understand an issue, solve a problem, or make a decision. The content can include explaining a certain offering from a B2B vendor or a new way to solve a nagging industry problem.
- **The format of a white paper** is ideally somewhere between a technical manual and a glossy brochure, between a dry-as-dust academic paper and an annual report. It can include a graphic cover and one or more business graphics inside to help explain the contents, but a white paper is still driven by text.

What are the industry standards for white papers?

Unfortunately, anyone can call anything a white paper. And people do. No laws or regulations can stop them. For instance, consider the length. Today's typical white paper is six to eight pages long, a little shorter than in past years. But I've seen everything from a 2-page flier to a 100-page book labeled as a white paper.

Consider the format. The typical white paper looks more appealing than a technical manual yet not as slick as a brochure. But I've seen white papers as dull as a memo and others as colorful as a cereal box. The typical white paper is distributed as a PDF on the web. But many are printed for sales calls, press kits, and trade shows, and some are posted online as HTML or split up to make microsites.

If no firm standards exist, don't white papers have at least a few shared conventions? Yes, I believe some conventions have been slowly emerging over the years. Seasoned writer Jonathan Kantor and I developed the following checklist. For us to consider any document a white paper, it must

- ✔ Be built from narrative text
- ✔ Be at least five pages long in portrait format
- ✔ Provide educational, practical, and useful content, not a sales pitch
- ✔ Provide well-researched facts, not just opinions
- ✔ Be used *before* a sale, not *after* a sale
- ✔ Include an introduction or executive summary

Everyone else may not be so old school. But I believe this tight definition works best. After all, if you can call any information published by any B2B vendor for any purpose a white paper, then why even bother with that term? Why not just call everything information or marketing bumf?

What else do people call white papers?

White papers come in many types, with no accepted system for labeling them precisely. Given this, the majority of white papers fall into one of the three main types I discuss in Part II:

- ✔ **Backgrounders** that describe the technical features and benefits of one particular product or service
- ✔ **Numbered lists** that provide a light and lively roundup of some highlights about some issue
- ✔ **Problem/solutions** that recommend a new, improved solution for a serious business or technical problem

Beyond these three, many other names can describe white papers, as shown in the *Acceptable Names or Document Types* column in Table 4-1. But remember, no rules or universal standards define what makes a white paper, so people use these labels somewhat randomly. Although you can find a lot of types of useful information, I don't consider all of them white papers.

Table 4-1	Other Names for White Papers
Acceptable Names or Document Types	*Unacceptable Names or Document Types*
Competitive review	Application guide
Discussion paper	Cheat sheet
Evaluator's guide	Installation guide
Executive briefing	Manual
Market overview	Optimizer
Position paper	Pocket guide
Product briefing	Reference
Special report	Troubleshooting guide

For example, Internet marketing guru Perry Marshall names 40-plus types of documents that he considers white papers, including all those in the *Unacceptable Names or Document Types* column in Table 4-1. Notice that the items in that column are all documentation used *after* a purchase to help install, master, or troubleshoot a system. Although those documents may be useful, they're not white papers. A white paper is strictly a presales document used for sales and marketing before a purchase, not for training or support after a purchase.

The label *white paper* has been overused in some sectors and never established in others. For some audiences, marketing teams may want to give these documents another label that resonates better. You don't have to change the contents at all; just consider using the label *executive briefing, guide, research report, special report,* or *technology backgrounder* instead.

What's the difference between white papers and other marketing materials?

B2B marketing teams generate all sorts of content to get the word out about their products or services, including blog posts, brochures, case studies, e-books, and, of course, white papers. Not everyone knows what sets each type apart from all the rest or when to choose one over another.

Table 4-2 provides a summary of the differences between white papers and other common marketing materials. In the following sections, I compare and contrast white papers with each of these other pieces.

Table 4-2   White Papers and Other Documents

Item	Blog Post	Brochure	Case Study	e-Book	White Paper
Focus	One person's opinion	An idealized view of how an offering can help buyers	One customer's true experience	A primer on some topic, or just about anything else	Benefits of a certain offering, highlights of a certain issue, or new solution to a problem
Length	~400 to 800 words	2 to 8 pages	1 or 2 pages (~750 to 1,200 words)	10 to 100 pages	~3,000 to 5,000 words
Production values	Online, often text-only	Printed or PDF, with great design and flashy graphics	PDF, color photos, multiple columns like a magazine	PDF, usually landscape orientation, often good design and graphics	PDF, sometimes good design and color graphics
Lifespan	A few months, then outdated	Until the offering changes so it's out of date	1 year, then update	1 to 2 years, then update	1 to 2 years, then update
Effort	Easy, anyone can write one	Difficult, usually requires a designer, photographer, and illustrator	Medium, usually requires a designer	Medium to difficult, depending on scope	Difficult, this form takes years to master, can require a designer and illustrator
When to use	Anytime, depends on contents	Early in the sales funnel, at trade shows or industry events	Later in sales funnel	Early in the sales funnel	Throughout the sales funnel
Why to use	To engage prospects, customers, partners	To generate leads, engage prospects	To reassure prospects	To generate leads, engage prospects	To generate leads, nurture prospects, close sales, or build mindshare
Closest analogy	Letter to the editor	Television commercial	Word-of-mouth testimonial	Slide deck	Well-researched article in industry journal

Comparing white papers and blog posts

Most people can tell the difference between a white paper and a blog post. For starters, a white paper is much longer. Beyond that, a good white paper is based on established facts and logical arguments, like a well-researched article in an industry journal. But a blog post can be sheer opinion or even a rant, like a letter to the editor. Table 4-2 sums up the key differences between a blog post and a white paper.

After you write a white paper, you can easily create blog posts from it. In fact, a good white paper contains enough ideas to fuel several posts. Here's the best way to use both together:

1. Publish an effective white paper.

2. Extract one key idea to blog about.

3. At the end of the blog, point to the landing page for the full white paper.

4. Repeat Steps 2 and 3 to cover all the key ideas in the white paper.

Using the SEO power of your blog helps build visibility and downloads for your white paper. However, don't expect an instant rush of web traffic. Some SEO enthusiasts get overexcited and say a blog can generate vast amounts of traffic and push your site to the top of Google. This rarely happens in B2B marketing. Business buyers take a good white paper far more seriously than a blog post. And to achieve what B2B marketers want — a steady trickle of warm, qualified leads — white papers are in a whole different galaxy beyond blog posts.

The easiest and most informal flavor of white paper is a numbered list with a title like "6 Things You Must Know about BI Software before You Buy." After you publish a white paper as a numbered list, make sure to blog about it. Your blog can present the bare list of numbered points and direct readers who want more details to the full white paper. Your white paper can present more detail, more evidence, and more logical arguments than the blog post. (For more about blogging and white papers, head to Chapter 16.)

Contrasting white papers and brochures

White papers and brochures are almost complete opposites. Brochures are sales documents intended to create interest and desire, often by pushing *emotional buttons,* such as fear, greed, envy, or vanity. Brochures are generally colorful, flashy, and filled with promises, using copywriting and advertising techniques.

White papers, on the other hand, are persuasive essays about a certain B2B product, service, technology, methodology, or new solution to an old problem.

White papers persuade through irrefutable facts, ironclad logic, impeccable statistics, and quotes from industry opinion makers. They're generally less flashy and more factual. A white paper should be more dignified, substantial, and informative than a brochure, using plain English and the occasional rhetorical device. Refer to Table 4-2 to see how brochures and white papers differ.

Some companies simply reformat an existing brochure and call the results a white paper. Doing so is a waste of effort that irritates most readers when they discover you've given them nothing but a sales pitch. Take the time to write a proper white paper, and you'll be rewarded with more leads, better word of mouth, and increased sales.

Spotting the differences in white papers and case studies

Case studies are extended testimonials on how a product or service helped someone in the real world. They're typically 750 to 1,200 words long, written in a journalistic style with many quotes from the customer. The classic format for a case study is before/after or problem/solution. Case studies tend to be used later in the sales cycle to reassure a prospect that other buyers just like them benefited from the same offering and are prepared to endorse the vendor.

White papers, on the other hand, are persuasive essays, generally 3,000 words or more, written in a somewhat academic style, with no direct quotes from the vendor. A white paper may use the problem/solution structure but rarely before/after. White papers tend to be used earlier in the sales cycle to help prospects visualize a possible solution to a nagging problem. At a certain point in the sales funnel, most prospects switch from looking at white papers to looking at case studies, and that's fine. Table 4-2 lists the key differences between the two.

You can include a brief case study inside a white paper, either as a sidebar, a proof point in the text, or a pull quote. You'll likely need to condense the case study and include only the bare outline of the story, such as the bottom-line results. But you can't include a white paper inside a case study; a white paper is just too long and too different.

Telling white papers and e-books apart

I'm not talking about an e-Pub version of the latest vampire novel for tweens or a 99¢ e-book on how to clean a fish in four easy steps. I'm thinking only of the e-books published by B2B companies as part of their marketing efforts. And these two marketing documents — an e-book and a white paper — are often the most difficult of all to tell apart.

When to use an e-book rather than a white paper

Here are three scenarios when an e-book may work better for your company than a white paper:

- ✔ **Your audience is especially prone to distraction.** They may be young or often on the road. An e-book may sound like more fun than a white paper, which may sound like a lot of work.

- ✔ **Many of your competitors publish white papers.** If you're trying to break through the noise of competing white papers, an e-book may sound different enough to be engaging. You may gain more traction by presenting the content as an e-book rather than a white paper.

- ✔ **You have superior design skills on hand.** If you're aiming to make a splash with an e-book, you need to make it look really good. B2B e-books benefit from the lack of standards, because so few formatting conventions constrain you. You can use different backgrounds, wild typefaces, animated graphics, and other visual flourishes that may turn off readers in a white paper.

The goals of many white papers and e-books are the same. An ideal e-book helps your target audience members understand an issue, solve a problem, or make a decision. If your content does that, you can call it an e-book, a white paper, or whatever, and your audience will still appreciate it.

Last year, I wrote a big e-book for a client. Before I started, I searched high and low for guidance on what makes a good e-book. How long should they be? How many graphics? Landscape or portrait format? Unfortunately, it looks like an e-book can be just about any length on just about any topic. Some experts say that e-books are just gussied-up white papers turned on their sides. In any case, Table 4-2 highlights the key differences between a B2B e-book and a white paper.

With no clear standards or conventions established yet for e-books, people call just about anything an e-book. An e-book can be anywhere from 10 to 100 pages long and packaged as a PDF, slide deck, or some lesser-known format. An e-book can have a lot of color and graphics, or not much at all. Fans of e-books call them "the hip and stylish younger sister to the nerdy white paper," while those of the opposite opinion say things like, "put some lipstick on a white paper and you've got an e-book."

Figuring Out Who Writes and Reads White Papers

Knowing the types of people and companies that get involved with white papers can help peel back another layer of the mystery. This section answers the frequently asked questions that start with *who,* such as who publishes white papers, who reads them, who hires people to write them, and who gets hired to write them.

Who publishes white papers?

B2B vendors publish white papers to help attract and nurture prospects, close sales, and get attention. White papers abound in the technology sector to explain the latest software and hardware products. But more and more white papers are written about many other types of B2B offerings.

In fact, any B2B vendor selling anything relatively new, complex, or expensive could likely benefit from a white paper. That definition includes many hundreds of thousands of companies in all the following sectors:

- ✔ Business services
- ✔ Computer and peripheral makers
- ✔ Construction companies
- ✔ Consulting firms
- ✔ Delivery and transport services
- ✔ Educational suppliers and private schools
- ✔ Electrical and electronic gear
- ✔ Energy companies
- ✔ Environmental or "green tech"
- ✔ Government, NGOs, and nonprofits
- ✔ Healthcare devices, products, and services
- ✔ Heavy equipment manufacturers, such as aerospace, factory systems, ships, transit systems, and trains
- ✔ Real estate (commercial)
- ✔ Technical services, laboratories, quality control, and testing

On the other hand, vendors of any relatively familiar, simple, and inexpensive B2C (business to consumer) products don't often publish white papers because they have little need for them. After all, most consumers don't want to read a six- or eight-page paper before they buy something. The exceptions, especially in the health and medical fields, include consumers who need or prefer to be extremely well informed about their choices.

Who reads white papers?

Almost any businessperson contemplating the purchase of a relatively new, complex, or high-priced product or service for his business may well read some white papers about it. White paper readers come from a number of roles in business, such as the following:

- Corporate executives (decision makers)
- Finance executives (financial recommenders)
- IT managers and staff (technical recommenders)
- Line-of-business managers (managers of potential users)
- User representatives (potential users)
- In-house supporters of the purchase ("champions")

In larger companies, up to 25 of these people may sit together on a selection committee that makes a collective decision. In smaller firms, some people may wear several of these hats and meet informally to discuss their purchase.

White papers are especially well read by IT managers. One survey showed that they read 30 white papers a year, and some read more than one a week! White papers used to be aimed strictly at IT professionals, but today, many less technical people are involved in major buying decisions, especially executives from finance teams. These people are seeking plain-language explanations with clear business benefits, backed up by convincing facts and arguments. And business people in any role routinely pass good white papers up and down the chain of command, both to their managers and their staff. They may also pass them to peers or partners in other firms.

Who hires people to write white papers?

In my experience, the business people who hire a contract white paper writer from outside a company are mainly marketing managers. Because most white papers are published as part of a content marketing campaign, the responsibility to produce and promote them falls naturally to the marketing department. Nearly all the requests for white papers that I get come from a marketing manager.

At times, a product manager in a large company may commission a white paper. Even rarer, the head of R&D or engineering or another technical manager may request a white paper to help explain some details about a complex offering. Even then, these executives most likely turn to the marketing department for help finding a writer, managing the project, and promoting the finished document.

Who writes white papers?

Professional or nonprofessional writers, either in-house employees or independent contractors hired from outside, can write white papers. The nonprofessional writers who produce white papers can be engineers, product managers, sales people, members of the management team, or even company founders. Recent surveys show that 50 to 60 percent of B2B companies that do content marketing outsource some or all of their efforts. Writing a white paper is likely to be outsourced because white papers are a difficult format that can take years to master.

Most of the independent white paper writers I've met have come into the field from three main paths. Some are experienced technical writers who were asked to write white papers for their company and became intrigued by these documents, which are more interesting to work on than technical manuals. Some are seasoned journalists who got laid off by a newspaper, decided to hang out their shingles as independent writers, and appreciate the factual nature of white papers. Others are skilled copywriters who decided to focus solely or partly on writing white papers so they could offer that as a new service to their B2B marketing clients. See Chapter 2 for tips on how to succeed in white papers if you come from any of these writing backgrounds.

Understanding Why White Papers Are So Useful

Here comes perhaps the most fundamental question of all: Why bother? This section answers the frequently asked questions starting with *why*. I address why companies publish white papers, why prospects read them, and why writers write them. These answers speak to the purpose of white papers and their tremendous effectiveness when they're done well.

Why do companies publish white papers?

In general, vendors publish white papers for three key reasons: to generate leads at the top of the sales funnel, to nurture prospects through the middle of the funnel, or to help close sales at the bottom of the funnel. Some publish white papers to attract attention, to redefine a market space, or to stake out a position as a leader in their industry. In the end, all these goals are measured the same: Are we attracting enough leads? And are we closing enough sales?

B2B vendors publish white papers for all these reasons:

- ✔ Gather leads for the sales force.
- ✔ Educate potential customers.
- ✔ Influence a selection committee.
- ✔ Educate the sales force or channel partners.
- ✔ Educate the media.
- ✔ Send to a trade publication or website.
- ✔ Redefine a market space.
- ✔ Build credibility or mindshare.
- ✔ Keep up with competitors who have white papers.

On a strategic level, white papers fit into the growing trend of "marketing with content." This model acknowledges that skeptical prospects are hungry for a vendor who can serve as a trusted advisor, not just a peddler of their wares. A white paper can serve this purpose remarkably well.

Why do prospects read white papers?

White paper readers are seeking useful information to help them understand an issue, solve a problem, or make a decision. This often involves learning about the features and benefits of a product or service they're considering buying. A survey of IT managers by Forbes.com and Bitpipe (now TechTarget) showed that they read white papers for the following reasons:

- ✔ To stay on top of new trends (76 percent)
- ✔ To get information about products and vendors (69 percent)
- ✔ To compare products (50 percent)
- ✔ To help justify buying decisions (42 percent)
- ✔ To develop a shortlist of qualified vendors (33 percent)

This list sounds realistic to me. Business people must try to stay current with their field, compare different vendors accurately, and make wise decisions. White papers can help them with all these challenges.

Why do writers write white papers?

Writers write white papers for three main reasons: the money, the change of pace, and the challenge.

✔ **For the money:** Doing white papers pays better than most other formats of B2B copywriting, such as autoresponders, brochures, e-mails, or web pages. You can earn more as a copywriter if you happen to write the control-busting sales letter of the year and get royalties on all the sales that letter generates for the next five years. However, something like that rarely happens. For most copywriters, getting paid $5,000 to write a six- to eight-page factual article is a big assignment at great pay. For some specific estimates of the earning potential in this field, see "How much can a writer earn doing white papers?," later in this chapter. For more on the overall opportunities for writers in white papers, see Chapter 2.

✔ **For the change of pace:** Technical writers often work on 200- or 300-page manuals that take months to complete (I speak from experience). Journalists regularly write short news stories or light fare focused on human interest or celebrities; they don't often get to sink their teeth into substantial subjects. Copywriters usually work on a steady diet of sales letters or web copy. A white paper gives a writer stuck in one of these ruts a welcome change to do a piece that may be longer, shorter, more interesting, more serious, more factual, or more persuasive than what they usually work on. This change of pace helps writers stretch their creative muscles, which many people appreciate.

✔ **For the challenge:** One of the most challenging assignments in B2B marketing is helping a company articulate the competitive features and benefits of an offering and how it can solve an old problem better than anything else. Doing the research to find enough convincing proof is one part of that challenge; another is choosing the most effective rhetorical devices to deliver the message.

Pinpointing the Wheres of White Papers

Location, location, location: That's certainly an adage in real estate, and it does drive the frequently asked questions starting with *where*. In this section, I touch on where prospects find white papers, where they read them, where white papers originally came from, and where they're likely going.

Where do B2B prospects find white papers?

In the old days, many business buyers got white papers sent to them by salespeople or handed to them at trade show booths. Today, business people tend to find white papers through online searches, social media, content networks, and vendor websites.

- ✔ **Online searches:** Most business people today start their research on any topic by doing an online search, mainly in Google, which gets the majority of all online searches. They may search for their problem as a complete phrase, something like "ERP software as a service." Or they may search with a shorter acronym, like "ERP SAAS."

- ✔ **Social media:** Blogs can be a great place to find out about a new white paper, and so can other popular social media used by business people, such as Google+, LinkedIn, Twitter, or YouTube. The jury is still out on how effective Facebook, Pinterest, and other social media are for B2B marketing.

- ✔ **Content networks:** Many B2B prospects use content networks like Bitpipe, KnowledgeStorm, TechRepublic, and others to find relevant white papers. You can be sure to find white papers on industry trends in these sources, which are most often linked to a whole armload of industry forums and publications.

  In fact, these content networks make it extremely easy to get an instant snapshot of their most popular white paper downloads. Here are three ways to check on the current hot topics:

  - Go to Bitpipe (www.bitpipe.com) and notice the similar list of Popular Topics. Then click Most Popular Reports to see the 50 most downloaded white papers for the day.

  - Go to KnowledgeStorm (www.knowledgestorm.com) and notice the list of Top Requested Categories.

  - Go to TechRepublic (www.techrepublic.com/whitepapers) and see the Hottest and Top Rated white papers.

- ✔ **Vendor websites:** Another likely place to find white papers is on the websites of vendors active in a certain field. Of course, you have to know their names in advance, so this approach favors the usual suspects — the top vendors in any field. Business prospects may be looking for a different approach, perhaps from some new vendor they've never heard of before.

Where do people read white papers?

Because white papers are about business, many people read them at work at their desks. But not everyone stays put all day long, so many business people access white papers from laptops and tablets while moving from one client site to another, during their daily commutes, or on airplanes or trains during longer trips. Some people catch up on their reading at home in the evenings or on the weekend.

In the old days, white papers were all designed to read as hard copy on paper. Today, more people read them right off the screen. Again, these screens may be large, such as on a desktop monitor; medium, such as on an iPad or other tablet; or pint-size, such as on a mobile phone. The design and content of an effective white paper must work well in all these form factors to truly reach all possible members of the target audience where they do business.

Where did white papers first come from?

Strangely enough, the term *white paper* is an accident of history. This term first arose early in the 20th century in Great Britain, when it was used to distinguish government report and position papers bound with white covers from longer reports and policy books with blue covers. I found a PDF of a white paper from 1907, and these documents were being published for some years before then.

White papers were often used in science and medicine during World War II, the 1950s, and the 1960s. With the rise of the personal computer in the '80s, white papers became quite popular in the IT industry. And in the '90s, the web provided an inexpensive distribution channel that sparked today's ongoing explosion of white papers. All in all, this long-form marketing document has been going strong for close to 100 years. For details about the history of white papers, see Chapter 3.

Where are white papers going in the future?

For the near future, white papers should continue to be popular with marketers and prospects. Over the longer term, new formats for delivering information will continue to be explored. For the kind of persuasive B2B content usually packaged as a white paper, I believe these new formats will include multimedia PDFs containing audio, animation, interaction, or video; microsites built around a core white paper; infographics with layered content for a viewer to browse on demand; and mobile apps that combine information and visuals with interaction.

Packaging B2B information for each of these channels will require different skills and production methods. Some may well offer a more engaging experience for certain audiences, especially members of the so-called Millennial Generation born after 1985, who grew up with the web and mobile technology — essentially enjoying "the world in their pocket." For more about the likely future of white papers, see Chapter 3.

Tracking the Whens of White Papers

No time like the present to get into the most frequently asked questions starting with *when*. In this section, I answer questions about when companies publish white papers, when prospects read them, and when each type is the most useful.

When do companies publish white papers?

Companies don't publish white papers in any special month or season. And a white paper isn't more effective at a particular time of the month or day of the week. A more useful way to analyze when companies publish white papers is to look at the sales cycle for any offering. The longer a B2B sales cycle — that is, the longer B2B prospects spend in the sales funnel — the more likely the vendor uses white papers to attract and engage them.

Problem/solution white papers are most effective early on, to draw fresh leads into the top of the sales funnel. Numbered lists can be used anywhere in the sales funnel to attract or nurture leads or attack competitors on the prospect's shortlist. Backgrounders are most useful near the bottom of the sales funnel to provide technical details an evaluator needs to help compare several offerings.

When do B2B prospects read white papers?

Prospects look at white papers before they make a purchase. Companies give these stages different names, such as Vision or Planning. People tend to read white papers when they need to

✔ Dream up a way around a pressing problem.

✔ Wonder whether anything could solve their problem.

✔ Look for something to satisfy their wish list.

✔ Research what's on the market.

✔ Make up a shortlist of qualified vendors.

Executives at the content network KnowledgeStorm encourage technology vendors to think of a sale in four phases, and white papers can help during the first three.

- ✔ **Stage 1 — Vision:** A businessperson struggles with a problem and imagines how to solve it. At this point, a problem/solution white paper can help him visualize a new way to solve the problem. Or a provocative numbered list can help gain his attention.

- ✔ **Stage 2 — Planning:** A prospect tries to map a set of functional requirements to a certain offering. That's when a more detailed, technical backgrounder can help him understand how a given solution would work in his environment. Or a numbered list can attack another vendor or reframe the buyer's checklist.

- ✔ **Stage 3 — Evaluation:** A prospect looks at a set of offerings from a shortlist of vendors. A backgrounder in the form of an evaluator's guide for a complex product can be helpful at this point. Somewhere in here, most B2B buyers start looking more at case studies about other customers than at any additional white papers.

- ✔ **Stage 4 — Acquisition:** A buyer purchases an offering. The customer may need added information at this point, but it's more accurate to call this production information, documentation, or training material. After all, the white paper has played its role and the sale has been made. Everything from this point on is after-sales training and support.

When should a company use each type of white paper?

Each type of white paper works best to deliver certain information at a certain time. Depending on your marketing challenge, you can pick the best type to meet that goal, as follows:

- ✔ To get attention with provocative views: numbered list

- ✔ To build recognition for your company: problem/solution

- ✔ To support a product launch: backgrounder

- ✔ To educate your sales force, channel partners, analysts, bloggers, or journalists: problem/solution

- ✔ To generate leads at the top of the sales funnel: problem/solution

- ✔ To nurture prospects in the middle of the funnel: numbered list

- ✔ To attack competitors anywhere in the funnel: numbered list

- ✔ To support a technical evaluation at the bottom of the funnel: backgrounder

- ✔ To help close sales at the bottom of the funnel: backgrounder

You can always combine a numbered list with either a backgrounder or a problem/solution to accomplish the same goal. For more on the three main types of white papers, see Part II.

Figuring Out the Hows of White Papers

Everybody likes to know how to do stuff. This section covers the most frequently asked questions that start with *how*. Here, you find answers for how long a white paper takes to create, how much it costs (if you're a marketing manager), how much you can earn writing white papers (if you're a writer), how to tell whether a company needs a white paper, and how many white papers are "enough" for any company.

How do people read white papers?

Almost everyone has more to read, more to remember, and more to do than he can possibly get to. For example, one study showed that the typical manager has more than 50 hours of work sitting right on his desk. He's certainly not waiting for another document to add to the pile.

No one reads white papers for fun; white papers are for work. And people don't read white papers the same way they read a novel by their favorite author, paying attention to every sentence. Instead, they tend to skim, scan, and skip — especially when they're reading on the screen. So a wall of gray text unrelieved by any graphics isn't likely to engage many white paper readers. Today, these documents must be carefully written and designed for business readers with limited time and attention.

White papers need to use visual breakers — bullets, graphics, headings, pull quotes, sidebars, and tables — to direct the attention of people who skim, scan, and skip. These visuals need to point out the key messages of the document in a way that's easy for today's busy readers to follow. For tips on how to design a white paper, see Chapter 18.

How long does a white paper take to create?

The typical white paper takes between 24 and 50 hours to complete, according to a survey of more than 600 writers in 2007. That means the equivalent of one to two weeks of full-time effort. But don't expect to complete a white paper in one to two weeks of elapsed time. This process doesn't happen in one smooth, continuous workflow; there are lags while the client and writer wait for one another and other team members.

Like any corporate writing project, creating a white paper involves interviews, research, outlining, writing drafts, and doing graphics and page design. The client will expect a few progress reports. And the writer will need to incorporate comments into at least two drafts, maybe more. If you manage this process well, writing a white paper can be smooth and efficient. If not, it can turn into the never-ending project that drags on and on and on.

The more experience a white paper writer has, the faster he tends to work, and the fewer missteps he takes. The survey showed that freelancers tend to produce significantly faster than in-house or nonprofessional writers.

In my own experience on close to 200 white papers, each project takes about six weeks of elapsed time. This span includes everything from the first discussions between the client and the writer through the entire 12-step process described in Part III up to the delivery of a finished white paper. And it can easily take longer, if subject matter experts travel a lot, take their time to do interviews or reviews, or manage to get deadlocked over some issue.

The research, writing, and approvals of the text alone take a minimum of four weeks, unless the project is put on an intense fast track; in this case, most writers will bill extra for a rush job. The design, illustration, proofing, and perhaps translation add at least another two weeks or more. And then the promotions begin and can run for many months, as described in Chapter 16.

The good news is, a B2B vendor can often continue using the same white paper — at least one structured as a problem/solution — for a year or more. This long life span helps achieve a positive return on the investment of so much time.

How much does a white paper cost?

Any way you look at it, a white paper is a significant project that requires a budget of thousands of dollars. Trying to do a white paper on a tiny budget of a few hundred dollars likely won't generate the kind of results you need — unless you're one of those Renaissance individuals who can research, write, design, and promote a professional-quality document all by yourself. And if you can do all of that, please give me a call; I want to hire you.

Here are the possible costs related to producing a white paper, which can be either outsourced or handled in-house:

- Researching, writing, and editing
- Illustration and design
- Translation, if required
- Printing, if required
- Promotions Ex: press release

Table 4-3 sums up all these costs of outsourcing a white paper in three possible scenarios. Remember these are only estimates, and your costs may well vary.

Table 4-3	Costs for Outsourcing a White Paper			
Item	*Price Range*	*Cut-Rate White Paper*	*Typical White Paper*	*Major White Paper*
Researching, writing, and editing	$2,500 to $10,000	$2,500	$5,000	$7,000
Illustration and design	$1,000 to $2,000	$0	$1,000	$3,000 total for three different versions
Translation	$1,000 per language	$0	$0	$2,000 for two
Printing	$1 to $2.50 per copy	$0 for 0 copies	$250 for 100 copies	$4,500 for 2,000 copies
Promotions	$500 to $10,000+	$500	$1,000	$10,000
	Total Costs	**$3,000**	**$7,250**	**$26,500**

The column marked *Cut-Rate White Paper* in Table 4-3 covers a low-end project: hiring an inexperienced writer, pressing him for graphics and design, and doing no promotions except a press release. Even with this barely acceptable quality, the costs add up to $3,000. You can see how unrealistic it is to expect a winning white paper from such a low budget, especially when most competitors are routinely spending twice as much.

The *Typical White Paper* budget covers a better-than-average writer, a professional designer, and printing 250 color copies for smaller events. But the paper isn't translated, and the company's left with only $1,000 to run a few promotions. The bottom line for this effort comes to $7,250. Any white paper produced on this kind of budget can do well, if the vendor makes sure to plan, produce, and promote it effectively.

The third scenario, marked *Major White Paper,* covers everything a B2B vendor could dream of spending on a white paper. This budget includes a top writer plus translations into two other languages, perhaps Spanish and French to cover the rest of the Americas. Design costs allow for three different versions, one in each language. The company can afford to print 2,000 copies in color for a big event, with another $10,000 for other promotions. The total budget comes to $26,500. For that kind of money — as long as the content is compelling and well targeted — a vendor should get one of the standout white papers of the year in its sector.

Counting the costs of researching, writing, and editing

Most writers do their own research, based on materials and directions given by the client. And very few writers pay for their own editing, so you can lump these three expenses into one. For pricing information, I drew on four sources: interviews with the content networks; estimates from AWAI, the country's largest copywriting training center; the latest annual *Writer's Market,* and the largest survey of white paper writers ever done. The average from all four sources is $4,180. I bumped that up to $5,000 to cover a better-than-average writer for the typical scenario, and to $7,000 to cover an expert writer for the major scenario.

Adding up the fees for illustration and design

Illustration and design cost significantly less than writing. Although these creative steps add tremendous value to a white paper, they take significantly less time than writing a white paper from scratch. For a round estimate, count on about $1,000 for several relatively simple graphics and a straightforward design of six to eight pages of content, a cover, and the rest of the front matter and back matter. For a major project with more illustration work, double that to $2,000. If the designer has to repour the translated text into each other version, count each translation as another job, because many pages will likely need tweaked.

Saving without scrimping on translation

Translation from English into other European languages is most often priced by the word. Don't scrimp here. And by all means, don't rely on machine translation for such an important marketing document. If you do, your carefully composed text could end up sounding silly, illogical, or even insulting in another language. Expect to pay about 25¢ a word for a white paper translation, which works out to less than $1,000 for any document up to 4,000 words. It's worth it.

Ideally, find a translator who is a native speaker of the target language, an accomplished communicator, who can work right in the source file from your designer, most likely an InDesign file. If you get lucky here, you can avoid sending each translation of the white paper back to your designer because your translator can return the InDesign file with the translated text right on the pages and everything looking sharp. Your translation budget may go up a little to pay for this expertise, but your design budget won't.

Most other languages run longer than English; for example, French takes 15 or 20 percent more characters to convey the same meaning. Spanish can be even more. So if you know your white paper will be translated into other languages, ask your designer to leave lots of white space at the bottom of columns and not cram in the headings. The extra space gives a design-savvy translator more room to work in. If your designer doesn't like that idea, consider switching to a more flexible supplier.

Factoring in the cost of printing

Printing costs depend on many variables: the number of pages, amount of color, paper quality, number of copies, binding, and any extras like covers. To check prices, I sent a typical 11-page white paper with modest color on every page to FedEx (formerly Kinko's) and Staples asking for quotes on 10 and 100 copies. With a plastic coil binding, quotes ranged from $1.20 to $2.20 a copy, depending on the paper, number of copies, and extras; taxes and delivery are extra.

Outsourced printing adds up, but it may be justified if your company routinely spends more than $100 to generate a lead, or if you're going to a big event like a trade show where you know your team will want to hand out your latest white paper.

Of course, if you need only two or three copies for a meeting, many business people just print them on their own color printers for a few dollars' worth of ink or toner. In fact, most prospects print their own white papers after downloading them, which is a key reason the use of white papers exploded with the web — vendors no longer have to pay for printing or distribution; prospects now serve themselves.

Pinning a price on promoting

Promoting a white paper can cost next to nothing, or it can exceed all the rest of the budget put together. Many companies stick to the no-fee or low-fee tactics, which don't run up any costs beyond the normal payroll for a marketing team. Others use some of the more high-cost tactics, such as syndicating a white paper on a content network or advertising in trade magazines (see Chapter 16). One cost that's easy to justify is sending out a press release about a white paper through a web-based service for a few hundred dollars. I consider this a must-do for any white paper, no matter how small the budget.

Accounting for in-house costs

One other cost is the soft cost for all in-house efforts, including the time it takes subject matter experts to answer questions and review drafts — perhaps two to four hours per reviewer — and the time it takes to manage a white paper project — likely six to eight hours. And finally, there's the time it takes marketing staff to plan and execute all the white paper promotions, which can vary from a few hours to several weeks. Because this cost is so variable and hard to calculate, I left it out of Table 4-3.

The more experienced the writer you work with, and the closer he sticks to the 12-step process explained in Part III, the lower those in-house efforts should be. That's because the writer will know how to engineer the project for success, interview efficiently, write a series of staged deliverables for your approval instead of jumping into the first draft too early, and generally avoid misunderstandings, false starts, and rework.

How much can a writer earn doing white papers?

White paper writers work either in-house or as independent freelancers, most often called copywriters. Unfortunately, labor statistics don't break out this full-time job as a separate profession; it's even lumped in with screenwriters and poets, who obviously work on quite different projects from white paper writers.

Working as an in-house copywriter

You don't likely have a steady diet of white papers to write. More likely, you write a mix of blog articles, case studies, press releases, tweets, and an occasional white paper as a big project. You may work either for a B2B vendor or for a creative agency that does the whole range of advertising, PR, and other campaigns.

According to several salary surveys, junior in-house copywriters in the United States typically earn $30,000 to $45,000, while senior copywriters can make up to $85,000. Intermediates rank somewhere in the middle, with benefits on top of salary in all cases. As so many other things do, these salaries fall into a bell curve, with most copywriters clumped in the middle and a few exceptionally high- and low-paid people at the edges.

Working as an independent copywriter

You can focus entirely on white papers, or you can write them as one of many types of documents and projects that you take on. Most full-time independent copywriters aspire to earn more than $100,000 because they must pay for their own benefits and retirement.

I've promoted myself exclusively as "That White Paper Guy" since 2005, yet I make only two-thirds of my income from white papers. The rest comes from writing case studies, coaching other writers, giving workshops, and even dabbling in writing mysteries. So expecting that you can write nothing but white papers as a self-employed independent is unrealistic.

Calculating your income from four factors

Four factors determine your income as a full-time white paper writer, and the good news is that you're pretty much in control of all four:

- How many white papers you can land
- How long it takes you to complete each project
- How much you work in a year
- How much you charge for each white paper

Here are three realistic scenarios for a beginner, an intermediate, and a senior white paper writer. Say you're a beginner in the field, without a developed network, an established presence, or any strong specialty you can claim. Because you're just starting to master the white paper format, the typical project takes you 60 hours, spread across four weeks or so. You're not booked solid and you spend a lot of time working on your website, your social media platform, and other marketing. And you charge a beginner's rate of $3,000 each. So all told, you do 12 to 15 white papers a year for $3,000 each to gross around $40,000. That's one possible scenario at the low end.

At the other extreme, suppose you're a seasoned freelancer who decided to focus on white papers a few years ago. With a strong network, an established specialty in a sector that uses many white papers, and great marketing, you now bring in as many projects as you can handle. Say you master the white paper format, so you get to the faster end of the spectrum where you can finish most of them in about 30 hours. So if you avoid distractions, you can comfortably finish one white paper in the equivalent of a week.

You take 6 weeks of vacation, so you work 46 weeks a year, although you still have to allow time to do some marketing, maintain your network, and manage your business. And you charge a realistic $6,000 per project. That means you can handily complete 30 white papers a year, for gross revenue of $180,000. Maybe you can push a bit to do a little more. Not bad at all!

There are two examples of possible freelance scenarios, at income levels of $40,000 and $180,000 a year. A third scenario, for an intermediate writer coming in somewhere between these two extremes, would mean revenues topping $100,000. You can surely earn that kind of money if you master the white paper format, bring in enough projects, complete each one diligently, put in an honest day's work, and charge a competitive rate for your efforts.

How can you tell whether a company needs a white paper?

You may work as a marketing manager and wonder whether your B2B company should be using white papers. Or you may be a white paper writer sizing up a possible client and wondering whether it could benefit from a white paper or two. Here are three simple questions that give you the answer:

- ✔ Does the company sell something new?
- ✔ Does the company sell something complex?
- ✔ Does the company sell something expensive?

If you can answer "yes" to at least one of these questions, the company could probably benefit from using white papers. If you can answer "yes" to two or three of those questions, the company can definitely use white papers.

Any B2B vendor selling anything relatively new, complex, or expensive probably needs one or more white papers to help tell its story. Whether the company sells a product, a service, a technology, or a methodology, it still needs one. Whether the company uses that white paper to gather leads, nurture prospects, undercut competitors, or cement sales, it still needs one.

Why these three questions? White papers help companies describe new innovations that are difficult to research anywhere else. White papers also help companies describe complicated offerings that take a little explaining to sketch in their features and benefits and how they solve an existing problem better than anything else. And white papers help nurture prospects through a long sales cycle, creating another touch point for the vendor and helping position the company as a trusted advisor that provides truly helpful information.

How many white papers does Acme NLP need?

No neat formula tells a company how many white papers it needs. So here's a sample company to consider. Acme NLP (Natural Language Processing) is a software startup with a smarter way to analyze English. The company seeks partners to embed its language processor into help systems and virtual personas. The marketing director wants to use white papers to get attention and generate leads. So how many white papers does Acme NLP need?

To find the answer, I run through all the questions I discuss in the "How many white papers are 'enough' for a company?" section.

✔ **Experience:** No one in the firm has ever created a white paper. So Acme NLP should probably start slowly with one or two, then review what it learned.

✔ **Market segments:** Acme NLP needs clients who create online help and virtual personas. Are these two segments so different that each needs its own white paper? If yes, the company needs two documents or one "cloned" into two versions.

✔ **Problems solved:** The language processor really solves one big problem, getting machines to understand natural language. So two papers will still be enough.

✔ **Competition:** The company has a couple of competitors and each has one white paper. So two will do for Acme NLP to hold its own against the competition.

✔ **Budget:** The marketing director can get the budget for two white papers in the next two quarters, giving Acme NLP the answer. For now, two white papers will be enough. Those two documents may be enough to do everything that Acme needs to attract partners and stay on track with its business plans. After that, the company can review the results and revisit this exercise to see how many white papers it needs for the following period.

White papers are now a standard part of the marketing arsenal for most technology companies. After all, many of their offerings are new and complicated, so that's two out of three right off the bat. And many businesses in other sectors, if they can answer "yes" to at least one of these questions, could well benefit from using white papers as the capstone of their content marketing.

How many white papers are "enough" for a company?

Marketing people often wonder: How many white papers should our company publish? How many white papers are really enough? The correct answer, of course, is "that all depends." You can figure out what that depends on in several ways.

For example, one of my clients asks me to write a white paper every time his sales force comes up against a serious objection. The more objections, the more white papers. After a few years, we've covered all the big objections his prospects have come up with so far. But isn't there a more scientific method? Yes, there is. And here's a list of factors to help you find that answer for your company or your client. (Also see the nearby sidebar "How many white papers does Acme NLP need?" for an example using these factors.)

- ✔ **Experience:** How many white papers has the company published so far? If the answer is none, it's probably best to do one or two to figure out the process.

- ✔ **Market segments:** How many markets does the company cover? It likely needs at least one new white paper for each significant market at a certain interval, such as two to four times a year. You can define these segments in the following ways:

   - By vertical market: Education, finance, retail, travel, or whatever

   - By size: Small, enterprise, Fortune 500, or Fortune 100

   - By volume: Number of employees, SKUs, transactions, or whatever

   - By role of prospects: Financial, line of business, management team, technical, user, or business owner

   - By product line

- ✔ **Problems solved:** How many big problems does the company solve? Does it need one white paper for each? Sometimes each "problem" has a separate product line with its own marketing team; in this case, you may want to treat each team as a separate company to work out how many white papers it needs.

- ✔ **Competition:** Does the company have aggressive competitors that publish white papers? How many? The scope and pace of competition can certainly be a factor here.

- ✔ **Budget:** How many white papers can the company afford to create and promote effectively? If the company has the budget for only one white paper per quarter, four a year may have to be enough.

A small company with relatively few competitors may need to produce only a couple of white papers per year. This small number likely fits the company's limited budget, staffing, and time resources, too.

A larger company with more aggressive competitors may clearly need more white papers. For example, a medium-sized company with three main markets may want one white paper for each market every quarter. In this case, 12 white papers a year are enough.

And a Fortune 500 company likely has many product managers, each wanting white papers for their individual products. For a company this size, there's no need to calculate how many white papers are enough. In this case, the real answer may be "as many as all those product managers want and can pay for."

Part II
The Three Flavors of White Papers

Vanilla:
The Backgrounder

Strawberry:
The Numbered List

Chocolate:
The Problem/Solution

Mash-up No. 1:
The Backgrounder
+
The Numbered List

Mash-up No. 2:
The Problem/Solution
+
The Numbered List

Illustration by Wiley, Composition Services Graphics

Go to www.dummies.com/extras/whitepapers to access the Cheat Sheet created specifically for *White Papers For Dummies*.

In this part . . .

- ✔ Find out how to choose the appropriate white paper based on your purpose and target audience.

- ✔ Understand how a backgrounder allows you to provide detailed information about your company's product or service. These straightforward documents are as predictable as vanilla ice cream.

- ✔ Discover how to use a numbered list to present information in an easy-to-read format that focuses on the highlights of your topic. These papers are often as light and lively as strawberry ice cream.

- ✔ See how a problem/solution uses facts and logic to present a new solution to a serious problem that afflicts a given industry. These papers are complex, but they're also as rich and satisfying as chocolate ice cream.

- ✔ Figure out how to mix and match different types of white papers to address two goals at once.

- ✔ Know the special elements to include in some white papers but to leave out in others.

Chapter 5

Picking the Perfect Flavor for Your Next White Paper

The world of white papers can seem pretty overwhelming. And most white paper "experts" don't help by insisting that there are eight or ten distinct types of white papers. That's a lot to remember and a tough decision to make every time you want to create a new white paper. But are so many distinctions useful? Is all that complexity really needed? I don't think so. In this chapter, I explain why I believe there are really only three main types of white papers, as different as vanilla, strawberry, and chocolate ice cream.

When you understand these three flavors of white papers and how to use each one, you gain more flexibility to deal with a wider set of marketing challenges. And you're more likely to provide your target audience with helpful information that they can really use. Otherwise, you may dish out a mishmash that confounds their expectations and leaves them scratching their heads — or even worse, clicking away to look for a white paper from a competitor.

In this chapter, I introduce the three main flavors of white papers, sketch in their key characteristics, and suggest a simple, three-step process for picking the perfect flavor for your next project. Plus I tell you which flavors you can mix together for a tasty treat and which ones you should always keep in separate bowls.

Recognizing the Three Purposes of White Papers

Until a few years ago, I agreed with every other white paper expert when they pointed to 8 or 10 (or even 40!) different types of white papers. Most people in the white paper world talked about papers focused on business benefits, technical benefits, or a hybrid of both. We talked about papers for executive briefings, technical evaluations, market overviews, corporate vision, and on and on. Thinking that we had a number of different white papers to work with made perfect sense. After all, we needed a big set of tools in our marketing tool chest; otherwise, how could we pick the right tool for the job?

Then one day, I was compiling a list of all the white papers I'd ever worked on and impressed even myself when the total reached nearly 100. (Since then, my list has grown close to 200.)

As I thought back over all those projects, I was struck by a new realization: They all fall more or less into three big buckets. And each type works best for one of the three key purposes that marketers seek to accomplish with white papers:

- Generate leads.
- Get noticed or stand out from competitors.
- Explain the benefits of a product or service.

To be fair, when you include all the combinations among my three biggies, you have seven possible flavors in all. (I know, I've checked the math — many times — to make sure I got it right.) But only five of those really work; the other two just make a mess.

The three flavors I introduce in this chapter and cover in detail in the rest of Part II are fun to explore, simple to remember, and easy to use. When I explain this in workshops, I see people's eyes light up as they realize the world of white papers is a lot simpler than they feared. You'll still hear lots of experts counting more types of white papers than that, but you don't have to listen to them. Take that, Mr. 40-Different-Types-of-White-Papers Guy!

Defining the Three Flavors: Vanilla, Strawberry, and Chocolate

Ice cream comes in dozens of different flavors, from banana cream to white chocolate crunch. Yet year after year, three flavors are more popular than any others, according to the International Ice Cream Association and the NPD Group's National Eating Trends. (Yes, some people actually track these things closely.) The top flavors are always vanilla and chocolate, and nearly every year, strawberry comes in third.

It's the same with white papers. White papers may seem to come in a bewildering number of varieties, but when you really analyze them, three main flavors are more popular than any others. And these three basic flavors of white papers are as easy to tell apart as vanilla, strawberry, and chocolate ice cream.

Why do you need to know about these three flavors of white papers? For one thing, if you don't recognize the distinctions between different white papers, you may always use the same type, no matter what the circumstances. As the old saying goes, "When all you have is a hammer, everything looks like a nail." But when you understand these distinctions, you can use different flavors of white papers for different marketing challenges and target them effectively at B2B buyers at the top, middle, or bottom of the sales funnel. With this understanding, you gain more flexibility to deal with a wider range of marketing challenges.

Another reason to study these three flavors is because when B2B buyers seek out a white paper, they know which flavor they want. When you understand how to create each flavor of white paper, you can meet these expectations and give your target audience what they want.

I call these three flavors of white papers the backgrounder (vanilla), the numbered list (strawberry), and the problem/solution (chocolate). Table 5-1 sums up many characteristics of these three flavors. The rest of this chapter gives you an overview of the three types of papers. In Chapters 6, 7, and 8, I provide all the details you need to know about each flavor and how to use it for best results.

Table 5-1	Three Main Flavors of White Papers		
	Backgrounder (Vanilla)	**Numbered List (Strawberry)**	**Problem/Solution (Chocolate)**
Definition	A detailed look at the features and benefits of a certain product or service	A numbered set of tips, questions, answers, or points about some issue	A persuasive essay that uses facts and logic to present a new solution to a nagging problem
Also called	Evaluator's guide; product briefing	List-based article; X (number of) questions to ask; X tips on; X things you should know about	Special report; executive briefing; market overview
Audience	B2B buyers near the bottom of the sales funnel	Anyone interested in the issue, generally in the middle of the sales funnel	B2B buyers near the top of the sales funnel; also analysts, bloggers, channel partners, and journalists who cover your market
Approach	A factual description of the technical or business benefits of a product or service	A light and lively roundup of points or highlights about some issue	Useful information about an industry-wide problem that educates readers and positions the vendor as a trusted advisor
When to use	To support your firm's position as an undisputed leader in the field To support technical evaluations To support a product launch	To get attention with provocative views To cast FUD (fear, uncertainty, and doubt) on competitors To nurture prospects through a complex sale	To generate leads To educate your market To build recognition for your company

	Backgrounder (Vanilla)	Numbered List (Strawberry)	Problem/Solution (Chocolate)
Length	8+ pages plus cover	5 to 7+ pages plus cover	8 to 12 pages plus cover
Typical contents	Introduction	Introduction	Executive summary
	Features and benefits of each feature	Numbered points (between 3 and 9)	Industry-wide problem
	Conclusions and call to action	Conclusions and call to action (optional)	Existing solutions and drawbacks
	About the company	About the company (optional)	New, improved solution
			Case study (optional)
			Buyer's guide
			Conclusions and call to action
			About the company
Leave out	Attacks on competitors, hype, marketing speak, groupthink	Product features, hype, marketing speak	Frequent product mentions, hype, marketing speak
Repurpose as	Press release (at launch), slide deck, demo, webinar	Blog post, guest blog, e-newsletter article, placed article	Slide deck, webinar, blog post, placed article, conference presentation

Zooming in on the product: Plain vanilla

The oldest form of B2B white paper is as predictable and reassuring as vanilla ice cream. The *backgrounder* first began as a detailed description of the features of some industrial widget. The audience for this flavor was mainly engineers and technicians allergic to any marketing spin or "fluff" in the content. The earliest versions of these papers were published by vendors who needed to explain their products in more detail than they could in a short brochure or data sheet.

This form evolved over the years to cover the business benefits of any B2B products, and today the backgrounder can just as easily cover any service or even a methodology or business process.

But the focus is always on the vendor's offering. A backgrounder usually goes deep into the guts of a product or service to discuss how it can outperform, outlast, or undercut the competition. In this white paper, the product is firmly in the foreground, and the product name is often in the title.

A backgrounder is most useful at two points where a vendor's message must be extremely clear and crisp:

✔ To support the launch of a new product by explaining it to the vendor's sales force and channel partners plus any journalists, analysts, or bloggers who cover that space

✔ Near the bottom of the sales funnel, to help a technical evaluator size up the product or service against the competition

The leading firms in any market often use backgrounders to describe their offerings. You can find out much more about backgrounders in Chapter 6, including the pros and cons of this flavor and how to build and repurpose one for best results.

Making points quickly: Scrumptious strawberry

A second popular flavor of white paper is as light and refreshing as strawberry ice cream. This white paper is a *numbered list* built up from a set of questions, answers, issues, points, or tips about a particular topic. This format was likely modeled after those magazine articles with titles like "5 Tips on Getting Better Mileage" or "6 Ways to Keep Weight Off" or "7 Things to Ask before You Buy Life Insurance." This flavor also owes a nod to David Letterman's Top Ten Lists, a popular fixture on late night TV since 1985. A list-based approach appeals to anyone who wants a quick study on some issue, the bottom line on some controversy, or some inside tips on how to succeed in some area.

Readers appreciate the fact that a numbered list is, by definition, quick and easy to scan. The framework is clearly visible in the numbered points themselves, so you don't have to delve deep to see where it's going. This flavor is the fastest and easiest of all to write and the easiest to reuse as a guest blog or a placed article in a trade journal or industry website.

A numbered list works best for three purposes:

- ✔ To get attention with a provocative approach to some issue

- ✔ To cast FUD (fear, uncertainty, and doubt — a classic marketing technique) on competitors

- ✔ To nurture prospects through the middle of the sales funnel by keeping them engaged and mildly entertained

This flavor can cover the widest range of topics, including a product, service, technology, methodology, market, trend, issue, or debate. Just remember to keep it as light and lively as a dish of strawberry ice cream. You can find out much more about numbered lists in Chapter 7, including the pros and cons of this flavor and how to build and repurpose one for best results.

Finding a solution: Rich chocolate

The third main flavor of white paper is as rich and satisfying as a big dish of chocolate ice cream — with hot fudge, roasted almonds, whipped cream, and a cherry on top. This *problem/solution* white paper describes a nagging business problem and how to solve it. A white paper in this flavor has three main parts:

- ✔ The problem

- ✔ The existing solutions and their drawbacks

- ✔ A new, improved solution

The problem can be technical, financial, organizational, or anything else — as long as it's big, nasty, and recognized by your target readers. The existing solutions part rounds up all the conventional ways to deal with the problem and why none of them are truly satisfactory. That's how this flavor sets up and then knocks down all the competition. The traditional solutions aren't identified by vendor, but as generic categories, classes, or genres. Finally, this flavor shows what an ideal solution to the problem looks like and then — as late as possible in the document — identifies the vendor and its offering by name as a new, improved solution to the problem.

A good problem/solution white paper is truly useful to readers because it helps them see a nagging business problem in a more thoughtful way or gives them a better understanding that they can apply on the job. This flavor is the most educational because it explores an industry-wide problem, not just one vendor's product or a superficial take on some issue. Because of all the research and thinking that goes into this flavor, it's the most challenging to write. The upside is that the problem/solution white paper generates the best return on the time and money invested in it. And it's the longest lasting, too; many problem/solution white papers continue to get good results for years.

A problem/solution white paper works best for three purposes:

- ✔ To generate leads at the top of the sales funnel
- ✔ To educate your market
- ✔ To build recognition for your company

You can use a problem/solution white paper to educate your own sales forces, channel partners, and any analysts, bloggers, and journalists who cover your space. The whole content of a problem/solution white paper is driven by facts and logic, not by marketing hype or fluff. When it's truly effective, this flavor of white paper delivers all the rich satisfying taste of a big dish of chocolate ice cream. You can find out much more about problem/solution white papers in Chapter 8, including the pros and cons of this flavor and how to build and repurpose one for best results.

Making two tasty mash-ups

Just as strawberry goes well with either vanilla or chocolate, you can combine a numbered list with either other flavor of white paper for tasty results:

- ✔ Numbered list + backgrounder
- ✔ Numbered list + problem/solution

In either case, the liveliness of a numbered list can lighten up and streamline the more detailed presentation of the other flavor. For example, a white paper can discuss five key features of a certain product, combining the liveliness of a numbered list with the many product details of a backgrounder. Or you can organize a problem/solution white paper around three questions or three steps, lightening up the deep research of a problem/solution with the easy-to-read appeal of a numbered list.

Getting messy with other flavor combinations

Two mash-ups don't turn out so well. Combining the high-level overview of a problem/solution with the microscopic focus of a backgrounder is nearly impossible. Also, consider the purpose of these two flavors: A problem/solution white paper works best to generate leads at the top of the sales funnel, while a backgrounder helps support prospects close to making a buying decision at the bottom of the funnel. How can you address both ends of the funnel at once? In this case, vanilla and chocolate don't mix. Instead, keep these two flavors separate and produce two distinct white papers aimed at different audiences.

And don't even think about creating the white paper equivalent of Neapolitan ice cream: a three-way combo of vanilla, strawberry, and chocolate. How can you possibly layer a numbered list — ideal for the middle of the sales funnel — onto the other two flavors? How can one document possibly engage prospects at the top, middle, and bottom of the sales funnel all at once? Again, you're better off separating your messages into three better-targeted and more effective documents.

The simplest way to avoid either mess is to just keep the vanilla away from the chocolate. Neither flavor of white paper mixes well with the other.

Choosing the Right Flavor

Talking about these three main flavors of white papers and studying their characteristics is all well and good, but which one do you pick for your next white paper? How do you find the right tool for the job? Decisions, decisions.

Actually, deciding which white paper to use isn't that tricky when you think about it in three steps:

1. Reflect on the main purpose of your white paper.

2. Consider the preferences of your target audience.

3. Do a reality check on your target sector, industry, or vertical market. (In other words, ask yourself: Will this be the first white paper anyone ever used in that sector?)

Although this process may feel a little overwhelming right now, after you get the hang of it, you'll find you can pinpoint the best flavor in just a few minutes. Don't rush through these steps, though, because picking the right white paper for the job is a significant decision that can make or break your results. The following sections outline the steps in detail.

Reflecting on your purpose

To pick the perfect flavor for your next white paper, the best place to start is your intended purpose. Your white paper can do one or two things, but it can't do everything. If you want to attract fresh leads at the top of your sales funnel, the same document can't very likely help technical evaluators at the bottom of the funnel. Trying to do both at once only creates a mash-up that doesn't work (see the earlier section, "Getting messy with other flavor combinations").

So, first of all, you need to pick one purpose that's more important than any other. For best results, stick to just one. Don't dilute your efforts by trying to do two or three different things with one document. The more you can focus your efforts, the more effective your white paper will be.

Table 5-2 lists the most common purposes for a white paper and which flavor works best for that purpose. To use this table, find your main purpose in the left column, and then look at the options in the right column. You may see two or more possibilities, any of which can work nicely. These possibilities become the working options for your white paper flavor, which you confirm or refine in the next couple of steps.

Table 5-2	The Best White Paper Flavors for Various Purposes
Purpose	*Best Flavor(s) to Use*
Support a product launch.	Backgrounder
	Numbered list + backgrounder
Educate sales force, channel partners, analysts, bloggers, and journalists.	Problem/solution
	Numbered list + problem/solution
Generate leads at the top of the funnel.	Problem/solution
	Numbered list + problem/solution
Nurture prospects in the middle of the funnel.	Numbered list
	Numbered list + problem/solution
Support technical evaluations at the bottom of the funnel.	Backgrounder
	Numbered list + backgrounder
Cast FUD on competitors or knock competitors off a shortlist of vendors.	Numbered list
Build recognition for your company.	Problem/solution
	Numbered list + problem/solution
Get attention with provocative views.	Numbered list

Many companies working on their first white paper try to do too much. They often try to pack everything plus the kitchen sink into one paper. But publishing three slimmer, more focused documents is much better than publishing one hulking tome that tries to be everything to everyone. Besides, when you break down that monster into smaller pieces, you also get more kicks at the can — two or three chances to reach your potential readers rather than only one.

What about "thought leadership"?

Whenever a prospect tells me, "We want to use this white paper to develop some thought leadership," I feel like screaming. As a former hardheaded journalist who read dozens of white papers for background research, I believe *thought leadership* is one of the most meaningless buzzwords ever devised. What is it, exactly? How do you get it? And how do you measure it to know whether your white paper helped you get more of it? That's why I don't include this term in Table 5-1.

Think for an instant: What is a leader? To me, a leader is the leader of a company, the head of state for a nation, or the most successful, most respected, most innovative company in its market. Leaders aren't shy and retiring; they're out there leading parades, giving speeches, and kissing babies. If your company is already a leader in your industry, everybody knows it. If not, you can't just hire a writer to create a single white paper and "develop some thought leadership." It's not going to happen. More likely, no one will care what you say, and your white paper will be quickly forgotten. I want to help you avoid that.

In recent years, marketing has evolved from one of the last holdouts where results weren't measured in numbers. In the old days, marketers were measured by how good the company logo looked or how funny the TV ads were. Today, marketers are held to account for their return on investment (ROI) on every campaign, and a white paper is no different. You can account for the number of leads generated, the number of prospects nurtured, or the total value of sales booked with the help of a white paper. But how do you account for thought leadership?

Instead of chasing such a vague goal, I urge you to pick a more specific and achievable goal. At the very end of Table 5-1, you see *build recognition* and *get attention*. These terms are as close as I get to *thought leadership*. These goals are synonyms for mindshare, which can actually be expressed as a number, as in "64 percent of our target audience has heard of our company." Admittedly, not all companies take this kind of survey. But do you know any way to measure thought leadership? To my mind, thought leadership is a contrived notion that non-data-driven marketing types use to sound important, hoping no one will notice what flimsy ground they're standing on. Don't fall for it. Don't use it as a goal for any white paper — ever.

Considering your target audience

Suppose you've already fixed on your unswerving purpose, which has led you to two possible flavors, one of them a mash-up with a numbered list. Next, consider the preferences of your target audience. Are they stolid and conservative 50-ish bean counters, like CFOs? Are you trying to impress them with how responsible your firm is and why they should deal with you rather than the other upstarts in your field? Then perhaps using a provocative tone in a numbered list isn't the best approach. For a conservative audience, you may decide instead to aim more for the factual details of a backgrounder or the dignified tone of a problem/solution.

On the other hand, what if your target market is mainly young, hip entrepreneurs running web-based startups, most of them not yet 30? Are they going to mind some quick tips or a slightly tongue-in-cheek approach? This audience will more likely appreciate the easy-to-scan format and the witty tone of a numbered list.

Or you may have other factors to consider. For example, if you're writing for doctors, you know they often read articles in medical journals to learn the findings of complex research projects. For an audience like this, a numbered list may not provide the scientific rigor they're looking for. You may even want to format your white paper more like a journal article than a business document. I've done that a few times.

In any case, use your understanding of your target audience to help narrow down your choices. Most important, decide whether your audience is likely to appreciate a numbered list.

Thinking about your target sector

For a final reality check on your decision, consider your target sector, industry, or vertical market. Ask yourself whether readers in this field are used to seeing the white paper flavor that you're thinking of creating for them. One way to check is to look at what your competitors are doing with white papers. Are the key players in your market all publishing the same flavor? Look at analysts, associations, consultants, and trade journals that publish white papers for your industry. What flavors predominate on their sites? You can follow the herd and use the common flavor (not necessarily a bad thing), or you can break away from the pack and shake things up a bit by choosing a less-common flavor for your white paper.

For example, certain vertical markets, such as finance, government, healthcare, insurance, and security, tend to be quite staid and conservative. After all, a key preoccupation in these industries is to protect their customers' money, health, or physical security. For industries like those, you can always use a numbered list with more serious content and dial down its informal tone. Or, if you want to be seen as an innovative vendor that pushes the envelope, you may deliberately decide to publish a different flavor with a more cheeky tone to help your firm get noticed. Just do a little homework first to make sure you're not going in a direction that's really out of sync with your target sector.

Choosing between a pure flavor and a mash-up

But what if your choice comes down to one pure flavor and one mash-up of that flavor plus a numbered list? How do you decide between them? Let your content drive that decision. If a numbered list doesn't emerge naturally from your material, don't try to force it; stick with the backgrounder or problem/solution. However, you can easily try out some ideas for numbered lists to see whether they make sense.

For example, suppose your white paper is all about automated parking meters on city streets. You want to show how using these meters saves a lot of money versus paying parking meter collectors; how they're more convenient because they enable people to pay by using debit and credit cards; how they reduce crime and shrinkage because no one is carting around hundreds of dollars' worth of change; and how they're a proven technology that many cities already use. In short, many good reasons support using automated parking meters. Do you think this content would be a good case for a numbered list? Of course it would! You already have four good points here, and coming up with another three or four would likely be easy. This example shows how a numbered list can naturally emerge from your content.

In fact, I can already start to glimpse three possible angles:

- ✔ "8 Benefits of Automated Parking Meters" would be a pure numbered list, showing eight points in a straightforward, easy-to-scan format.

- ✔ "7 Questions to Ask Your Automated Parking Vendor" would be a backgrounder–numbered list, highlighting seven strengths of this one vendor's automated meter products and casting FUD on all competitors.

- ✔ "6 Ways Automated Parking Helps Municipalities Avoid Budget Crunches" would be a problem/solution–numbered list, where the problem is that cities are facing tight budgets, and the new, improved solution is the cost savings and higher revenues that automated parking meters can help generate.

Depending on the purpose and audience for your white paper, and where they are in the sales funnel, you can pick one of these possibilities or continue to tweak your ideas until you have one that works better than any other.

Figuring out what to do if your idea doesn't fit any flavor

These 3 flavors and 2 tasty mash-ups will probably fit 9 out of 10 — even 19 out of 20 — white papers that you're likely to encounter or need to create. What about that weird outlier, that 5 percent that doesn't fit any of these flavors? All I can say is, don't sweat it. These three flavors aren't intended as ironclad categories. To paraphrase Captain Barbossa from the *Pirates of the Caribbean* movie, these three flavors are more what you'd call guidelines. Feel free to mix up another flavor if you need something different to reach your target audience.

You can create a white paper about any topic, for any audience, using any approach under the sun, as long as you remember this key mantra: A truly effective white paper helps business people understand an issue, solve a problem, or make a decision. If your content does all of that, your readers will thank you — and they won't give a hoot what flavor you call it.

Developing Your Topic

Beyond picking the best flavor to achieve your purpose and reach your target audience, you need an engaging topic. Likely, you already have some inkling of a good topic or perhaps a set of topics that you can develop into white papers. The short example on automated parking meters (in the "Choosing between a pure flavor and a mash-up" section) hints at the process for focusing your topic. Again, go back to your purpose, your audience, their sector, and the half-baked ideas you already identified. Which of these would accomplish your purpose best? Which would reflect best on your company? Which would be freshest, most unusual, and most helpful? In the following sections, I help you narrow down your topic.

Sizing up your ideas

One thing to watch out for is picking an idea that's either too big or too small. You want to focus on something you can cover in about 5 to 12 pages, depending on the type of white paper you're writing.

For example, an idea that's really too big for one white paper is "How Cities Can Solve Their Budget Crises," which probably calls for congressional hearings and a report thousands of pages thick. The flip side of this topic is one that's just too small for a white paper, such as "How to Position Automated Parking Meters on City Streets." This topic sounds more like a section from an installation manual or perhaps a blog post, probably not an idea that justifies putting together a six- to eight-page white paper. Just like Goldilocks, you need to find an idea for your white paper that's not too big, not too small, but just the right size.

Giving readers something new

A truly effective white paper helps readers gain a better overview of an issue, provides helpful insights on how to solve a problem, or gives useful pointers on how to make an important decision. You want to avoid any ideas that have already been done to death, covered repeatedly by sources such as trade magazines, industry associations, and other vendors. You don't want to rehash the same tired material as everyone else. No one gets excited about a white paper on the same topic as one they read two years ago. Even if prospects start reading your paper, if you don't give them a fresh take on a topic or something new, useful, and educational, they're bound to be disappointed.

The surest sign of a floundering marketing team is a "Me Too!" white paper on the same topic everyone else is writing about, a document that adds nothing to the literature and casts no new light on the issues. Some vendors are so uninspired that they steal white paper ideas — and sometimes whole chunks of text — from competitors. (Of course, no one reading this book has ever done anything like that!) For people who take such a lazy approach, all their effort will likely come to naught. Truly creative, inspired, turned-on marketers have more ideas than they can ever possibly implement.

You can quickly check how much has already been published in the same area by Googling a few phrases close to your working topic. In fact, doing so is a great way to get some preliminary research and find some initial sources that you may be able to quote in your white paper. Don't wait until you're in the formal research stage; do some web searches early on, while you're still shaping your idea.

A client once asked me to review a white paper published in Europe that it was considering republishing in North America. Unfortunately, the topic — how to pick an enterprise resource planning (ERP) system — was extremely old hat. Twenty years ago, this topic would have interested a great many business people. But ERP is now a very mature type of enterprise software. If you Google "how to pick an ERP system" you get 16-plus million hits! I was forced to tell my client that he shouldn't bother with such a tired topic for a white paper. The client wasn't happy about that because he had no other ideas and no budget to develop any. But he had to admit I was right.

Getting ideas from prospects and clients

If you're stuck for ideas, you can always turn to a ready source: anyone in your company who talks directly to prospects or clients. For most companies, that includes the sales force, channel partners, customer service, technical support, and possibly marketing. Sit down with a few of these people and ask them some simple questions: What are the prospects and clients you deal with asking about? What are they curious about? What big problems are they grappling with? What do they need help with? Listen carefully to the answers, and you'll hear some rich topics for possible white papers.

What's more, this conversation doesn't have to be a one-way street. If you have a customer advisory board, user group, focus group panel, or any other way of getting hold of some typical prospects or customers, try out some possible white paper topics on them.

Chapter 6

The Backgrounder: As Basic As Vanilla

To delve deeper into the three flavors of white papers that I outline in Chapter 5, the natural starting point is the backgrounder. This flavor is as plain and predictable as vanilla ice cream. But just like vanilla, it's amazingly popular. For example, all the leading technology companies with household names like Apple, Google, Hewlett-Packard, Oracle, and so on produce mainly this flavor.

In this chapter, I define this original flavor of white paper, show how to recognize it, and reveal when to use it for best results. Then I sketch in the pros and cons of backgrounders and provide a sample list of contents and recommended page counts. I also cover how to repurpose a backgrounder into other types of content, especially a press release, slide deck, demo, or webinar.

Introducing the Granddaddy of All White Papers

You don't get any surprises when you order vanilla ice cream. The same applies to a backgrounder. Your readers know what to expect when they pick up a white paper of this flavor. You can think of the backgrounder as a "deep dish" about the features and benefits of a certain product or service. Best used for prospects near the bottom of the sales funnel, a backgrounder pitches the technical or business benefits of a vendor's offering.

To many marketing executives, the backgrounder is what white papers are all about. Once upon a time, all B2B white papers came in this flavor. In those days, white papers were used mainly to deliver technical information to prospects. By now, marketing has come a long way, B2B buyers have evolved, and new flavors have emerged that are better suited for certain marketing challenges. But a backgrounder can still be powerful if you use it at the right time for the right purpose.

In the following sections, I explore the ins and outs of the backgrounder, including how to spot one and why certain B2B buyers like this flavor best.

Defining a backgrounder

A backgrounder is a B2B white paper with a tight focus on one offering from one vendor. This offering is most often a product or service, but it can also be any sort of methodology or business process. The backgrounder is also known as an *evaluator's guide* or *product briefing*.

A backgrounder does one or more of the following:

- ✔ Explains the key features, functions, and benefits of an offering to give B2B buyers more detailed information than they can find in a brochure, data sheet, or website
- ✔ Explains a new, unfamiliar, or misunderstood technology to a technical audience
- ✔ Supports a product launch by explaining a new offering to the world

Prospects deep in the sales funnel download product backgrounders to get technical details they can't find anywhere else. They don't want brochure-style copy; they're looking for precise technical details. But they don't want 120-page operations manuals, either. The trick is to be selective and hit the high points without getting bogged down in arcane details that matter only to your own engineers, not to your prospective buyers.

A backgrounder is relatively easy to prepare because it includes mostly technical information that's easy to find within your own company. The tone is factual, and the graphics can be simple boxes and arrows. (No need for special effects; "all we want are the facts, ma'am.") If you think *vanilla* when you think of a backgrounder, you can't go far wrong.

Spotting a backgrounder

To identify a backgrounder, look for a product or service name in the title and a lot of information about that offering in the body. In fact, the actual name of the product or service likely occurs dozens of times, often more than once a page. Also look for descriptions of proprietary features, functions, interfaces, methodologies, modules, technologies, workflows — the kind of technical details that used to be called *feeds and speeds.* If you see all of that, you can be sure that you've spotted a backgrounder.

You won't likely find much discussion of any industry-wide problem or much attempt to point out the drawbacks of any other vendor's solution to that problem. You won't find any levity, provocative language, or trash-talking about the competition. And you won't see many question marks in the title or section headings. A backgrounder is all about facts, figures, throughput, total cost of ownership, return on investment, new features and innovations, and how that offering does what it does better than anything else on the market.

Understanding this flavor's appeal to sales and marketing types

Backgrounders appeal to sales and marketing types within a company for an obvious reason: They mirror the way these people usually think, focusing on their company's offering and how it's the best thing on the market. A backgrounder highlights the unique selling points (USPs) and competitive advantages that they're always talking about. The first instinct of most sales and marketing people who've never worked on a white paper before is to create a backgrounder. Because it's what they know, it's the most natural flavor to use.

Of course, this instinct isn't always correct. Sometimes a backgrounder is the right flavor to use; other times, not so much. In the next section, I describe three specific situations where a backgrounder can work very well. In any other circumstances, think twice before you pick this flavor — even if you have to push back against other people in your company. The white paper you save may be your own.

Deciding When to Use a Backgrounder

To me, nothing is like a scoop of vanilla ice cream melting all over a big piece of fresh-from-the-oven strawberry-rhubarb crumble — unless you're talking a double scoop of vanilla melting over a big piece of warm pumpkin pie. No doubt you have your own favorite ways of eating vanilla ice cream.

In the same way, a backgrounder can be the best flavor to pick in three specific situations:

- ✔ To promote an undisputed leader
- ✔ To support a technical evaluation
- ✔ To supplement a new product launch

Promoting an undisputed leader

Is your company an undisputed leader in your field? Are you working for a Fortune 500 company that's a name brand already lodged firmly in every prospect's mind? Are you so well known that you usually end up on the shortlist of B2B vendors being considered for any purchase in your market?

If so, you're among the fortunate few, including companies in B2B technology, such as Cisco, Dell, Hewlett-Packard, and IBM; in software, Adobe, Microsoft, Oracle, SAP, and Symantec; in telecom, AT&T, Sprint, and Verizon. Every sector of the economy has a few leading lights — the powerful standout companies that everyone knows.

For this select number, publishing backgrounders makes a lot of sense, because most B2B buyers naturally check out what these firms can offer to help them with their business problem. In many cases, all that one of these big, well-known companies has to do is lay out its wares and wait for the prospects to flock to them, like children around an ice-cream truck. And the best way for a well-known B2B company to lay out its wares is often by publishing a vanilla flavor of white paper, a backgrounder.

Supporting a technical evaluation

As explained in Chapter 1, you can look at the sales process as a funnel. During a complex B2B sale, prospects enter the sales funnel at the top, gain the information and reassurance they need in the middle, and ultimately make a buying decision at the bottom. Throughout the process, every vendor competes against the rest to win the buyer's business.

A backgrounder isn't effective at generating leads at the top of the funnel and is only mildly effective for nurturing prospects through the middle, simply because it's too early in either case for B2B buyers to think about any product specifics. They're still mapping out their requirements, formulating a budget and a timeline, and getting everyone on the selection committee to agree on a shortlist of vendors.

But when prospects finally reach the bottom of the funnel and want to do a final evaluation of their shortlist of vendors, a backgrounder can be just the ticket. Often, a knowledgeable staff person on the prospect's side is assigned to evaluate a handful of competing solutions, weigh them against one another, and come back with some recommendations. A backgrounder packed with details on the technical and business benefits of a vendor's offering gives that person exactly what he needs when he needs it. At that point, you can imagine how much a vendor with a backgrounder gains over those without. In fact, any vendors with no explanatory white papers may find themselves dropped from the shortlist of possible suppliers.

Supplementing a product launch

A backgrounder can be useful to round out a product launch when a vendor needs to explain a new offering to analysts, bloggers, channel partners, journalists, and perhaps even its own sales force. This is the one time when you can expect a certain amount of interest in the product itself, especially if the new product or service represents a departure from conventional approaches or any significant improvements on the past. A backgrounder can focus on what's new and how this product or service delivers more benefits for B2B buyers.

If your company is launching a product or service in a new category, with a new approach, or anything a little unconventional, publishing a backgrounder to support it is a good idea, no matter how big or small your company may be. You can also publish a white paper of another flavor at the same time, but to help tell the story of your new offering, you should likely create a backgrounder.

Looking at the Pros and Cons of Backgrounders

Nothing in this life is perfect, and the same applies to white papers. Like every flavor, backgrounders have certain strengths and limitations. On the plus side, because backgrounders are so focused, they're relatively easy to research and write. On the downside, they have a short life span and aren't effective at generating leads. Understanding the pros and cons of this flavor, which I address in the following sections, helps you decide when you should use a backgrounder for best results and when to choose another flavor that's a better match for the challenge you face.

Pro: Easy to research

A backgrounder is the easiest of all flavors to research, mainly because all your sources are already inside the company. Everyone you need to line up as a subject matter expert (SME) and all the material you need to gather comes from inside the company — most likely from the team that designed and created the product or service in the first place. When you speak to those experts, they'll tell you about what they know best: the features, functions, philosophy, and benefits of the offering they just created. In a short time, they can dish out more source materials, including all sorts of market research, slide decks, product plans, and use cases about that offering, than you can possibly use.

For a backgrounder, you won't likely have to do any web searching, compile any external research, or keep track of any footnotes. Of course, you still have to gather the facts you need to present the offering in a compelling way, but your research should be clear and straightforward. That makes a backgrounder the easiest of any flavor to research.

Pro: Easy to write

A backgrounder can be quite easy to write because it has a simple structure and a tight focus. The structure of a backgrounder is pretty straightforward:

- ✔ Here's the offering.
- ✔ Here are the key features.
- ✔ Here's how these features can benefit you.
- ✔ Call us if you want to talk.

You may want to do an entire backgrounder about one specific aspect of an offering, such as security, robustness, total cost of ownership, or whatever. In this case, you can arrange the list of features into some sort of logical pattern so that each one builds on what you discuss earlier in the paper.

Or a backgrounder can take the opposite approach with a modular structure. With this approach, when you cover four discrete features and their benefits, you don't have to link them all together into a grand design, with each point following logically from the one before; you can just talk about one, another one, the next, and then the last.

With either approach, you should arrange your points in logical order, starting and ending your list with strong, memorable features. If you have one or two less-exciting features, tuck those into the middle to de-emphasize them. Beyond that, there's no trick to writing a backgrounder. Just stick to the facts and explain the offering in clear terms.

Con: Short-lived

Of course, any document tied so intimately to a specific product has a limited shelf life, roughly equivalent to the life span of that release, version, or model. As soon as the product or service changes or gets an update, the white paper may be out of date. At that point, long after the initial excitement of the launch, justifying the resources to update and rerelease that white paper may not be easy. You may have more interesting marketing tactics that you can use to promote the new version of the product, especially if it's now at a mature point in its lifecycle or no longer considered different or unconventional. You may as well expect a backgrounder used at a product launch to have a short life span, about as long as that product generates any initial buzz. After that, it may be time for that document to go to that big recycling box in the sky.

Con: Not good for generating leads

Using a backgrounder can be tempting in certain situations where it's not the wisest choice, such as when trying to generate leads. Some sales and marketing people may be tempted to say, "If we just tell people how great our technology is, they'll want to buy it!" But this flawed thinking doesn't match how most B2B buyers operate in the real world.

In fact, using a backgrounder to generate leads is like dipping into an almost empty tub of ice cream: You're just not going to come up with much. The only prospects likely to encounter a backgrounder are the ones already exploring your offering by name. Whenever I interview executives from white paper content networks, like KnowledgeStorm or TechTarget, they confirm that mentioning a product name in a white paper title dramatically cuts downloads, generally by 50 percent or more. That's because most prospects aren't looking for this flavor of white paper. They know backgrounders are completely focused on the nitty-gritty details of one specific product, not on an overview of the particular business problem they're grappling with. And they know any white paper with a product name in the title is likely a backgrounder.

Think about how B2B buyers actually encounter your white paper. Any prospects low in the sales funnel who already know your product by name and who search on your website for more information may well find your backgrounder. But this number touches only a tiny fraction of your universe of possible buyers. What about all the other prospects out there who don't know your product by name or aren't even in your funnel yet?

Many more B2B prospects at the top of the sales funnel search the web for the solution to a nagging problem or for help understanding an issue. Because a backgrounder doesn't answer these questions, the majority of your prospects never encounter it in their search engine results and never know it exists. That's why a backgrounder just doesn't draw many prospects into the top of the funnel where leads are generated. If you try to use one for that purpose, you'll likely be disappointed.

If your company is an industry leader that doesn't have to work hard to attract prospects, the backgrounder can be an ideal white paper. Smaller vendors, be warned: If your firm has to work hard to attract recognition and if you're seeking to generate as many leads as possible, don't use a backgrounder to achieve those goals. You can get much better results from a problem/solution white paper (which I discuss in Chapter 8) or even a numbered list (which I cover in Chapter 7).

Planning a Backgrounder

Publishing any white paper involves three major phases: planning, producing, and promoting. Parts III and IV of this book go into each of these phases in great detail, even breaking them down into a step-by-step plan. This section covers key areas in planning a backgrounder, namely the following:

- Gathering the essential information you need
- Allocating pages
- Choosing an appropriate title
- Setting the right tone

Gathering essential information

This section is all about the background you need for your backgrounder. (I could get all postmodern about that, but I'll restrain myself.) In any case, you need to know five key things to help plan an effective backgrounder:

- Your intended reader(s)
- The purpose of the backgrounder
- The key features of the offering
- The key benefits of each feature
- The call to action at the end

The following sections discuss each of these items in turn. Until you uncover these items and make a plan for your backgrounder, don't even think about starting to write. You write during Phase 2 (see Chapter 13) when you actually produce your white paper.

Your intended reader(s)

To help target your backgrounder to the right audience, identify your ideal reader as specifically as possible. You can use the following four categories to help specify your target readers:

- ✔ **Company:** Find some sense of the size, vertical market or sector, and location of the company where your intended reader works. For example, your reader may work at a Fortune 500 company in the Midwest that makes finished wood products, like doors and windows.

- ✔ **Demographics:** Dig up hard facts, such as the age, sex, education, and job title(s), of your target readers. For example, your readers could be C-level executives in their 50s, most often male with engineering degrees or MBAs. To find these kinds of facts, ask your sales, marketing, customer service, or technical support teams, or anyone else who has daily contact with your actual customers.

- ✔ **Psychographics:** Sketch in some of your target audience's attitudes, such as their experience, interest in your offering, and workaday stress. For example, your readers could be aware that their teams are drowning in paper but skeptical of hardware solutions and not keen to make any new capital expenditures. Because everyone is different, your guesstimates here may be all over the map. That's okay, because thinking about these things is better than remaining blissfully ignorant of them.

- ✔ **Technographics:** Imagine how your target readers will likely access the backgrounder — whether through a desktop, laptop, tablet, or mobile device. For example, you may assume that 80 percent of your target executives never leave their office until they're done working for the day and don't own an iPad or any other kind of tablet; in other words, the vast majority of your target readers will view your white paper on a desktop or as a printout. If you really have no idea, it's probably fair to say that some will use each class of device.

The main difference between a desktop, laptop, tablet, or mobile device is that each device has a smaller screen than the one before it, so someone reading your white paper on a desktop with a large screen has a much different page view than someone reading from his mobile phone.

Remind your white paper designer of these technographics during the design phase. Knowing how readers will likely view your white paper onscreen may well affect how the designer formats the pages, how many columns and graphics he uses, the colors he chooses, and so on.

If you have any secondary audiences — those who have the backgrounder passed along to them or are desirable but not essential readers — define them as well. For example, your secondary readers may be female department managers in their 30s and 40s whose teams are buried in paper files and forms. You may consider these readers secondary because they're not in a position to buy from your company, but they may be in an ideal position to recommend a purchase to help solve their department's problems.

The purpose of the backgrounder

You must have a clear goal you want to achieve with your white paper. Do you want to support an evaluation? Train your sales force or channel partners? Knock a competitor off a buyer's shortlist of vendors? Help close sales? Note that "generate leads" isn't on this list because a backgrounder isn't the best at attracting new prospects. Your white paper can do one thing, but it can't do everything.

The key features of the offering

List the most unique and powerful features of the offering in some purposeful order, such as from the most important to the least, the most familiar to the least, the newest to oldest, by workflow, or by some other scheme. Don't try to cover everything in one backgrounder. You're not creating a specification or manual that provides a definitive list of everything the product can do. Be selective. Four to six features are often plenty.

In fact, some backgrounders are built around a single feature. And some describe a bundle of features related to one function, such as security, work-flow, or whatever. Note that you don't have to dig down into the details of any feature at this point; you just need to put together an initial working list of the features you intend to cover in your backgrounder.

The key benefits of each feature

Features without benefits have little appeal. Not every reader can visualize how each raw feature can help in his environment. To make your backgrounder more persuasive, describe the benefits for every key feature slanted toward your target audience(s). One way to make benefits clear is to introduce a running example, perhaps a fictitious company like Acme Scanners, as I do in this book. For enterprise software, you can even show dummy data from Acme in every screenshot.

The call to action at the end

What do you want your ideal readers to do after they read your document? Don't simply send people to your home page to wander aimlessly. Instead, send them to a specific landing page. Point them to a short presentation or demo. Invite them to use an interactive calculator. Have them call a toll-free number or request a free trial. In general, the more specific the call to action, the more effective it will be and the easier it is to measure the results.

Allocating pages

This section describes the typical contents most often included in a back-grounder in the recommended order. As shown in Figure 6-1, a backgrounder is typically eight or more pages, not counting an optional cover and executive summary. A backgrounder can even run 25 or 30 pages without losing any readers, as long as all the material hangs together and provides useful, factual information without a spec of marketing fluff.

A backgrounder can run longer than any other flavor, mainly because of its role at the bottom of the sales funnel. After all, if an engineer or technician is told to evaluate a product for possible purchase and he gets his teeth into a good product description with lots of technical details, he likely won't complain that the document is too long when he reaches the ninth page.

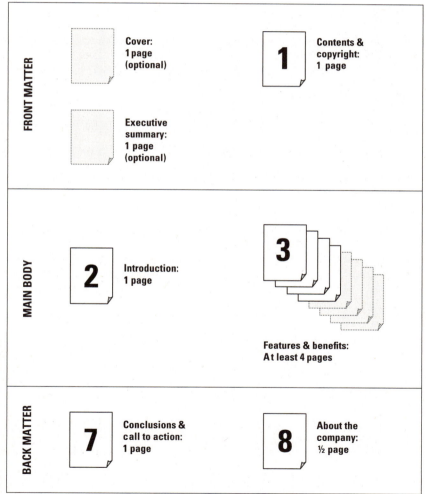

Figure 6-1:
The typical page count for a backgrounder is 8+ pages plus an optional cover.

FRONT MATTER

Cover:
1 page
(optional)

Executive summary:
1 page
(optional)

1 Contents & copyright:
1 page

MAIN BODY

2 Introduction:
1 page

3 Features & benefits:
At least 4 pages

BACK MATTER

7 Conclusions & call to action:
1 page

8 About the company:
½ page

Illustration by Wiley, Composition Services Graphics

Knowing your target readers

The first rule of any good communicator is to know your audience. Having a clear idea of the age, sex, education, job role, size of company, industry, location, experience, interest, stresses, and viewing devices of your ideal target readers gives you a better shot at reaching them with language and imagery that resonates with them.

For example, many men in business — especially old-school men — appreciate the language of combat and sports: bashing, crushing, defeating, stomping, winning, and so on. But to many women, these metaphors are a complete turnoff. Worse yet, people from other cultures may not even know what you mean by football or NASCAR. If you know in advance, for example, that 50 percent of your audience for a backgrounder are women in Europe, would you still use that same language? Or would you appreciate the chance to find another frame of reference?

Another even simpler example is readability. People's eyes begin to change around age 40. As most people get older, they find it harder to resolve small print. So your designer should be aware of the intended age of your audience. If your readers are all 20-something, you can probably get away with gray text at a smaller point size. But if they're all 50-something executives, your designer should pump up the point size and make all the text crisp black on white.

Knowing your audience isn't about being sexist and ageist; it's about having a better clue of how to tailor your message to make it easy to decipher and understand.

A backgrounder, like all white papers, includes three parts: front matter, main body, and back matter. The following lists discuss briefly what to include in each part of a backgrounder and how many pages each should run. For more tips and discussion, see Chapter 10. You can also check out sample backgrounders at www.thatwhitepaperguy.com/sample-white-papers.html.

Front matter: One to three pages

The front matter of a backgrounder shows what your paper is about and how it's structured and includes the following elements:

- A **cover page** is optional in a backgrounder, and you can often combine the cover with the contents and copyright page. A text-only cover page shows the title, subtitle (if any), vendor, and sometimes the date the paper was published. You can include all this info in a few lines of text or expand it typographically to fill an entire page. Some backgrounders have visual covers, with a photo of the offering in action, the intended reader, or something else that suggests the contents.

- The **contents and copyright** sections often appear on the same page, sometimes with the cover page. The contents section provides a quick overview of your document that many readers use to skip to the pages they want. It usually takes up about half a page, certainly no more than one page. In the contents, you typically list the main headings and perhaps the secondary headings, if any. In a longer document, you may want to list all the tables and figures; in a shorter one, you can leave them out. You can then tuck your copyright notice at the bottom. Legal teams from most vendors want to insert a disclaimer along with the copyright notice. Work with them to keep it short and sweet.

✔ An **executive summary** is optional in this flavor and serves to "tell them what you're going to tell them." In a longer backgrounder, you may want to sum up the whole paper in just a few paragraphs at the start to help readers scan or cut-and-paste from your overview. In a shorter backgrounder, no executive summary may be needed, especially if the list of contents shows clearly what's covered in the paper.

Main body: Five or more pages

Here's where you get to the tastiest bits of the backgrounder, including the following:

✔ The **introduction** sketches in the intended audience, the scope of the white paper, and the level of technical detail throughout and points to any other related documents from the same vendor or elsewhere. The introduction should take up about one page. If you include an executive summary in the front matter, you may not need an introduction, but some backgrounders have both.

✔ The **features and benefits** of the offering itself should span at least four pages of meaty content; otherwise, your backgrounder will be too short to look like much of a white paper. Describe each feature in as much detail as required, and translate each feature into a benefit that your target audience can appreciate. Benefits make any backgrounder much more persuasive than a mere list of technical features because they link the abstract to the concrete, the technical to the real world. In the features and benefits section, you deliver the key messages of the white paper, or in other words, you "tell them."

The best strategy is to stick to the facts and prove your assertions with benchmarks or test results, industry awards, reviews, or comments from acknowledged experts. If you have any such sources to reference, include them either as *footnotes* at the bottom of the page or *endnotes* gathered together on a separate page at the back of the white paper.

Back matter: Two pages

The back matter wraps up all the helpful info in the earlier sections with the following elements:

✔ A brief set of **conclusions,** no more than half a page, rounds out a backgrounder nicely and "tells them what you told them." The conclusions should cover the take-away messages that you want all readers to remember.

> ✔ At the very end of the conclusions, include your **call to action** — the next step you want your ideal readers to take. It can be as short as a single sentence.
>
> ✔ Nearly every backgrounder features a brief section **about the company** to show the standard boilerplate from the vendor. Include company contact information here.

Choosing an effective title

Unlike other flavors of white papers, mentioning a product, service, or company name in the title of a backgrounder is acceptable. In fact, it's hard not to. If you have a large product family, you can specify a certain model or model range in the title to avoid confusion. Beyond that, a good title clearly conveys the contents of the white paper, the audience, and the benefits of reading it.

Here are some possible formats for a backgrounder title:

> ✔ How the Acme ScanOMatic 3000 Provides Network Security
>
> ✔ Evaluator's Guide for the Acme ScanOMatic 3000
>
> ✔ Product Briefing: Acme ScanOMatic 3000
>
> ✔ Unattended Scanning with the ScanOMatic 3000

Another useful tactic is to use a subtitle to name the ideal reader's job title or industry that clearly indicates who the backgrounder is aimed at, such as "A White Paper for CFOs from Acme."

You don't have to finalize your title during the planning stage of your backgrounder, but having a working title is useful to bandy about the office, especially if your team routinely works on more than one white paper at a time. If nothing else, you can call this something generic, like "that backgrounder on the ScanOMatic 3000," or a tad more specific, like "that backgrounder on unattended scanning with the 3000."

Setting a factual tone

If you had to come up with just one word to describe the tone of a backgrounder, that word would be *factual*. On every page of your backgrounder, make sure the text is clear, crisp, and accurate. You don't need a lot of flowery language or adjectives in this flavor. You're describing a product or service that exists now, designed for a certain purpose, and aimed at a certain target market. That offering has certain features, and each feature has an intended benefit. Where's the need for any hot air? Just describe what's there and what it does, using plain English and industry-standard names for various items. And when you claim a benefit, don't be outlandish.

Here's another reason to be factual: Your white paper is going out in the world to represent your company. If you try to trick your readers, obscure the facts, or make claims you can't substantiate, that reflects poorly on your company. Part of the task of a technical evaluator is to sniff out the specific strengths and weaknesses of any offering, true. But another part of his work is to form an impression of the various vendors on his shortlist.

Suppose an engineer reports back on his research like this, "Well, Acme has okay products, but the company makes a habit of exaggerating its performance. The white paper on the ScanOMatic 3000 makes some awfully dubious statements that it doesn't back up. I'm not sure we can really trust this company." Imagine the reception from the buying committee: Raised eyebrows, puzzled frowns, and likely a thick black line through Acme's name as they cut it from the shortlist. That's not what you want!

Most of all, remember your audience. For a product launch, your audience includes your channel partners and the journalists and analysts who cover your space. For a technical evaluation, your audience includes technicians and engineers trying to size up your offering. These people are all trained skeptics who can see through any smoke screen you can possibly throw up. So keep the tone in your backgrounder factual, clear, and informative. Your readers will appreciate it.

Going Beyond Text in a Backgrounder

Besides having clear, crisp, and factual text, most backgrounders benefit from graphics to help convey detailed information about a vendor offering. Every white paper needs at least one good concept graphic to show an overview of the key points in a way that's easy to scan and simple to remember. In the future, you can expect to see more rich media, like animation, audio, and video, in backgrounders, although this flavor may well be the last one where these become commonplace. In the following sections, I discuss both types of added visuals: graphics and rich media.

Adding graphics

Most backgrounders include at least a few graphics to help explain the content. Although black-and-white graphics are acceptable, the added contrast and emphasis of color is always nice. Either way, graphics in a backgrounder must be clear and simple. You can choose from block diagrams, flow diagrams, network diagrams, screenshots of software products, actual photos of a hardware product, or anything else that communicates a significant idea at a glance.

Not all white papers are printed, and of those that are, not all are printed in color. Test-print your final PDF in black and white to see how the color looks that way. If you use colors that are too close in tone or density, they may look the same in black and white. Where those colors are significant, like in a pie chart, not being able to tell them apart in black and white can be irritating. If you see this happening in your test printout, go back to the graphics and change one or more colors to make them easier to tell apart in black and white.

Don't just take whatever graphics the engineers give you and plunk them into your backgrounder. Many engineering-style diagrams are disasters that don't give up their messages without 20 minutes of scrutiny. Can you really expect that much effort from any reader of your backgrounder? Expect to edit every graphic the same way you edit text to make it more comprehensible and easier to scan for your target audience. In fact, you may need to use an original image from an engineer as the starting point to create a simpler diagram for your readers.

To fix a drawing that's too dense, try to separate the various messages into two or three separate graphics and use each one at the appropriate place, or not at all. Or see whether you can drop two-thirds of the information packed into one graphic so that what's left makes a useful illustration.

A backgrounder isn't the place for any fancy, overproduced graphics. Many engineers distrust anything that looks too "slick." And you don't want to include any "smug shots" of happy business people working together in peace and harmony; these images give your whole paper an aura of fakeness, which isn't what you want. Instead, you want all the graphics in a backgrounder to say, "Here's our product out there working in the real world!"

To find out more about the types of graphics and how to use them, check out Visipedia from the graphic software publisher SmartDraw at `www.smartdraw.com/resources/glossary`.

Using rich media

Using rich media, like animation, audio, or video, in a backgrounder isn't yet a common practice, as I explain in Chapter 3. Rich media will likely become more common in backgrounders over the next few years, but if you can't use it today, don't worry. The last thing you want in your backgrounder is anything that looks gimmicky.

Several reasons contribute to the slow uptake of rich media in backgrounders. To start, rich media hasn't yet become an industry standard in B2B marketing, so few white paper sponsors or creators even think of using it. Backgrounders are generally prepared by using the media assets, like graphics and slide decks, that a vendor already has on hand. If a vendor has no rich media suitable for a backgrounder, no one will likely create it just for this purpose. Also, rich media can swell the size of a PDF so it takes longer to download, which every-one wants to avoid.

Finally, consider the essence of a backgrounder. It's the oldest and probably most conservative of all flavors. A backgrounder with rich media is like a dish of vanilla ice cream with gooey caramel sauce and colorful sprinkles on top. Why would people pick vanilla if they're really after something as exciting as all of that?

Repurposing a Backgrounder

One way to get a better return on your investment in a white paper is to repurpose that content in other formats. Because a backgrounder is already focused on a particular product or service, you can usually repurpose it handily as a press release, slide deck, product demo, or webinar, as I explain in the following sections.

However, simply repurposing this content never changes its intended audience. No matter what format you use to present a backgrounder, it will only interest prospects near the bottom of the sales funnel. It won't work well as a webinar or in any other format intended to attract leads at the top of the funnel.

Press release

You can repurpose a backgrounder as a press release when the product is first launched and still has a certain amount of news value. At the start, a press release should position the product in its market space and describe the significance of the offering. After that, it can include direct quotes from a company executive that weren't included in the backgrounder. Then the press release can touch on the same set of features and benefits in the same order as the white paper. Finally, as a call to action, it can urge readers to download the entire white paper for more details.

Slide deck

The feature-by-feature structure of a backgrounder lends itself readily to being repurposed as a slide deck. You can give each feature a similar number of slides — three or four is usually ample — and handle them in the same order as in the white paper. Then work in another two or three slides at the start for the introducion and the same number at the end for the conclusions. Reserve the final slide for the call to action, which can be to download the entire white paper for more details or to take another step in the sales funnel. Sticking to these simple slides gives you a manageable slide deck that covers the highlights with no filler.

After you complete your slide deck, you can decide whether you want to post it on the web on a slide-sharing site, such as SlideShare (`www.slideshare.net`), SlideBoom (`www.slideboom.com`), or myBrainshark (`www.mybrainshark.com`). You can even plan to share your slide deck a few months after the initial product launch, after the initial buzz has dissipated and you're not giving away anything to competitors.

Don't make the mistake of too many presenters — starting the show with six or eight slides "to give you a little background about our company." News flash: Nobody cares! People viewing your slide decks aren't interested in your company; they're interested in their own problem and wondering whether your product or service can solve it for them. Drop all those slides and give everyone who looks at that slide deck some welcome relief.

Demo

If your offering is software or some sort of system, tool, or hardware that can be shown in action, consider repurposing your backgrounder as a product demo. For software, you can do screen captures of using all the main features described in the backgrounder. For any physical product, you can take videos of some colleagues or actual customers using each feature. Perhaps you can find some stock video or B-roll images that complement your slide deck nicely. You can still assemble your product demo as a presentation, perhaps building on your existing slide deck. You'll likely want the finished results to be packaged as a larger slide deck with rich media included and perhaps set up as a demo, download from your website, or a self-running demo to use in your booth at a trade show or industry event.

Webinar

A webinar naturally builds on the content of a slide deck and a demo. If you already have both, you don't need much more than a title slide and the infrastructure to start taking sign-ups for an online webinar. You can structure your webinar to move through each feature and benefit with your slides and then, from time to time, move to the demo to show this feature in action in the real world. This kind of pacing also keeps your webinar audience interested and awake, not drifting off to check their e-mail.

You want to record your webinar and make the recording available on-demand through your website. You can also consider posting the entire webinar, or some choice bits of it, on your company's YouTube channel.

Chapter 7

The Numbered List: As Fresh As Strawberry

Nothing says "summertime" and "the living is easy" better than a big serving of strawberry ice cream. After all, this flavor is based on a fruit that was traditionally in season for just six weeks in the summer. So when the strawberries came in, everyone enjoyed them in shortcake, summer pudding, with cream, or just plucked straight from the plants.

A white paper structured around a numbered list is like a dish of scrumptious strawberry ice cream: a light and lively treat that tingles on your tongue for an instant and then melts away into nothingness. Just like the fruit, a numbered list is extremely popular, easy to digest, and so versatile that you can use it for many purposes.

In this chapter, I define this ever-popular flavor of white paper. This chapter explains what a numbered list is all about, shows how to recognize it, and reveals when to use it for best results. Then I sketch the pros and cons of this flavor and show a sample list of contents and recommended page counts. This chapter also covers how to repurpose a numbered list into other types of content, especially a blog post, guest blog, e-newsletter article, or article in a third-party website or trade journal.

Introducing the Lightest and Liveliest of All White Papers

If you wonder where the numbered list comes from, just check out any magazine rack. Notice all the tag lines on different covers with one thing in common: a number. In women's magazines, these tag lines may be "35 Spring Looks Under $35" or "5 Ways to Tell He Loves You" or "7 New Exercises That Burn Fat Like Crazy." In men's magazines, they may look like "6 Ways to Reorganize That Messy Garage, Fast!" or "Our Top 5 Picks for the All-Stars" or "12 Minutes a Day to Your Best Abs Ever."

Although the content is quite different, each article is organized the same way: as a numbered list. These articles sound easy and fun to read, something you can zip through fast to pick up useful pointers. And this popular format has moved to the web and into B2B marketing in full force. Any white paper structured as a numbered list instantly conveys the impression of a light and lively read.

And it's the only flavor you can mash up with either of the others to make a tasty treat (more on mash-ups in Chapter 9). Anyone scanning through a numbered list is looking for a fresh perspective or some quick tips to help them solve a problem or do their job better. Readers may not spend long with this type of white paper, but if it's well done, they'll remember it.

In the following sections, I show you the details of a numbered list, how to spot one, and why it's such a popular flavor.

Defining a numbered list

A numbered list is a white paper organized around a set of tips, questions, answers, or points about some issue. This flavor provides a quick roundup of highlights that appeal to anyone interested in the issue, along with the welcome promise of an easy read. The topic can be anything under the sun: the dominant B2B product in its class, a whole product category, some hidden flaws in that category, or why you don't need it in the first place because it's about to be replaced by the new, new thing.

Everyone loves numbered lists. They appeal to a time-pressured, information-overloaded audience because they signal an easy read that delivers the bottom line without a lot of extra preamble. A numbered list works in the following ways:

✔ To attract attention with some provocative views

✔ To nurture a prospect through the long middle of the sales funnel

✔ To cast doubts on competitors

A white paper in the numbered list flavor is the fastest and easiest to create, the easiest to repurpose as a blog post or web article, and the simplest to place in a magazine or website (to see other ways you can use a numbered list, check out the "Repurposing a Numbered List" section, later in this chapter). When time is short and you absolutely must create a white paper to meet your editorial calendar or any other marketing commitment, consider using this flavor.

Spotting a numbered list

Identifying a white paper structured as a numbered list couldn't be easier. Look for a title like "4 Best Practices . . ." or "5 Questions to Ask . . ." or "6 Things You Must Know . . ." Scan through the pages and check for content broken into chunks, with each chunk set off with a number in consecutive order. Bingo! These are the sure signs of a numbered list flavor.

You won't likely find a lot of deep research or any high-level overview in a numbered list. A numbered list is more like a set of spoons prepped for a food-fight battle that you can fling at any level of any issue. The content isn't likely to strain your brain or even stretch it much. Like strawberry ice cream, a numbered list is intended to be light and refreshing, not heavy and complex.

Five reasons numbered lists are popular

Everyone from the most old-school marketer to the youngest reader loves white papers in the numbered list format. Here's why:

1. **They're quick and easy to scan.**

   You can check a heading, decide whether you want to read that point, and, if not, skip ahead to the next. Even if you don't read a numbered list carefully, you can still gather all the key points quickly. Anyone with too much to read appreciates this format.

2. **You always know where you are.**

   The numbering system itself is like a gauge that measures your progress, so you can always see how far you've come and how much farther you have to go.

3. **They give you a break from heavier material.**

   In an age of information overload, when most people have too much to read, too much to remember, and too much to think about, a numbered list is fast and simple to understand.

4. **The structure is clear.**

   You don't have to waste any effort figuring out the message because the key points are already broken out of the text. All the main points are lying right on the surface, where they're totally accessible.

5. **You've been trained for years to appreciate them.**

   Countless magazines, blogs, and e-newsletters all use this format, not to mention David Letterman's Top Ten List every night for more than 25 years. Everyone's used to seeing numbered lists by now.

Deciding When to Use a Numbered List

A numbered list really shines when you need some quick content to promote in a blog, e-newsletter, or magazine — or to meet some commitment in your marketing calendar. Numbered lists, in fact, are the quickest and easiest flavor of white paper to create. They can present an almost random set of points held together by the numbering system alone, without demanding any deep logical explanation that connects all the dots. When time is short but you really need some content, consider a numbered list.

In particular, a numbered list is likely the best flavor to pick in three specific situations:

- To get attention with provocative views
- To nurture prospects already in the funnel
- To cast FUD — fear, uncertainty, and doubt — on competitors

Getting attention with provocative views

One fun way to use a numbered list is to come up with a new, slightly racy, or provocative twist on some issue. As your list is picked up, retweeted, and commented on, it can attract a lot of attention that your company never had before. You can even use a sarcastic or comedic approach that pokes fun at some sacred cow or unchallenged belief in your market space. Here are a few examples of possible provocative white papers done in this flavor:

- "5 Issues to Remember about Team Building"
- "6 Gotchas in Disaster Recovery"
- "7 Things Hackers Know about Your Network That You Don't"
- "8 Secret Ratios Wall Street Uses to Stonewall Your Company"

Don't be provocative just for the sake of being provocative. Each of your items should make a real point that can help your target reader understand an issue, solve a problem, or make a decision. Of course, the ultimate decision you want them to make is to buy from your firm, but you can help them by publishing useful information, not just sensational, silly fluff.

Nurturing prospects already in the funnel

The middle of the sales funnel can be a lonely place. The selection committee has to draw up a list of requirements and beat the bushes for any possible vendors who can likely meet their needs. Often each vendor needs to send in a multipage answer to an RFP. Then each vendor must be vetted and their offering evaluated. For a major B2B purchase, this process can take months, and for a truly major purchase, even years.

A light and lively numbered list can be just the thing to send to prospects stuck in the waiting game at the middle of the funnel. Doing so enables your firm to "ping" prospects again to help them remember you. And it gives you another chance to position your firm as a company that B2B buyers can trust and even enjoy working with. At this point, a numbered list may get noticed when a heavier white paper may not. After all, who doesn't have time to look at a numbered list?

Casting FUD on competitors

Tearing something down is easier than building it. I should know; I've torn down rotting cottages that came apart like cardboard. You can apply this maxim to a numbered list designed to undermine your competitors: All you have to do is tear down someone else's offering, not build a better offering yourself. This approach touches on the classic marketing tactic of tainting your competitors with FUD — fear, uncertainty, and doubt.

Virtually, every big corporation at some point resorts to FUD. To use FUD, you suggest that dark, stormy consequences will befall anyone who buys from the competition, but only blue skies await for people who buy from you. This tactic is most useful when you and a competitor are locked in a battle for market share and repeatedly find yourselves on the same shortlist of B2B vendors. A numbered list can do a lot to knock the other guy off the list, or at least help you shoulder your way ahead of him. Here, I touch on each of these elements in a little more detail.

✔ **Fear of failure and embarrassment:** B2B buyers are in it for their companies, sure, but they're also in it for themselves: their own careers, bonuses, raises, and achievements. Buying the wrong thing can be a major career-limiting move. No one wants to be known as "that goof who caused all those problems by picking the wrong system." If a numbered list can succeed at raising concerns about the other solutions that B2B buyers are considering, those buyers will take note.

✔ **Uncertainty about hidden flaws:** Every vendor wants to reassure B2B buyers that it's a solid outfit they can count on. If a numbered list lobs a few giant boulders that manage to crack the carefully constructed foundations of a competitor, it's doing its job. One effective way to do this is to uncover any operating limits or unintended consequences of other solutions, stating that your white paper is out to reveal the "truth" about these flaws. A numbered list can actually cast itself in the role of a buyer-protection service, out to save B2B buyers from making a big mistake.

✔ **Doubt about claims and features:** An effective numbered list can keep up a steady barrage of sniping questions about the claims and features of other vendors: "What about this? What about that? What about the other?" Again, simply casting doubt around these issues is enough. With these questions, a numbered list can shift the reader's attention toward any perceived weaknesses in the competing solutions — and away from any perceived weaknesses in your own. Done skillfully, this approach can tilt the entire playing field to your own advantage.

I never advocate that someone lie, fabricate evidence, or even stretch the truth beyond recognition in any white paper. Each flavor of white paper must use facts and logic to make its point. If FUD is distasteful to you, don't use it. But be aware that your competitors may not feel the same way, and they may hit you with a numbered list carrying a huge payload of FUD.

Looking at the Pros and Cons of Numbered Lists

Critiquing a bowl of strawberry ice cream seems a little pointless. It's there; it's yummy, so why not dive in? But just like every ice-cream flavor, numbered lists have certain strengths and drawbacks. On the plus side, numbered lists are the easiest of all to write, the fastest to read, and the simplest to repurpose. On the downside, a numbered list can be dismissed for being superficial. And some companies, publications, and writers go overboard, using this format for almost everything they produce. In fact, you can have too much of a good thing, even strawberry ice cream. In the following sections, I reveal the pros and cons of this flavor to help you decide when to use a numbered list, when to mash it up with another flavor, and when you can accomplish your purposes best with a different flavor.

Pro: Easiest to write

A white paper formatted as a numbered list doesn't actually write itself, but it can almost feel that way. After you get your list of points worked out, writing a numbered list can be as easy as filling in the blanks. What's more, you can handle each point as a stand-alone chunk of text. That makes writing, say, a five-point white paper feel more like writing five short articles rather than one long document. With the numbered list as a framework, you don't have to make any logical links or graceful transitions. You don't have to construct a continuous argument. And you can use whatever process or workflow feels right to you. Perhaps you feel like banging off the easier points first and then nibbling away at the more difficult ones over the next few days; well, you can. Because you don't need to develop a high degree of continuity, you can write the parts of a numbered list in any order and assemble them later.

Pro: Fastest to read

A numbered list is the fastest flavor of all to read, for several reasons. Numbered lists are most often the shortest white papers. The entire structure is clearly evident in the list of points, questions, or tips. And a white paper in this modular format is remarkably easy to scan. Most readers scan through the list of points, stopping at the ones that interest them and skipping the rest. You have little overhead in terms of front or back matter and fewer sources or footnotes than in a problem/solution, all of which makes for a zippy reading experience.

This flavor works especially well for reading on-screen. Web visitors tend to skim, scan, and skip their way through text. A numbered list is ideal for that type of quick read. After readers get one point, they can quickly skip on to the next, which is already broken out with a subhead. They never have to search for the next link in the argument. Reading a numbered list, on paper or on-screen, is as easy as one-two-three.

Pro: Easiest to repurpose

Because numbered lists are so popular with readers and so straightforward in their content, they're the easiest of all white papers to repurpose into another format or to place on a third-party website or magazine. Editors and bloggers understand the appeal of numbered lists. They know readers love them because they're so accessible. Because numbered lists are usually quite concise, editors know they won't take a lot of work to edit and republish. In many cases, when you suggest an article in this format, editors and bloggers jump at it. For more on how to repurpose this flavor and how to approach editors, see the section "Repurposing a Numbered List," later in this chapter.

Con: Most superficial

One downside of a pure numbered list is that it's the most superficial of any flavor. With a breezy, scatterbrained approach, a numbered list can't provide the deep detail of a backgrounder. And with a shorter length and shallower focus, a numbered list simply can't offer the same in-depth understanding as a problem/solution flavor. The numbered list is very much a sweet and sugary treat. It may be tasty, but it's not what you'd serve to anyone expecting a hearty helping of knowledge to muse on for the next few days.

The obvious way to give a numbered list more gravitas is to combine it with another flavor. Ideally, this type of mash-up gains the best of both flavors: either the product detail of a backgrounder plus the easy-to-scan structure of a numbered list, or the deep insights of a problem/solution plus the lively approach of a numbered list. Strawberry goes with either vanilla or chocolate to create a tasty treat. Head to Chapter 9 for more on combining different flavors of white papers.

Con: Easiest to dismiss

A numbered list can be full of sound and fury without signifying much, so it's the easiest flavor to dismiss out of hand. The short length and shallow focus of a numbered list — the very things that make it so appealing — can also work against its credibility. Although every flavor needs a certain grounding in fact, a numbered list doesn't have to be as well researched as either other flavor. Many numbered lists, especially those published on blogs, are based on only a dollop of concrete information, with all the rest filled in with witty opinions, innuendo, rumormongering, and other rhetorical devices. Unfortunately, all this empty rhetoric can backfire when readers sense it, and they can dismiss the entire document for making too many claims or criticisms backed up by too few facts.

Con: Can be overused

Sometimes copywriters and marketing people complain that too many numbered lists are being cranked out. Sometimes a naysayer even compiles a list like "5 Reasons to Stop Writing Numbered Lists." This feeling has a certain validity; at times, the whole world seems to be drowning in this flavor.

Here's what Canadian novelist Farzana Doctor had to say about this format in a recent posting on the Open Book blog:

"Numbered lists make for lazy writing, but people love them. Some of my most popular posts were numbered lists. For example, '10 Things I Wish I'd Known 10 Years Ago: Letter to My 30-Year-Old Self' got over 1,050 hits. If I could find a way to write a novel as a numbered list, I'd do it."

I think her words sum up the issue nicely: At times, I don't want to see everything reduced to a numbered list — but because this format is so popular, people will likely keep on using it ad infinitum.

On the other hand, the opposite view is just as valid. As long as everyone, from established publishers to informal bloggers, continues to dish out this flavor and readers continue to lap it up, what's the harm? Would you criticize friends who prefer strawberry ice cream over any other flavor? Or would you make some allowance for their taste?

Planning a Numbered List

Publishing any white paper involves three major phases: planning, producing, and promoting. Parts III and IV of this book go into each of these phases in great detail, breaking them down into a step-by-step plan. In this section, I cover how planning a numbered list is a little different from any other flavor, including the following:

✔ Gathering the essential information you need

✔ Allocating pages

✔ Choosing an appropriate title

✔ Setting the right tone

Gathering essential information

As with any white paper, you need certain information before you can start creating a numbered list. Your project will go much more smoothly if you clarify these five items during your planning:

✔ Your intended reader(s)

✔ The purpose of the numbered list

✔ The topic or issue

✔ The high-level numbered points about the topic

✔ The call to action at the end

Make sure to research all these items before you jump in to write your list. Writing comes during Phase 2 (Chapter 13), when you actually produce your white paper. Otherwise, you'll be like the writers in David Letterman's back room, chugging coffee and chain-smoking as they frantically try to come up with the last couple of items to round out the night's Top Ten List. Now I ask you: Is that any way to write a white paper?

Your intended reader(s)

The ideal reader for a numbered list can be anyone interested in the topic it covers. But you'll likely want to narrow down your intended audience. You can use the following four categories to help specify your target readers:

- **Company:** Get a sense of the size, vertical market or sector, and location of the company where your intended reader works. For example, your reader may work in a medium-sized company anywhere in the world with too much paper clogging up its processes.

- **Demographics:** Find some hard facts, such as the age, sex, education, and job title(s), of your target readers. For example, your readers could be department managers in their 30s, split 50-50 male-female, who rely on their in-house IT departments to maintain their computers. To find these kinds of facts, ask your sales, customer service, or technical support teams, or anyone else who has daily contact with your actual customers.

- **Psychographics:** Sketch in some of your target audience's attitudes, such as their experience, interest in your offering, and workaday stress. For example, your readers could be aware that their teams are drowning in paper but skeptical that computers can really solve this problem. You may have to rely on some broad guesstimates here. That's okay, because grappling with these questions is much better than ignoring them.

- **Technographics:** Will your target readers likely access the numbered list through a desktop, laptop, tablet, or mobile device? If you expect your numbered list to go viral and be picked up, commented on, and retweeted a lot, many of your target readers will likely see it online. A bare-bones numbered list displays fine on a mobile device, so that's not a problem. That's a hint, though, to keep it short and not bother with a lot of graphics that will make your message harder to see.

If you have any secondary audiences — desirable but not essential readers — define them as well. For example, your secondary readers may be associates in their 20s and 30s working on one of those teams overwhelmed by paper. These readers may not be in a position to buy from your company, but they may be in an ideal position to recommend a purchase to help solve their department's problems.

The purpose of the numbered list

Without a purpose, your white paper could end up being nothing more than a random collection of numbered points, so make sure to identify what you want the paper to achieve. Some likely purposes include attracting attention to your company, nurturing prospects at the middle of the sales funnel, or casting doubts on competitors (see the earlier section "Deciding When to Use a Numbered List" for details). You may also want to train your sales force on how to overcome objections, block sales of the competition, or help close sales for your company. But a single numbered list can't do everything. Pick a top priority and stick to it.

The topic or issue

Be sure to choose a hot-button topic for your intended audience or a burning issue in their industry. Ideally, your topic is something that irritates them or keeps them awake at night. In B2B, these topics typically revolve around money, employees, productivity, costs, waste, risk, change, or the future. You may want to suggest that your numbered list shows readers the inside track, clarifies a fuzzy area, or gives them the bottom line on a key issue. By following the concerns of bloggers, forums, news reports, and trade journals, you can keep your finger on the pulse of your market space and dream up many relevant ideas for numbered lists. Then pick the topic that's likely to create the most noise, be the most amusing, or cause the most devastation for your competitors.

When you choose your topic, you don't have to know in advance what to say about it. You only have to know that it's an issue your readers will respond to. After that, you can develop your points.

The high-level numbered points

You may have to do some research to help come up with any solid points about your topic. Or your whole list may come dancing out of your mind as if by magic. Most likely, what happens will be something in between: The first few points come bubbling out, and then you have to work harder to pull out the final few.

One useful brainstorming method is to list all the points you could possibly include, no matter how crazy. Then use your existing points as springboards to further ideas, asking yourself, "Could I push that further? What about the opposite of that? Is that one idea or two?" Sometimes you can break up a big, nebulous item into two smaller, more focused points.

If you're tackling preconceived notions about your topic, you can negate those notions either by arguing directly against them or by labeling them as myths that need reexamining. For example, suppose your company is fighting the perception that "all scanners are pretty much the same." To argue against that, you can call your numbered list something like "6 Things You Should Know about Fifth-Generation Scanners" and then introduce the point that "not all scanners are the same." To explode that perception, you can frame your whole list as "5 Common Myths about Scanners," list "all scanners are the same" as a myth, and then show why it doesn't hold water.

Coming up with good points will take some thinking and perhaps some discussion with your team members. Stop when you reach 15 or 20 points, which is more than enough for one numbered list. Then pare down your list and keep only the best until you have seven or eight very strong points.

The call to action at the end

A numbered list doesn't always contain an explicit call to action, especially if it's shorter. But you must have a clear answer to this question in mind: What do you want your ideal reader to do after reading your white paper?

If you decide to include a call to action, you can wrap it up in one sentence, according to my formula:

> To find out more about how you can gain *[key benefit]* with *[product or company name]*, *[do something]*.

Or for a numbered list that warns about the dangers or hidden flaws of some competing solutions, you can express the call to action as a negative:

> To find out more about how you can avoid *[key pain point]*, *[do something]*.

If your call to action points readers to your website, don't simply send them to your home page on a wild-goose chase. Instead, send them to a specific landing page that you created just for readers who finish this white paper. Point them to a short presentation or demo. Invite them to take a survey or use an interactive calculator. Have them call a toll-free number or request a free trial. In general, the more specific the call to action, the more effective and the easier it is to measure the results.

Allocating pages

As shown in Figure 7-1, a numbered list typically runs five to seven pages plus an optional cover. Above all, you want to keep this flavor short and sweet; otherwise, you're working against the inherent strength of the list format. Many of the elements listed in this section are optional to help you keep your numbered lists as short as possible.

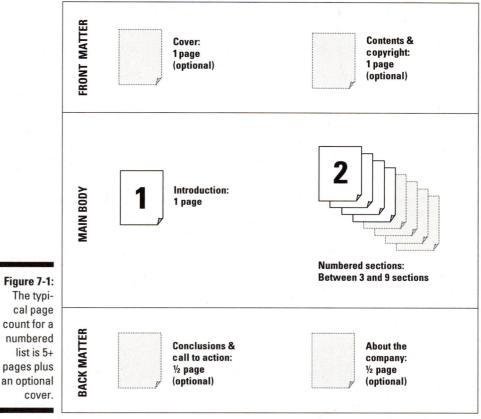

Figure 7-1:
The typical page count for a numbered list is 5+ pages plus an optional cover.

Illustration by Wiley, Composition Services Graphics

A pure numbered list is generally the shortest of any white paper. That's not a bad thing; people love to skim and skip their way through a brief numbered list, picking up quick tips or perspective on the way. When in doubt, leave it out of this flavor.

Pagination is important in any white paper but perhaps most of all in a numbered list. In a longer document of this flavor, where each point fills two-thirds or three-quarters of a page, consider asking your designer to break out a separate page for each numbered point instead of pouring the text in a continuous stream onto the pages, running right over page breaks. Doing so can make a big difference in a longer numbered list.

A numbered list, like all white papers, includes three parts: front matter, main body, and back matter. The following lists discuss briefly what to include in each part of a numbered list and how many pages each should run. For more tips and discussion on using these elements to cook up a white paper, see Chapter 10. You can also check out some sample numbered lists at www. thatwhitepaperguy.com/sample-white-papers.html.

To keep a numbered list brief, much of the front and back matter can be condensed, merged, or dropped altogether. You can dispense with a cover, table of contents, and info about the company and keep the introduction and conclusions short, just two or three sentences each. Slimming these items down can save four pages or so and give you a "skinny-mini" version of your numbered list.

Front matter: Zero to one page

Although not all numbered lists include front matter, you may choose to include the following elements:

- A **cover page** is optional in a numbered list, especially if you want to keep your document as slim as possible. If you do use a cover, the same rules apply as for any other white paper: Keep the title above the fold (on the top half of the page), use a big photo that shows your target audience or target market, keep your logo small, and don't clutter it up with any extra text. Make your cover inviting so your target readers can't wait to start scanning through your list.

- If there's one page you can easily leave out, it's the **contents and copyright page.** A pure numbered list doesn't gain much from a table of contents. After all, the contents are self-evident — the numbered points or questions, perhaps with an introduction at the front, and some conclusions at the end. And you can easily insert the copyright bug — © 2013 by Your Company Name — in the footer for every page. If you don't want to go that far, you can handily combine the cover with the contents and copyright page to yield just one page of front matter. Legal teams from most vendors want to insert a disclaimer along with the copyright notice. Work with them to keep it short and sweet.

Main body: Four to ten pages

The main body includes the fun and interesting parts of the numbered list white paper — the introduction and list of points!

- Most numbered lists include a brief **introduction,** just to set the scene, but it can be short. The introduction can simply touch on the intended reader and the urgency of the issue being covered. In the introduction for a longer paper, you can include all the numbered points as bullets to "tell them what you're going to tell them." In a shorter paper, a couple of sentences may be enough, with no need to preview the list of points before the reader gets into it.

- ✔ Offer **between three and nine numbered points.** Any less than three isn't much of a list, and any more than nine can be too long. Don't settle on an even ten points; doing so makes you sound like a David Letterman wannabe. Hey, after churning out a Top Ten List every night since 1985, Letterman owns the number ten. But everyone knows a few of Letterman's items are going to be groaners that are there only to pad out the list to a full ten items. So cut your weakest point to end up with a stronger list of nine items.

If you list more than about a dozen points, you risk tiring out your readers. If you end up with anywhere close to 20 points, consider splitting your list into two and issuing two separate documents. You can perhaps call these something like "9 Questions to Ask . . ." and "8 More Questions to Ask . . ." Splitting up your points gives you two chances to engage your target audience plus a simple call to action in the first paper that directs readers to the second paper.

- ✔ What about the **proof** in a numbered list: Can you get away with less research for this flavor? Well, no. The points in any white paper, including a numbered list, must be based on facts and logic, not opinions, fluff, or name-calling. As you put together your numbered list, you still need to research the topic, listen to various points of view, drill down for solid facts or convincing proof, and put together a compelling argument.

One of the key benefits of a numbered list is that it's modular rather than linear. After you dream up all your points, you don't have to connect Point A to Point B and on to Point C in a coherent argument. Of course, you still want to use some sort of rhetorical approach, such as moving from an overview to the details or from the most familiar to the least familiar. If you can impose any logical order on your points, do so. You'll help your readers understand and remember your key points.

Don't be afraid to work with your original list, adding, deleting, combining, rephrasing, and reordering your points to make your list as compelling as possible. To deliver on the promise of a numbered list, make sure every single point is clear, crisp, and easy to scan.

- ✔ **Sidebars** generally have no place in a numbered list, unless they're extremely short, on the order of a definition for a term. Longer sidebars can dispel the urgency of the numbered list, distract the reader, and undermine the effectiveness of the entire document. Use sidebars cautiously in numbered lists.

Back matter: Zero to one page

The following elements of back matter are optional in a numbered list; if you choose not to include them, the final numbered point can stand alone as your ending:

✔ After the numbered sections, you may want to provide a half page of **conclusions** to wrap up your paper. Keep this section short and sweet. There's no need to repeat the whole list of points. You can even keep your conclusions down to a single sentence.

✔ At the end of your conclusions, include a brief **call to action,** describing what to do next, where to find more information, or how to move deeper into the sales funnel.

✔ In the final section, **about the company,** you can simply use the standard boilerplate from your company's website. If the one on your website is longer than 100 words, trim it down to a few sentences by chopping out phrases. Then finish that section by providing your company's website address.

Of course, you probably also want to include contact details, like the company phone number, e-mail address, fax, Twitter feed, and company LinkedIn or Google+ pages.

Choosing an effective title

The title is more critical for a numbered list than for any other flavor. After all, the title gives the number of points, the issue being covered, and a good sense of a white paper's viewpoint. Numbered lists can be more provocative to attract attention, more entertaining to keep prospects engaged, or more critical to attack competitors. However you slant your document, that intention should show in the title so readers can tell at a glance what they're getting.

In fact, here's a handy formula for expressing the title for a numbered list:

[Number from 3 to 9] + [Benefits / Concerns / Gotchas / Issues / Problems / Questions / Reasons / Things / Tips / Ways] + [You Must / You Should / to] + [Ask / Avoid / Consider / Know / Remember / Think / Watch Out for] + [about / in / on / to / When / with] + [specific issue being covered]

Try it and see all the possible titles you can easily create, like the following:

✔ 3 Gotchas You Must Avoid When Switching ERP Vendors

✔ 4 Issues to Consider with Unattended Scanning

✔ 5 Problems to Remember about Your WAN Security

✔ 6 Questions to Ask Your Multimedia Production Firm

✔ 7 Reasons You Must Think About RFID

✔ 8 Things You Should Know When Developing with Open Source

✔ 9 Tips to Remember When Writing Numbered Lists

Cooking up an intriguing title is much easier than actually researching and writing a solid numbered list. Whatever title you pick, your content must deliver on the promise it makes. Don't be like one vendor who published a white paper titled "79 Tips on E-mail Marketing" — but when I counted up the tips, I couldn't find more than a dozen! Matching the numbers in your title to the items in your main body is obvious. Beyond that, make sure you cover what the title talks about. Don't pull a bait-and-switch where you get readers interested with a provocative title but then lapse into a sales pitch about your product.

Don't be afraid to break your regular style and express the initial number in your title in numeric form, as in the preceding examples. Why? Because people can scan numbers in a list faster than words, so your title gets noticed more, and because computers sort numbers to the top of a list, so your title shows up earlier. For example, in a list of search results — everything else being equal — "8 Questions to Ask . . ." will appear much earlier than "Eight Questions to Ask . . ."

Setting a provocative tone

Of all the flavors, a pure numbered list is where you can get away with the most provocative tone. After all, you're not using this flavor to present the details of your flagship product or the insights from months of groundbreaking research. You're using it to get attention, to keep the attention of existing prospects at the middle of the funnel, or to throw mud on your competitors. When you publish a lighter numbered list, your firm stands out from competitors who only dish out the heavy flavors that work at the top and bottom of the funnel.

For example, here are actual titles of numbered lists:

- "6 Things to Consider before You Rely on Open Office" (critical tone from Microsoft)
- "7 Infectious Diseases of Marketing — and Their Cures" (tongue-in-cheek tone from B2B marketing consultant Kathryn Roy)
- "8 Reasons You Should Kiss Excel Goodbye" (provocative tone from B2B software vendor 3PL Central)

These titles immediately set the expectation that these documents are lively, sarcastic, or tongue-in-cheek. And that's fine. No one expects a numbered list to be the last word on any issue or a definitive guide to any subject. It's enough for it to be brief, lively, and thought provoking and to undercut the offerings from competing vendors. If you can do that with style, pizazz, and a touch of humor, this flavor will win over readers.

Going Beyond Text in a Numbered List

Although I generally like to see at least one concept graphic in every white paper, a numbered list can be the exception. The organizing principle of the numbered list is so powerful and so accessible that you may not even need graphics to retain your reader's attention. In the future, you can expect to see more rich media, like animation, audio, and video, in numbered lists, although this flavor may not be where these first occur. In the following sections, I discuss how to use graphics and rich media in a numbered list.

Adding graphics

Graphics are normally included in white papers to clarify concepts and hold the reader's attention. But not many readers fall asleep in the middle of a numbered list! The liveliness of a numbered list diminishes the need for graphics. Of course, you may want to include a flowchart or process diagram to illustrate one point or another. Tables, charts, and other text enhancements are appropriate in a longer numbered list.

Because a numbered list is built up from discrete points arranged in a modular framework, you may never find any one photo that adequately sums up the whole document. You may prefer to use one or more photos to illustrate individual numbered points, instead of trying to convey the overall message of the document as a whole.

One approach a designer can take with a numbered list is to format the numbers themselves as graphic elements. Making the numbers big, bold, and colorful helps break up the text and reduces the need to search for a photo to match every point of the white paper.

Because a cover for a numbered list is optional, you may not even need a cover photo. If you do use one, look for a photo that sets the stage by showing the target reader, the target market, or some symptom of the issue being covered. For example, if your numbered list talks about six ways to relieve paper burden with unattended scanning, consider a cover showing an office worker buried in paper. As with any flavor, photos of the real world build more credibility than clip art or custom graphics.

Using rich media

Using rich media, like animation, audio, or video, in a numbered list is not yet common, as discussed in Chapter 3. These forms will likely become more common over the next few years, but it may take some time to wash over the numbered list flavor. Rich media can make an old-fashioned print document more compelling, but the numbered list format is already so engaging that it has less need for any added attractions.

On the other hand, the modular structure of a numbered list lends itself nicely to being supplemented with rich media. An existing video or a piece of B-roll may fit perfectly with one point in a numbered list, without needing any continuity with the other points. You may be able to use a bit of video in a tongue-in-cheek way, perhaps some retro scene from a black-and-white training film — as long as you always get proper permissions for any copyright material. The Internet provides many sources for free, public domain, Creative Commons, or inexpensive video snippets that you may want to use.

Repurposing a Numbered List

A white paper in the numbered list flavor is quite easy to repurpose as an article, blog post, or press release. Because magazines and websites thrive on numbered lists, they're the easiest flavor to place with a third-party publisher. Although some observers caution that numbered lists have been overused, readers and web surfers seem happy to keep looking at them. And where there are eyeballs, there is marketing. So you may as well recycle your numbered lists to the hilt. The following sections explain how.

Blog post

Repurposing a numbered list for a blog is simple. You can just take the whole paper, keep the numbered points intact, but cut most of the text supporting each point. Boil down the introduction (if any) to a couple of sentences, and then do the same for the conclusions. Many bloggers say that the ideal length for a blog post is 500 to 600 words, so you don't have any room to spare. If you use 50 words for the intro, 50 for the conclusions, and 100 each for five points, that's all you get. You just created a post from a numbered list in minutes flat. Next, post it on your blog, with a link to the full white paper for those who want an extended discussion.

Another way to repurpose a numbered list as a blog post is to take the first three or four points, keep some text with each one, and then point to the full white paper to see the rest of the list. But I don't recommend doing this. Showing the whole list and letting interested readers click through for more details is better for three big reasons:

1. Not playing hide-and-seek with your content shows more respect for your reader's time.

2. Showing just the bare list of points may sling as much FUD on your competitors as the full white paper.

3. A complete list has a better chance than a partial to be picked up, retweeted, and commented on.

Guest blog

After you create your original blog post, you can easily repost the same topic with a different intro and ending on any other blog that accepts guest sub-missions. You could try the blog from an association, trade journal, forum, or any interested blogger who follows your space. Send the blog post and a link to the full white paper on your website. Your fellow blogger may decide to comment on your numbered list blog, pick up part or all of it, or ask you to tweak it a little so the search engines don't find exactly the same text in two places, which is a no-no for SEO. Your guest blog may become one of that blog's most interesting and controversial posts ever.

To approach a blog where you want your company to be featured, simply drop the blogger an e-mail, something like this:

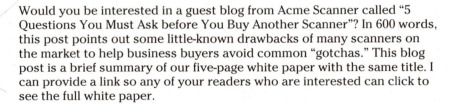

Would you be interested in a guest blog from Acme Scanner called "5 Questions You Must Ask before You Buy Another Scanner"? In 600 words, this post points out some little-known drawbacks of many scanners on the market to help business buyers avoid common "gotchas." This blog post is a brief summary of our five-page white paper with the same title. I can provide a link so any of your readers who are interested can click to see the full white paper.

Believe me, if that blog accepts guest posts, this approach will get noticed. You may well hear back on it in minutes.

E-newsletter article

If you publish an e-newsletter, you have another golden opportunity to repur-pose your numbered list. Depending on the structure of your e-newsletter, you can do this in several ways:

- ✔ **As a complete article**, where you republish your original numbered list white paper verbatim in the e-newsletter. The only problem is that the full white paper is probably too long to fit your e-newsletter format.

✔ **As an intro to the complete white paper**, where you publish just an intriguing snippet or the first few sentences of the white paper, with a link to download the entire numbered list PDF.

✔ **As a skeletal article**, where you publish your short, blog-style posting that gives the entire numbered list with only a little detail for each point. Then you invite readers interested in more detail to download the white paper in full. I prefer this format for the same reasons given in the "Blog post" section: This way, you're not making your readers play any guessing games or wasting any of their time.

Placed article

A *placed article* is an opinion piece, column, or article published in a trade magazine, newspaper, or on a website without any notice that it's coming from an outside vendor. Most often, a placed article gets a byline from a marketing executive from the vendor. To a B2B publisher, the obvious advantage is that this content is free. And because this piece was professionally written, the editor won't have to do much to get it ready. If your numbered list is based on credible facts with some provocative new twist, it can make compelling content for the people who read that journal or visit that website. And as the white paper sponsor, a vendor gets a wider platform for his ideas, so this is an all-around win-win-win.

As the old saying goes, "If you want an audience, start a fight." So if the placed article attacks some sacred cows or directs some zingers at other vendors in the field, that helps attract attention to the publication, the content, and the vendor.

If you've never done it before, you may be wondering how you place your numbered list as an article with a trade magazine or website. There's no magic here. Just call or e-mail the editor, tell him the title of the white paper, and say it's available as a bylined article for no fee. Many outlets will ask for exclusive rights to your placed article so that it doesn't pop up in the pages of a competing publication. That's okay as long as you start from the top, with the outlets with the biggest circulation. Don't start from the bottom and work your way up or you may give away the exclusive republishing rights to a much smaller outlet than necessary.

You really have only one good shot at placing a numbered list in a legitimate website or trade journal. After it gets out there on somebody else's website, no one else is likely to pick it up.

If editors or webmasters ask you to pay a fee to place your article with them, think twice. I'm old school enough to consider this request a questionable practice. I can't believe any credible outlet with much of an audience can get away with charging companies to run vendor-sponsored content like a white paper disguised as regular editorial. Readers aren't stupid; they're bound to smell something fishy when many articles come from some vendor or other. Unless the price is dirt-cheap and you're very hungry for exposure, move on and try the next outlet on your list. And if you're paying for exposure, don't give them an exclusive. You may still be able to place the same piece somewhere else for free and get double exposure.

Chapter 8

The Problem/Solution: As Complex As Chocolate

Chocolate is second only to vanilla among the world's most-loved flavors of ice cream. Many consider it the deepest, richest, longest-lasting, and most satisfying flavor of ice cream ever created. And just like chocolate ice cream, the problem/solution white paper has millions of devotees: marketing people who have tasted its wonders and keep on coming back for more.

In this chapter, I describe what a problem/solution white paper is all about, show how to identify one, and reveal when to use it for best results. Then I sum up the pros and cons of this flavor and provide the typical sections to include, along with recommended page counts. This chapter also describes how to repurpose the rich content of a problem/solution into other formats, especially a blog post, placed article, slide deck, webinar, or conference presentation.

Introducing the King of Content

The problem/solution white paper is like chunky chocolate ice cream: a rich and satisfying experience that lingers long after the moment is gone.

A substance in chocolate is said to mimic the feeling of falling in love, which may be why many find it so addictive. Readers of this flavor also experience a powerful mood-altering sensation as they gain deeper insights into some troubling business issue.

An effective problem/solution white paper is a persuasive essay that uses facts and logic to present a new solution to a serious problem that afflicts many companies in a given industry. With this soft-sell approach, a problem/solution white paper provides useful information that helps intended readers understand an issue, solve a problem, or make a decision.

This approach makes the problem/solution white paper the most powerful, most complex, and most challenging of all the flavors. I consider this flavor the undisputed king of content at the very top of the pyramid: No other piece of marketing material can consistently generate so many leads for so long and pay back so much on its investment. No other piece of marketing collateral can so dramatically change how a prospect views a vendor, so effectively define an entire market space, or so significantly elevate the level of respect for a B2B vendor across an entire industry.

In the following sections, I describe this complex yet tasty flavor of white paper, show you how to spot one, and explain why B2B executives find it so appealing.

Defining a problem/solution

Presenting a new solution to an acknowledged business problem in a convincing way is no small feat. A problem/solution white paper must be supported throughout by credible facts, convincing proof, and logical arguments. In many ways, this flavor is similar to the closing argument of a trial lawyer. The goal is to build an open-and-shut case that all right-minded people accept as fair and reasonable.

It's hard to say when this formula first originated. The problem/solution format was described by AdWords guru Perry Marshall in 2003 and refined by social media expert Michael Stelzner in his 2006 book *Writing White Papers* (WhitePaperSource Publishing). I've been promoting it as one of the three main flavors of white papers since before 2010. And the effectiveness of this flavor continues to be recognized by more and more B2B marketers around the world.

Problem/solution white papers are the toughest of all flavors and take the longest to create. They must provide truly useful content based on reliable research, engaging ideas, and compelling conclusions. But just like any challenge you overcome, problem/solution white papers are the most rewarding. And the rich content of this flavor makes it the most versatile to repurpose in many other ways.

Spotting a problem/solution

Identifying a problem/solution white paper can be challenging. It doesn't dwell on product information; instead, it tends to focus on a broad industry problem and a better way to solve it, as implemented in a certain product or service. That specific solution is only mentioned late in the document, after discussing the drawbacks of every other possible approach to solving the problem. In this subtle way, a problem/solution white paper positions an offering in a market space and argues for its superiority. But that structure makes this flavor the hardest of any to spot.

In a pure problem/solution, you won't find content structured as a set of numbered points or any number in the title. You also won't see many details on the features and benefits of one particular offering with the product name in the title. A classic problem/solution starts off by describing a big problem and eventually gets around to introducing a new, improved solution. If you see those two elements, you're most likely looking at some version of a problem/solution flavor.

Understanding why this flavor appeals to executives

By definition, an *executive* is someone who makes things happen. Executives can make things happen best when they understand the space they're operating in, weigh several possible courses of action, and pick the most effective option. Always remember that a truly effective problem/solution white paper helps a businessperson understand an issue, solve a problem, or make a decision. Notice how those imperatives line up perfectly with the challenges facing all executives.

If you're beginning to suspect that the problem/solution flavor was designed to appeal to executives, you're probably right. C-level executives, especially, don't have any time to plow through a backgrounder about the inner workings of a specific product or to sort through lightweight numbered lists looking for solid information. That makes the problem/solution the preferred flavor for the vast majority of juicy B2B prospects.

Deciding When to Use a Problem/Solution

The problem/solution flavor is gaining popularity all the time as more marketing people realize how effective this format can be. Using this flavor makes sense for any B2B company seeking to build recognition and attract as many prospects as possible. You can use this flavor to share the high-level benefits of a new, improved approach with stakeholders, including your sales force and channel partners. You can use the same paper to influence any analysts, bloggers, and journalists who cover your industry. If your company wants to redefine a market space, this flavor is the only one with enough depth to accomplish that. If you have the time and the resources to pour into developing a problem/solution, it can really pay off in a big way.

In particular, a problem/solution is the best of all flavors to pick in five specific situations:

- ✔ To generate leads at the top of the sales funnel
- ✔ To educate salespeople and channel partners
- ✔ To educate analysts, bloggers, and journalists
- ✔ To redefine a market space
- ✔ To build mindshare

Generating leads at the top of the funnel

Hands down, a problem/solution is the best flavor to generate leads at the top of the sales funnel. This flavor enables a company to cast the widest possible net and harvest the biggest catch of fresh leads. (To understand how this works, see the later section "Pro: Generates the most leads.")

Because a problem/solution white paper is best aimed at prospects near the start of the buying process, this flavor can't come across as a sales pitch. Unlike a backgrounder, this flavor uses a soft sell to inform prospects about an issue and position the sponsor as a trusted advisor. When the time comes to buy, B2B prospects feel so positive about your company that they're inclined to do business with you.

 Any smaller company that struggles to generate leads and fights to get onto vendor shortlists should consider publishing at least one white paper in the problem/solution format. By the same token, any large company addicted to backgrounders should publish a few problem/solution papers to round out its library and pull some fresh prospects into the funnel.

Educating salespeople and channel partners

For any company moving into fresh territory, the sales force puts the boots on the ground. Your salespeople need to understand the point of your offering, the problems it's designed to solve, and the drawbacks of every other way of doing things. A problem/solution white paper can give your salespeople all the background they need to discuss the problem in a more informed way. It can also serve as a send-ahead or a leave-behind, a conversation-opener or a deal-closer. Ideally, a problem/solution white paper gives you a way to elevate your company so far above other vendors that your salespeople can sell without hearing any objections about pricing, features, delivery dates, or anything else.

All these benefits apply equally to channel partners. If you have a network of consultants, retailers, or value-added resellers (VARs) that help generate revenues, send them all your white papers. An effective problem/solution white paper can make the difference between being remembered or being forgotten when your channel partners are in front of a client. Imagine channel partners trying to explain the benefits of a product with no white papers versus a product with a highly effective problem/solution flavor they can study and hand out to their own prospects. Which product do you think they recommend and sell more often?

Boosting sales with a creative twist

When I was VP of Marketing of a tech startup, I oversaw the creation of a special-report white paper focused on a fictional manufacturing firm, Acme Tricycle Works. In the white paper, two executives, in the roles of the decision maker and the technical recommender, stopped by several departments to discuss the problems they used to suffer and how much our new, improved offering had helped their company. We printed this creative twist on the problem/solution format as a small booklet in full color. That made it a relatively expensive project for a small company, about $25,000 all told.

Here's how our West Coast sales manager put the results: "Whenever I go into a meeting and put out a copy of our handbook for everyone at the table, our company shoots right to the top of their vendor list!" That little publication meant instant credibility for our firm, even though we were far smaller than most of our competitors. That problem/solution booklet helped us sell $20 million worth of software over the next two years. This is the king of content in action.

Educating analysts, bloggers, and journalists

A problem/solution white paper is a powerful item to send to opinion leaders in your space, including analysts, bloggers, journalists, and anyone who runs a website that your B2B buyers consider influential. In this context, you aren't necessarily expecting those opinion leaders to pick up your content to republish or even to comment on it publicly. (Of course, both are valid promotional tactics to try.) But even if they look at your white paper as "deep background," it can help shape their perceptions of your market from then on.

Imagine how opinion leaders see one company that regularly sends them helpful and well-informed white papers versus another that doesn't. Who do you think they'll mention, quote, and seek out for further opinions? By feeding the media and other opinion leaders your best thinking in the form of a problem/solution white paper, you're taking your best shot at influencing the influencers. As publicists have long known, getting editorial coverage has an incredible multiplying factor. If you get a favorable notice from one blogger with 5,000 subscribers, you've just generated 5,000 hits of positive word of mouth. If you get a notice in a magazine with 50,000 readers, that's 50,000 possible new hits. You can't buy that kind of publicity.

Redefining a market space

Occasionally, a B2B vendor may seek to redefine an entire market space, perhaps to enlarge it by showing how it overlaps with nearby spaces, perhaps to limit it by showing how it has certain unique and specific requirements. Perhaps you want to introduce a new acronym or do something else to tilt the entire playing field in your favor. Which flavor do you suspect would be best for these purposes? You guessed it: a problem/solution. A numbered list may hint in passing at some of these ideas without the depth to develop them. A backgrounder is too busy navel-gazing at your own offering to achieve this kind of profound effect. But a problem/solution is the only flavor than can grapple with this challenge of redefining a whole market space.

In this case, the *problem* is likely that every other vendor looks at the market space the wrong way, creating difficulties, limiting results, and wasting money. The *new, improved solution* can be as basic as a change in perspective so that readers see the market space in a new light. If your company ever reaches that historic moment when you need to redefine your market space, the problem/solution is the best flavor to use.

Building mindshare

An effective problem/solution white paper can do wonders to build more recognition for your company. Ideally, this flavor is so thoroughly researched and well expressed that it has ample credibility. Those qualities can propel your white paper up and down the food chain, passed from one executive to another within the same company and even between peers and friends in different companies. You may find your problem/solution white paper being commented on and recommended via social media. All this pass-along publicity helps to build mindshare by reaching B2B executives who may not have heard of your company before. Better mindshare helps smaller companies work their way into the inner circle and on to the vendor lists along with the big guys.

Looking at Pros and Cons of Problem/Solutions

Almost everyone loves chocolate ice cream. But despite what some 5-year-olds may tell you, you can't have it with every meal. And sometimes chocolate ice cream just won't work — like at the end of a huge Italian wedding dinner, when you can't possibly hold another bite, except for perhaps some light, melt-on-your tongue lemon gelato.

Just like every other flavor, the problem/solution has its strengths and its limitations. In some situations, a problem/solution white paper works better than others. On the plus side, this flavor routinely generates the most leads, lasts the longest in active duty, and returns the most on your investment. On the other hand, a problem/solution is the hardest flavor to create, takes the longest to complete, and, in rare circumstances, can even heighten an internal conflict that can't be resolved. In the following sections, I explore each of these pros and cons to the problem/solution flavor.

Pro: Generates the most leads

Every business needs new prospects to fill the sales funnel, which is where a problem/solution really shines; it draws more fresh leads into a vendor's funnel than any other flavor. To understand why, think about how most B2B buyers use search engines like Google to get the answer to a question or to find help understanding an issue. Do they Google the name of some product or search for a top-ten list? Or do they Google their actual problem or question and see what pops up in the search results that looks interesting? Of course, people search for answers to their real issues, which is precisely why a problem/solution generates the most leads.

By grappling with a serious business problem that afflicts an entire industry — and inserting appropriate keywords that convey how business people express that problem — this flavor turns up in search results at the best possible time: when business executives are actively looking for help. Even if those readers have never heard of your company before, when they download a white paper that provides useful advice and an enlightening perspective, they begin to see your company as a trusted advisor, which is exactly what you want.

Pro: Lasts the longest

As long as the same nagging problem remains unsolved for many companies and as long as B2B buyers search for help and find your white paper, your problem/solution can continue to work for you. Done properly, a document in this flavor can have a long and happy life: at least one year, often stretching into several. After all, what harm is there in leaving an effective white paper available on your website for a couple of years, as long as people are still downloading it? Many times, you can update or refresh a problem/solution and use it for another year.

You need to update or take down a problem/solution white paper only when most companies have already solved the problem it describes, when new categories or alternate solutions exist that you didn't cover, or when your own offering has evolved so much that it doesn't resemble what you were talking about in your original document. Otherwise, leave it up, and let it keep on working to generate leads.

Pro: Makes the best investment

This long life, coupled with its supreme lead-generating powers, makes the problem/solution white paper the best investment of any flavor. Why? Because marketers calculate the total number of leads generated by a campaign as follows:

$$\frac{\text{Total number of leads generated by a campaign}}{\text{Total cost of campaign}} = \text{Average cost per lead}$$

Time after time, marketers find that leads generated by white papers are much less costly than leads generated with advertising, direct mail, trade shows, or other traditional marketing methods. And an effective problem/solution white paper generates more leads for longer than any other flavor. Where a backgrounder looks under the hood at a single product, a problem/solution surveys an entire industry. While a numbered list is often quickly forgotten for its frivolity, a problem/solution is taken seriously for years to come. Even though the costs to produce a problem/solution are slightly higher, the results make it worth every penny.

Con: Hardest to create

Despite the many strengths of a problem/solution, it's the most difficult flavor of white paper to create. This flavor demands that marketing and sales executives take a break from their regular habits of pitching and selling. Instead, they must provide clear, compelling answers to some fundamental questions, like these:

- What problem does this offering solve?
- What other solutions have been tried in the past?
- What drawbacks do other solutions suffer from?
- How does this offering overcome these drawbacks to solve the problem best?

Another challenge: A problem/solution white paper must present a mountain of proof. For B2B buyers, proof points include specific numbers from impeccable sources, persuasive comments from acknowledged experts, compelling testimonials from delighted customers, and ironclad logic that ties it all together with chocolaty goodness.

Some marketing teams find these challenges daunting. They may want to retreat back to a backgrounder, which is much easier to research simply by speaking to your own in-house people. But it's usually better to push on to complete a problem/solution white paper that can generate many leads and serve your company for years to come.

Con: Slowest to create

Because of its ambitious scope, a problem/solution white paper takes longer than any other to create. It takes time to compile detailed research, to analyze all the traditional solutions, and to include a buyer's guide of what to look for in an ideal solution. And it takes time to write a coherent narrative that links together all this content in a compelling way, without veering off into a sales pitch. No other flavor aims this high or takes this much in-depth research or nuanced writing. I estimate a minimum of four elapsed weeks for creating a problem/solution: one week each for planning, researching, writing, and reviewing. And these tasks can often take six to eight weeks, especially when numerous interviews or reviewers are involved. When you need a white paper in a big hurry, don't pick a problem/solution flavor.

Con: May heighten internal conflicts

Believe it or not, some white papers don't get completed because various people can't agree on some fundamental point! The most common split is engineering versus sales. One side thinks the key point of some offering is obviously *this,* while the other declares that anyone in his right mind knows it's *that.* Having to set down in writing the key problem that the offering is designed to solve and how it does it somehow brings up such strong differences of opinion that the white paper gets stalled and even abandoned.

This situation doesn't happen often, mind you, but I have encountered it — most often with a problem/solution. Conflicting opinions don't seem to happen so much with a backgrounder, which simply describes how an offering works, or with a numbered list, which can usually flit around any heavy issues. If you've heard any serious internal conflicts about a product, get them sorted out before the writer starts interviewing people.

Planning a Problem/Solution

Publishing any flavor of white paper involves three major phases: planning, producing, and promoting. Parts III and IV of this book go into each of these phases in great detail, breaking them down into a step-by-step plan. In this section, I cover how creating a problem/solution is a little different from any other flavor, including the following:

- ✔ Gathering the essential information you need
- ✔ Allocating pages
- ✔ Choosing an appropriate title
- ✔ Setting the right tone

Gathering essential information

You can't make chocolate without getting some cacao beans. By the same token, you can't write a problem/solution white paper without gathering some basic information about the project. You likely need a little research to dig up these items and establish the frame of reference for your document, and that's fine. Every project goes much more smoothly if you clarify these seven items during your planning process:

- ✔ Your intended reader(s)
- ✔ The purpose of the problem/solution
- ✔ The industry-wide problem
- ✔ The traditional solutions and their drawbacks
- ✔ The new, improved solution
- ✔ What to look for in an ideal solution
- ✔ The call to action at the end

The writing comes during Phase 2 (see Chapter 13), when you actually produce your white paper. If you're working with an in-house writer, he can be involved in every stage of this research. You're more likely working with an outside writer, so you have a choice: Do all this research without the writer and hand it over, or involve the writer in your research with you.

I always appreciate when clients think about these issues before speaking with me, but I still want to walk through all these matters in a conference call with all their reviewers, just to make sure everyone is on the same page. This step is a recommended best practice that helps avoid the dreaded "scrap and rework" that can occur when a hidden reviewer pops up late in the process and declares, "You're doing it all wrong! Go back! Do it my way!"

Your intended reader(s)

To help target your problem/solution to the right audience, identify your ideal reader as specifically as possible. You can use the following four categories to help specify your target readers:

- ✔ **Company:** Get a sense of the size, vertical market or sector, and location of the company where your intended reader works. For example, your reader may work at an engineering company in the southeast that specializes in managing major construction projects, such as highways and power plants.
- ✔ **Demographics:** Dig up hard facts, such as the age, sex, education, and job title(s), of your target readers. For example, your readers could be

managers in their 30s or 40s who are 60-40 male-female, all with civil engineering degrees. To find these kinds of facts, ask your sales, customer service, or technical support teams, or anyone else who has daily contact with your actual customers.

✔ **Psychographics:** Sketch in some of your target audience's attitudes, such as their experience, interest in your offering, and workaday stress. For example, your readers could be aware that their engineering drawings aren't always where they should be and that lost documents cost time and money. They may be open minded about using some sort of web-based system to solve those problems. Summing up the attitudes of a whole audience can be difficult, but wrestling with these questions is much better than ignoring them. The insights you gain can be important.

✔ **Technographics:** Will your target readers likely access the problem/solution white paper through a desktop, laptop, tablet, or mobile device? Perhaps the vast majority of your target readers will hear about your white paper by doing a Google search and then viewing it on a laptop or tablet while they travel between sites (as a passenger, of course, not the driver). That's useful information to know.

Remind your white paper designer of these technographics during the design phase. Knowing that readers will likely view your white paper on-screen may well affect how the designer formats the pages, how many columns and graphics he uses, and so on.

If you have any secondary audiences — desirable but not essential readers — define them as well. For example, your secondary readers may be female clerks in their 20s and 30s who are responsible for using outdated systems to manage engineering libraries. You may consider these readers secondary because they're not in a position to buy from your company, but they may be in an ideal position to recommend a purchase to help solve their problems.

The purpose of the problem/solution

What are you trying to accomplish with this flavor? Some likely purposes include generating leads; educating salespeople, channel partners, analysts, bloggers, or journalists; redefining a market space; or building mindshare. A problem/solution white paper can do a lot, but it can't do everything. Pick your main goal and stick to it.

The industry-wide problem

Before you can write a problem/solution, you must pinpoint the precise problem you intend to address, which should be an acknowledged issue that causes daily pain for many companies within a certain industry. Don't pick an insidious problem that may be wasting resources but remains out of sight and out of mind — like a leaky water pipe underground. Pick a problem that's aboveground and noticeable, more like those unsightly piles of paper files cluttering up the entire company's headquarters. And make sure it's a problem you have an offering to solve: a product, service, technology, methodology, or vision.

If you're wondering what makes a good topic for this flavor of white paper, here are just a few of the many problems I've written about in the past year:

- Engineering firms have trouble managing all the plans, drawings, and documents that pile up for major construction projects.
- Most companies spend too much on mobile phone services for employees.
- Drug development teams get stuck for years trying to generate acceptable test results for FDA approvals.
- Many private-school administrators don't understand the electronic data security standards that apply when they begin to accept credit cards.
- Business process software can't help most organizations run more efficiently, because it wasn't designed for their type of operations.

Notice how this flavor can address a vast range of organizations, sectors, and business challenges.

The traditional solutions and their drawbacks

Draw up a list of all the possible ways to solve this problem. Don't forget to include what many people do, even in business: Ignore it and hope it goes away. In your final white paper, you can spell out the huge cost of ignoring the problem as it festers and grows. Work through the following steps to create your list:

1. **Include using manual methods, forms, spreadsheets, or any other type of homegrown or do-it-yourself system.**

2. **Add all the current solutions on the market.**

   Simply listing all the competing companies and products at this point is okay. Ultimately, you'll need to create a set of buckets to sort these solutions into various categories, classes, genres, or types.

3. **Think of the failings, limitations, or unintended consequences of each category of existing solution.**

   Here, you get to set up every possible alternative to your offering and give each one your best shot. You don't have to know all these details right off the bat, but the more you can list at this point, the faster your writer can get on with his research.

The new, improved solution

You already know all about your offering and how superior it is. But now, you need to shift out of your regular thought patterns and consider your offering in more generic terms. What category, class, genre, or type of solution is it, exactly? Where does it fit in your market space: Is it a dominant product or a new challenger? Did your company create a whole new category? Or did you redesign and rethink an existing category with some breakthrough innovations? Can you accurately label it the "next generation" or "version 2.0" of an existing paradigm? Why does it work better than anything else on the market? What proof do you have for that claim?

When you start thinking this way, you get ready to face the toughest challenge of your problem/solution white paper: providing some truly educational information for your readers, positioning your offering accurately in its market space, and showing how it works better than anything else ever designed.

What if your offering really isn't better?

What if your solution really isn't any better than anything else on the market? What if it's only cheaper, easier to use, saves energy, or is made from 95 percent biodegradable items sourced from fair-trade farmers? Well, each of these benefits — or any other unique selling point — can be enough to drive a problem/solution white paper.

For example, consider pricing: Many companies admit that they're drowning in paper. Some have even calculated how much they spend to handle every paper invoice, check, form, and other items on paper instead of electronically. Say the best way to solve this problem, in many cases, is to route e-mail attachments directly to a fifth-generation scanner that can run unattended and convert those attachments into structured data, all set to import flawlessly into a spreadsheet, database, CRM, ERP, or Big Data analytics system. Who wouldn't want that? The only problem is, this service is extremely expensive.

Say Acme Scanners has just released a cost-reduced scanner that can do almost everything that one of the high-end models does, but it costs only one-tenth as much. This offering can work well for a problem/solution white paper. In this case, the problem can remain the devastating costs of paper burden. But then you can move on to the related problem that the ultimate solution has already been invented, but it's been priced far beyond the reach of many organizations. What's needed is a scanner that can do everything the high-end machines do, only at a much lower price point. There you have it. Acme Scanners to the rescue, with a scanner priced for everyone.

Similarly, the problem could be that unattended scanning is too difficult to set up, that it sucks up too much energy and air conditioning, or that the existing models all use certain rare earth chemicals sourced from nasty warlords in downtrodden countries that are impossible to recycle. As long as your offering has at least one unique selling point that makes it better than the competition in any way, you can still write a problem/solution white paper around it.

What about the worst-case scenario, when your offering doesn't have a single competitive advantage but is only a "me-too" copy of someone else's product? If your offering isn't better, cheaper, faster, more rugged, more energy efficient, more powerful, or more something, more anything, then using a problem/solution flavor of white paper may not be realistic. In this case, you can still use a white paper; just think about doing a backgrounder or a numbered list instead.

What to look for in an ideal supplier

Still thinking about your offering and your company in generic terms, list all your key competitive advantages, unique selling points, or all the things that only you can rightfully claim. This list will eventually turn into a page of bullet points. Compile what you can of these points for now, remembering that you'll have to fill it in later.

Every company in the world can make nebulous claims like, "We believe in excellent customer service." But that's not good enough for a white paper. Have you won the top industry award for best customer service for the past five years in a row? Now that's proof! In this case, you can write your bullet point for this item like one of these options:

- ✔ "Award-winning track record for top customer service"
- ✔ "Recognized for industry-leading customer service"
- ✔ "Industry's top customer service for five years running"

That makes it a lot harder for any competitor to say, "Me too! Me Too! We do that, too!" If anyone wants to challenge this claim, the most obvious questions are, "Awards from whom? Recognized how? Who says you're the top?"

The call to action at the end

What do you want your ideal reader to do after reading your white paper? Don't refer busy people to your home page to wander around looking for the right place to click. Instead, send them to a specific landing page. Point them to a short presentation or demo. Invite them to use an interactive calculator. Have them call a toll-free number or request a free trial. Ideally, you can build the call to action into your sales cycle as a natural next step. In general, the more specific the call to action, the more effective and easier it is to measure the results.

Allocating pages

As shown in Figure 8-1, a problem/solution white paper is typically nine pages or more from start to finish. About half of the document is the actual content; the other half is the wrapper around the content. To stay in today's sweet spot, a problem/solution can run a little shorter or a little longer, but not by much. Even more than the page count, pay attention to the content. A white paper in this flavor must provide reliable research, engaging ideas, and compelling conclusions. If you can give your readers all of that, they won't care much about the length.

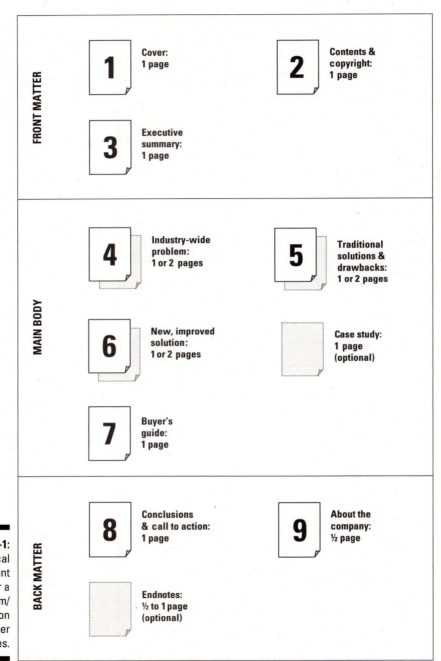

FRONT MATTER

1 Cover:
1 page

2 Contents &
copyright:
1 page

3 Executive
summary:
1 page

MAIN BODY

4 Industry-wide
problem:
1 or 2 pages

5 Traditional
solutions &
drawbacks:
1 or 2 pages

6 New, improved
solution:
1 or 2 pages

Case study:
1 page
(optional)

7 Buyer's
guide:
1 page

BACK MATTER

8 Conclusions
& call to action:
1 page

9 About the
company:
½ page

Endnotes:
½ to 1 page
(optional)

Figure 8-1:
The typical
page count
for a
problem/
solution
white paper
is 9+ pages.

Illustration by Wiley, Composition Services Graphics

Like all white papers, a problem/solution includes three parts: front matter, main body, and back matter. The following sections discuss briefly what to include in each part of a problem/solution flavor and how many pages it should run. Remember that these page estimates are only guidelines. You can expand most of these sections or condense some of the front and back matter into fewer pages. For more tips and discussion on building a white paper, see Chapter 10. You can also check out some sample problem/solution white papers at www.thatwhitepaperguy.com/sample-white-papers.html.

Front matter: Two to three pages

The front matter for a problem/solution is more significant than for any other flavor and usually includes all the elements in this section.

A **cover page** sets up the serious matters under discussion. For best visibility, keep the title to the top half of the page. Show your logo but keep it small; acknowledging that your white paper is sponsored content from a vendor is fine, but you don't want prospective readers to think they're about to get clobbered with a sales pitch. If you prefer not to use a visual cover, you can combine a text cover with the contents to eliminate one page of front matter.

With so much competing for the attention of your target reader, a visual cover gives your white paper better odds of getting noticed. For the cover photo, use an appropriate shot that shows the target audience or the dire consequences of the problem being tackled. If you make your cover look as inviting as a magazine — so that members of your target audience are itching to download it — it's working.

A **contents and copyright page** shows the document's framework at a glance. This page also adds to the academic feel of your white paper, suggesting its scholarly depth of research. You can just tuck your copyright notice and any company contact information beneath the table of contents. Don't clutter up your copyright notice with any extended legal verbiage about how this content "cannot be stored or transmitted in any electronic system now known or invented in the future anywhere in the universe . . . blah blah blah. . . ." That phrasing is counterproductive. In fact, you *want* B2B buyers to copy the heck out of your white paper, pass it around their companies, and send it to all their peers, colleagues, and friends in the same industry. Don't let the lawyers write your marketing materials; they're terrible at it.

A one-page **executive summary** sums up what to expect from the rest of the paper. This summary serves to "tell them what you're going to tell them." If you prefer, you can consider the executive summary as part of the main body and not the front matter.

My colleague Jonathan Kantor wisely points out two types of executive summaries: a *preview* of selected highlights intended to attract readers to the full document, or a *synopsis* that provides a complete summary of the paper. With a preview, you're asking busy executives to tolerate playing peek-a-boo with your ideas. I prefer the synopsis, because it lets you lay out your entire argument in brief. If B2B buyers read only that one page, at least they see your whole argument in a nutshell.

Sometimes, prospects copy the executive summary from a problem/solution for other members of the selection committee. Or they may photocopy the first page to include in a report to a C-level executive or capture the text from your PDF and paste it into an e-mail. Think about it: A manager asks a staffer to look into how their company can solve some nagging problem, so the staffer finds a problem/solution white paper full of helpful tips and insights. Why not give his manager a taste by pasting the executive summary right into his report? What could be better for a vendor than to have that one-page distillation of your ideas in the hands of everyone at the boardroom table?

Don't make your executive summary any longer than a page, and if you can keep it to half a page, so much the better. Everyone appreciates conciseness.

Main body: Four to eight pages

The main body of the problem/solution is where you "tell them"; it's where you cover all the gritty details of the problem, describe the failings of all the traditional solutions, and present your new, improved solution.

Start this part with a **serious, nagging problem** that afflicts companies in your target market. Describe it in some detail, showing its nasty consequences and how it robs otherwise worthy companies of their profits. Make sure it's a problem that has gone unsolved for some time, ideally a problem that your target reader is suffering from at this very moment. Use statistics, anecdotes, and quotes from recognized experts, publications, or trade associations to confirm the severity of this problem.

This section should be at least one page long, perhaps two. If you go on much more than two pages, you may tire out your readers; after all, they're looking for solutions, not an extended discussion of a problem they already know well.

Sketch in all the **traditional solutions** that were tried over the years for this problem. These represent all the competing notions cluttering up your B2B buyer's mind, and your job is to clear them all away. Include anything a prospect can do besides use your offering, such as doing nothing and letting the problem continue to eat away at the foundations of the company. This section could include developing some homegrown system or using existing office software and designing forms or spreadsheets to fill in on paper. Include every single possibility, leaving nothing out.

Express these traditional solutions as categories, classes, genres, or types of offerings, not specific products from named competitors. Doing so keeps the tone elevated to a higher, more analytical level where you can consider an entire market space, not just a certain grab bag of products. Then list the drawbacks of each category you identify, taking your best shot at every competing solution to clear the field for your recommended solution.

This section is usually one or two pages long, although it can be shorter. Often, you can set up and knock down an alternate approach in a single sentence, or two at most. For example, in a problem/solution white paper about engineering companies struggling to manage their files, I dismissed every existing solution in just a few words:

> Paper files are so easy to lose or misplace that most firms prefer to manage their files electronically. According to an IDC study, paper is a major source of information overload, and seven out of ten knowledge workers prefer to deal with digital information.

Dispensing with whole categories this way keeps your white paper much shorter than considering a whole parade of individual products one by one. From this point on, you want your readers to lump any competing product into one of the categories you dismissed in this section. You want to shake their faith in that approach, permanently.

Describe your **new, improved solution** but only in generic terms. Staying generic may feel strange, like speaking about your offering at arm's length, but it provides the key educational value of your paper instead of resorting to a sales pitch. Talk about your offering as a new category, class, genre, or type, or even a new generation, or at least a significant upgrade or major tweak to what came before. Put off mentioning your offering by name in this section, even though that may feel counterintuitive. Your goal is to remain as vendor-neutral as you can for as long as you can.

A **buyer's guide** is a powerful element to include in every problem/solution white paper. It doesn't have to be elaborate; you can format the buyer's guide as a set of bullets, listing what to look for in an ideal solution. Of course, you want to make sure every bullet focuses on some unique selling point of your offering, something that only you can do that gives you a definite competitive edge.

White paper author Michael Stelzner coined the phrase *buyer's guide* for this section, and he calls it "the most powerful and persuasive element of the entire white paper." This section is powerful because it can tilt the entire playing field in your favor without making a blatant sales pitch. Remember that every B2B selection committee needs to draw up a list of requirements. If you give them a list for the taking, odds are your list will influence their thinking; in the best case, they simply take your list and use it for their own. And then your offering is bound to score highly against their requirements!

Mention your offering by name only after the buyer's guide — and then only to confirm that it's an *ideal* solution that matches every bullet in the buyer's guide. Whatever you do, don't devolve into a sales pitch for your offering, because that can undo everything you achieved by using the problem/solution flavor.

A **case study** that highlights the positive experience of an actual customer with your offering is optional, but it can be powerful. You can include a case study as a full page, a brief sidebar, or even a tiny text box. You can include more than one or skip them entirely. Always compress case studies down from their original size. If you originally published a customer story as 800 words over two pages, boil it down to 100 words, or even 50 if you can, and then use it more like a proof point.

Or if you want to feature a longer, more complex case study in a longer problem/solution, set it up as a one-page sidebar with a graphic, a different typeface, or a light tint of color behind it. For more tips on designing sidebars, check out how magazines like *Time* or *Scientific American* handle them.

Back matter: One to three pages

The back matter in a problem/solution white paper often includes these elements: a set of conclusions, a call to action, info about the company, and a list of the sources used in the paper.

A set of **conclusions** brings your problem/solution to a satisfying end by "telling them what you told them." This section briefly retraces the main thread of your argument, accomplishing two things: It reinforces the main messages for those who read all the way through, and it provides another statement of the paper's scope for those who flip to the back first. Your conclusions should be half a page to a page, max.

At the very end of the conclusions, include a brief **call to action**. What do you want the ideal reader to do after reading your white paper? The answer is your call to action, which can be as short as a single sentence to suggest what to do next, where to find more information, or how to engage with your company to move deeper into the sales funnel.

Include a section **about the company,** drawn from the standard boilerplate on your company's website. Of course, at the very end, you probably want to include contact details, such as the company phone number, e-mail address, fax, Twitter feed, and company LinkedIn or Google+ pages.

If you use **endnotes,** they generally fall at the end of your document, if only because Microsoft Word puts them there, and struggling with that software any more than necessary is no fun. Some prefer to give references in footnotes at the bottom of each page; others like to gather all references together at the end of the document as endnotes. Your writer can do either and format them according to your preferred style. In a problem/solution, always include endnotes, footnotes, or at least a list of sources so your readers know where your references come from. Using credible sources gives B2B buyers a higher opinion of your company — exactly what you want your white paper to accomplish.

Choosing an effective title

Coming up with a title for this flavor of white paper is critical. A poor title can sink your efforts and limit your downloads, no matter how strong the actual content. A good title gives your white paper a fighting chance to get noticed, get downloaded, and make a difference. What distinguishes a good title from a bad one? A good title spells out the issue being discussed, specifies the target reader or industry, and includes the benefits the reader will gain by downloading and reviewing your document.

Knowing the problem, how nasty it is, and why your solution is better than anyone else's equips you to develop an effective title. Play around with these elements by stating the problem and giving some new hope of solving it in your title. If you can do so in a way that sounds natural, include any keywords you've identified as likely search terms that will lead your target readers to the white paper.

You don't have to come up with the ultimate title when planning your problem/solution white paper, but having a working title can be helpful, especially if you're juggling more than one white paper at once. Unlike a numbered list, no formula exists for writing the title for a problem/solution white paper, but here are some possible formats and examples:

- A leading question: "Is Your Enterprise Buried in Paper?"

- A how-to: "How to Gain from Unattended Scanning"

- A metaphor: "Slaying the Paper-Burden Dragon"

- An imperative with clear benefits: "Save Time and Money with Today's New Generation of Unattended Scanners"

- A call to action: "The Time Is Right for Automated Filing with Fifth-Generation Scanners"

You can help generate leads by including a subtitle to clearly identify who the white paper is aimed at. Pick the most compelling and unifying factor about your target audience, such as your ideal readers' job title, the industry they work in, their attitude toward the problem, their region, or anything else that ties them all together. For example:

- ✔ "A White Paper for CIOs Being Asked about Unattended Scanning"
- ✔ "A Special Report for Insurance Companies Suffering from Paper Burden"
- ✔ "An Executive Briefing for ISP Executives"
- ✔ "A Research Report for Deans in Ivy League Colleges"

In a recent workshop, I handed out a half-finished white paper and asked participants to give it the worst title they could possibly imagine. The hands-down winner was "Acme and You." This title still makes me chuckle because it's so awful in every possible way. It gives no hint about the contents, no clue about the target audience or industry, and no whiff of any benefit to readers. If you take exactly the opposite approach, you're on the right track to naming your problem/solution white paper.

Setting a dignified tone

To achieve the goals you expect from a problem/solution white paper, your document must maintain a certain tone: calm, logical, and, above all, dignified. Where a numbered list can engage in sardonic commentary or imaginative flights of fancy (see Chapter 7), a problem/solution must stand firmly on solid ground, citing expert opinions and impeccable statistics in the manner of a trial lawyer. Where a backgrounder can zoom in on the inner workings of a certain offering (see Chapter 6), a problem/solution must offer a sweeping vision of a nagging challenge that faces many companies. The tone of a problem/solution white paper must be engaging, of course, but never bombastic, comedic, or over-the-top in any way.

Finding this middle ground isn't easy for some writers, especially those steeped in writing advertising copy or sales letters. A problem/solution white paper explains a big issue in the manner of a magazine article and persuades by using facts and logic, not calls to emotion. A seasoned writer experienced with expository text should be able to hit the right tone: not too flippant, not too plodding, but just the right mix of facts, logic, imagery, and persuasion.

Because problem/solution white papers are aimed at business executives, they're often passed up and down the corporate ladder within companies. It may help to visualize your target readers and write as though you're giving a presentation in their boardroom or having a discussion in their office. Don't write as though you met up for beers — that's just too informal for this flavor.

Going Beyond Text in a Problem/Solution

The problem/solution flavor cries out for more than just text. Not everyone learns best by reading, and your target audience has far too much to read, too much to remember, and too much to deal with. In fact, the typical executive has more than a full week's work sitting on top of his desk at any given time, not to mention constant interruptions from staff, higher-ups, and customers, plus a daily flood of e-mails and phone calls. My colleague Jonathan Kantor calls these readers "time- and attention-challenged," and he's right. Do you really think your message can get through all those distractions and lodge firmly in the mind of your prospect if you present it as a wall of text?

I believe effective graphics make all the difference in a problem/solution white paper. And in the future, rich media, like animation, audio, and video, will likely become popular additions to this flavor — just the same as toasted nuts, colorful sprinkles, or chunky bits add even more excitement to a scoop of chocolate ice cream. In the following sections, I discuss the role graphics and rich media can play in a problem/solution white paper.

Using graphics in a problem/solution

Every problem/solution white paper needs at least one concept graphic that clearly lays out the central argument of the document. This graphic could be a flow diagram that sums up a process, a before-and-after diagram that contrasts old and new approaches (see Figure 8-2), or a glorified block diagram that shows the parts within the whole. Or you could use a two-part diagram, where the first part shows the problem and the second part builds on the first to show how the new, improved solution solves the problem.

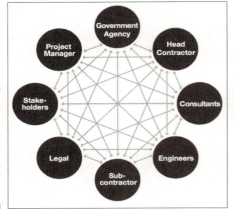 

Figure 8-2:
An example
of graphics
that show
the before
and after
approaches.

Illustrations courtesy of Aconex

White papers have evolved quickly over the past decade to become much
more visual. Today, at least half of all problem/solution white papers have
visual covers (see Figure 8-3), and this trend is bound to keep on growing.
You should plan on doing a little photo research to find a good stock image
that sets the scene for the content inside your white paper.

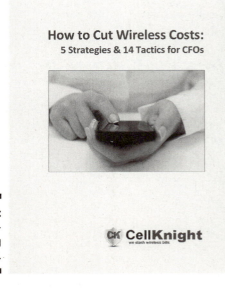 

Figure 8-3:
Two eye-
catching
covers.

Illustrations courtesy of CellKnight, Aconex

A good source for stock photos with reasonable pricing and a good indexing system is www.istockphoto.com. In just a few minutes, you can find an appropriate cover photo for a problem/solution white paper.

I'm always amazed to see companies, large and small, invest thousands of dollars to put together an effective problem/solution white paper but then neglect to create a single graphic to go with it and not even bother with a photo for the cover. What were they thinking? This thoughtless lack of graphics can sink the effectiveness of the whole document.

When you're designing or reviewing a white paper, think of it as a magazine that's supposed to include a mix of text and graphics. Every page should have something to break up the text, and the best way to break up a sea of gray is to include a graphic that sums up and illuminates much of the surrounding text. And don't discount sketches or ideas you come up with on restaurant napkins or white boards because they're not "pretty" enough. Instead, give your rough sketches to a professional artist or designer who can make them, literally, as pretty as a picture.

Using rich media

Using rich media, such as animation, audio, or video, isn't yet commonplace in problem/solution white papers, as discussed in Chapter 3. But I firmly believe rich media is coming to the world of white papers, and the problem/solution is the most appropriate flavor to use it. You can package rich media in many ways with narrative text, using a PDF as a "container" for all types of content. In this way, the white paper remains a single file that's easy to download, e-mail, or otherwise share with colleagues.

The effects of rich media in white papers will be profound. Instead of static images, graphics could be animated in full color to show flows, cycles, or growth and decline. Some or all of the text could be spoken as audio through a mobile device to become the soundtrack for another activity, like commuting, exercising, or gardening.

Imagine a clickable sidebar where B2B buyers can view a short video on some aspect of the problem or watch the vendor's CEO giving the executive summary. Toward the end of the piece, a video testimonial could provide a case study from a satisfied client, or a well-spoken executive could state the conclusions and invite interested readers to take the next step.

This next generation of white papers will be thrilling indeed, and the problem/solution white paper will be the flavor that leads the way into these exciting developments. For more on the possible futures of white papers, see Chapter 3.

Repurposing a Problem/Solution

The problem/existing-solutions/best solution approach of this flavor provides thought-provoking content you can readily repurpose in several ways. For example, you can extract a few specific ideas to create a blog post or placed article. You can create a slide deck and then use it for a webinar or for a presentation at an industry conference. Some marketing teams now create stand-alone videos to highlight the key ideas from a problem/solution white paper and urge viewers to download it. The rich content in a problem/solution flavor makes all this repurposing possible, as I explore in the following sections.

Blog post

An effective problem/solution white paper contains so much interesting content that you can use it to generate a multipart series of blog posts. For example, one post can describe the industry-wide problem and show how serious it is. The second can explain why the existing solutions on the market don't truly solve the problem. The third can introduce your new, improved solution in a generic way, without a lot of product mentions. You can even do a fourth post that lists what to look for in an ideal solution. Each post in the series can link back to the earlier posts and ahead to the next. And each post, of course, should contain a link to find out more by downloading the entire white paper.

You probably don't want to paste every word from the white paper into your blog. Four blog posts of 600 words each don't quite equal your entire white paper. Plan to leave extra details in the full white paper for those who download it.

Placed article

A *placed article* is an opinion piece, column, or article published in a trade magazine, newspaper, or on a website without any notice that it's vendor-sponsored content. Most often, a placed article gets a byline from a marketing executive from the vendor. A placed article becomes a win-win for both publisher and vendor: The publisher gets interesting content for free, and the vendor gets a wider audience for its views.

You may find that placing a problem/solution white paper is more difficult than placing a numbered list. If you happen to create a mash-up of a numbered list–problem/solution — as in "6 Ways Paper Burden Is Slowly Strangling Your Company and What to Do about It" — that should prove interesting to editors and bloggers. (See Chapter 9 for details about mashing up white papers.)

Start at the top when you're trying to place your problem/solution white paper. Many publications ask for an *exclusive,* meaning you can't place the same piece with anyone else. Why waste your single shot on a blog with 1,000 subscribers when you can shoot for a magazine with 50,000 readers?

If you've never tried to place an article, check out the section about placed articles in Chapter 7. That advice applies just as well to placing a problem/solution; so do the tips about paying for publication.

Slide deck

Any problem/solution white paper can be repurposed as an effective slide deck. Let's face it, most slides are pretty boring. Your deck for a problem/solution white paper should break out of this mold. Instead of the usual plodding introduction, why not start off your deck with a bang: a visual slide that illustrates the problem in gruesome detail.

Bad news travels fast, so when you start off a presentation by tackling an industry problem head-on, most audience members sit up and take notice. If that's a problem they're wrestling with, you'll have their undivided attention. Then use a couple more slides to show the extent of the problem by extracting quotes or factoids from your white paper. Then set up each alternate solution on a single slide, and knock it down on the same slide, or perhaps the next one. All of this will keep your deck moving along quickly in a logical way.

Finally, introduce your new, improved solution, but *don't* plaster your product name all over the screen. Talk about your solution in a generic way as a new category, class, genre, type, generation, or innovation. Show how it's better, and prove it the same way you did in the white paper. Then include a slide for a buyer's guide. And only after you do all of that, unveil your offering by name and confirm that it meets all the criteria in the buyer's guide.

Reserve your final slide for the call to action. If you're giving the presentation in person, have copies of the white paper available for handouts — but only after your presentation is finished. If you're building the deck for an online demo or to run unattended at a trade show, the call to action can be simply to download the white paper for more details.

After you complete your slide deck, you can decide whether you want to post it on the web on a slide-sharing site, such as SlideShare (`www.slideshare.com`), SlideBoom (`www.slideboom.com`), or myBrainshark (`www.mybrainshark.com`).

Never start off your presentation with six or eight slides "to give a little background about our company." Doing so is a gold-plated invitation to your audience to start checking messages on their mobile devices. At this point in your show, nobody cares about your company! They want to hear about their problem, why what they're doing doesn't work, and what else they can possibly try. First, give them useful content. Then, tell them about your company when they have a reason to be interested.

Webinar

After you build an interesting slide deck, a webinar is a natural follow-up. You don't need much more than a title slide to welcome people to the webinar, and the associated infrastructure to start taking sign-ups online. You can follow your slides to move through the problem, each traditional solution and its drawbacks, and your new, improved solution in exactly the same order as in your white paper. One benefit of an online webinar, if you enable this feature, is that anyone in your audience can type in a question as you go, and you can make sure to answer it.

Record your webinar and make the recording available on-demand through your website. You can also consider posting the entire webinar, or some choice bits of it, on your company's YouTube channel.

Conference presentation

If a problem/solution white paper is chocolate ice cream, a slide deck is toasted nuts, and a webinar is whipped cream, then a talk at an industry conference must be the cherry on top. With your white paper for a handout or download after your talk, an executive from your company can use your slide deck to give a thought-provoking presentation at an industry event. That talk may stir up some controversy about the drawbacks of the traditional solutions, but if your research was thorough, your presenter should be able to hold his own against any questioners.

Presenting at industry conferences can be a big credibility builder for smaller firms, so don't overlook this likely way to get even more return from your problem/solution white paper.

Chapter 9

Mashing Up Different Flavors

● ●

In This Chapter

▶ Combining white paper flavors to meet your needs

▶ Studying two flavor mash-ups that turn out well and two that don't

▶ Fixing a mash-up that goes wrong

● ●

*B*ased on the three main flavors of white papers, you can create four possible mixed flavors, or mash-ups. You can combine each flavor with one other, or you can mix all three flavors together:

✔ Backgrounder (vanilla) + numbered list (strawberry)

✔ Numbered list (strawberry) + problem/solution (chocolate)

✔ Backgrounder (vanilla) + problem/solution (chocolate)

✔ Backgrounder (vanilla) + numbered list (strawberry) + problem/solution (chocolate)

However, you must be careful about what you mash together. Not every flavor goes well with all the rest. A numbered list (strawberry) adds a light contrast that mixes well with either other flavor. But a backgrounder (vanilla) and problem/solution (chocolate) don't go well together, because each has a completely different flavor. And trying to mix all three flavors together generally turns into a mess, with too many discordant flavors fighting for supremacy.

In this chapter, I describe when you may need to use a mash-up and give some examples of how these mash-ups can be useful. Then I look at each of the four possibilities, showing why two of these mash-ups turn out to be tasty, while the other two usually make an unhappy mess. Finally, I explain how to tell whether you've made a mess and how to fix it if that happens.

Understanding Why You Need Mash-Ups

In an ideal world, marketers would have as much time, money, and energy to publish as many white papers as they ever wanted to. That would be a kind of heaven where people could eat as much ice cream as they wanted all day long, in every flavor under the rainbow. But in the real world, people have only limited time, money, energy, and attention. We can pile only so many scoops on an ice-cream cone before they start melting all over our hands or toppling over to fall on the street. Mash-ups can be a good solution to the real-world problem of constraints by enabling your company to, in effect, get a two-for-one deal: a single ice-cream cone holding scoops of two different flavors.

You can work from your white paper's intended purpose to zero in on the ideal flavor for your particular challenge. But sometimes a "pure" flavor can't do everything you need. It's easy to say, "Pick one main goal and stick to it," but what if you can't? What if you have two goals you want to accomplish but not enough in the budget for two separate white papers? Or what if your manager tells you both goals are the same priority, so you can't just pick one over the other? What if you'd love to do two white papers, one for each goal, but you simply don't have the time or resources to manage that? What if you can't decide between chocolate and strawberry, but really, really want some of each? In any of these cases, a mash-up can be exactly what you need.

The following sections offer examples of how you can address two goals in one white paper. However, don't think that the goals I talk about here are the only ones you can combine. You can mix and match any goals in one white paper. The challenge comes in knowing which ones fit well together and which ones are best avoided. I address those concepts later in the chapter.

Supporting a product launch, plus attracting attention

Suppose you need to support a product launch and, at the same time, attract attention to your company as an up-and-coming vendor in your niche. You realize that a backgrounder is the best flavor to accompany a product launch (see Chapter 6), while a numbered list is best at attracting attention with provocative views (see Chapter 7). But you can't afford to do two separate white papers.

In this case, think about combining both flavors to produce a mash-up with a title like, "6 Must-Have Capabilities of Unattended Scanning" or "5 Things to

Look for in Your Next Enterprise Scanner." To support your launch, organize this kind of white paper as a numbered list focused on the specific innovations that your new product provides. At the same time, you can declare these features must-haves that any competitive product in your niche must provide, a provocative stand that can help attract attention to your firm.

The liveliness of the numbered list format can help this white paper circulate more widely than if it were a pure backgrounder with your product name in its title. Meanwhile, the detailed product information — perhaps a checklist confirming that your product delivers every breakthrough capability — helps support the launch and educate your market space about your new product. In these ways, creating this mash-up helps you accomplish both goals at once.

Generating leads, plus raising your company's profile

Suppose you have two goals, one short-term and one long-term: to generate immediate leads now and, at the same time, to help your company get noticed by potential buyers in the future. And say you're in the commercial insurance market where every deal has a lengthy sales cycle of a year or more. In this case, getting your company on a buyer's radar now can mean getting a request for proposal (RFP) six months from now. Both goals amount to the same thing: building sales and revenues. You understand that a problem/solution is the best flavor for generating leads (see Chapter 8), while a numbered list is best to help your company raise its visibility (see Chapter 7). But you just can't manage two separate white paper projects on top of all your other marketing campaigns.

In this case, consider combining both flavors in a mash-up with a title something like "3 Profit-Sinks of Paper Burden and How to Avoid Them" or "5 Simple Solutions to the High Cost of Paper Files for Insurers." You can structure this kind of white paper as a numbered list that deals with several dimensions of a major problem, positioning your company as a trusted advisor. This mash-up can generate leads by pulling prospects into the top of your sales funnel, both now and for months to come. And this mash-up can also appeal to prospects at the middle of the sales funnel, helping your company earn a place on the short-list of vendors to receive the RFP they eventually send out.

Consider the advantages of this type of mash-up. The sparkle of the numbered list can help this white paper attract attention by promising a quick read on an essential topic. At the same time, the serious nature of the problem/solution can help this white paper get taken more seriously and have a longer life span than a pure numbered list. Creating this mash-up helps you accomplish both goals at once.

Creating Tasty Mash-Up #1: Backgrounder + Numbered List

One mash-up that can be quite successful is a backgrounder (vanilla) with a numbered list (strawberry). The lightness of the numbered list can make a backgrounder more appealing to a wider audience at the middle of the sales funnel, not just the bottom. Remember that vanilla and strawberry mix well together, because both are relatively mild flavors that complement one another nicely. In the following sections, I explore the background–numbered list mash-up.

When to use this mash-up

Try this flavor combo when you want to lighten up and extend the reach of a backgrounder with the appeal of a numbered list or to spread FUD (fear, uncertainty, and doubt) on all the competing offerings — and when you can't spare the time, money, or attention to do two separate white papers.

For example, I wrote one of these mash-ups called "EFM Evaluation Guide: 20 Must-Have Capabilities for a True Enterprise Feedback Management System" that listed a set of desirable features for this particular genre of software. It included a checklist to confirm that the white paper sponsor had the most capable offering on the market, casting doubt on every other product in that category. You can see this white paper at www.thatwhitepaperguy.com/sample-white-papers.html.

What to include and what to leave out

In a backgrounder–numbered list mash-up, you probably want to include a cover and perhaps a contents and copyright page as front matter. These items signify that the paper is somewhat more ambitious than a pure numbered list, where the front matter is more limited.

In the main body, make sure to include a brief introduction and then provide a lot of specific details about the features and benefits of your offering, all structured as a numbered list. For example, this type of mash-up can be organized as a set of must-have features every buyer should check for, a list of capabilities of the most advanced offerings in your niche, a number of items not to overlook, or a set of questions to ask every vendor, along with your answers for your offering. For back matter, include some brief conclusions, your call to action, and some brief boilerplate about the company.

Leave out any sweeping analysis of industry-wide problems and the failings of competing products, except for brief mentions or short sidebars. In this type of mash-up, you likely won't need any buyer's guide, footnotes, or endnotes, which are chocolate-flavored elements that can overwhelm this type of white paper with too much complexity.

Creating Tasty Mash-Up #2: Problem/ Solution + Numbered List

The second mash-up that can work well is a problem/solution (chocolate) with a numbered list (strawberry). The lightness of the numbered list can undercut the seriousness of the problem/solution and broaden its reach with the promise of a quick read. This mash-up can also appeal to prospects at the middle of the sales funnel, not just the top. Remember that chocolate and strawberry go well together, with the strawberry serving as a light contrast to the richness of the chocolate. The following sections show how to make a problem/solution–numbered list mash-up work.

When to use this mash-up

Try this mix when you want to use the appeal of a numbered list to provide a lighter take on a widespread problem and how to solve it or to reach out to prospects both at the top and in the middle of the sales funnel — and when you don't have the time, money, or attention to do two separate white papers to achieve these goals.

For example, I wrote one of these mash-ups called "3 Critical Challenges on any ARRA Construction Project" that explained three common pain points that companies were experiencing with U.S. stimulus projects after the financial meltdown in 2008. The rest of the paper discussed the drawbacks of every other solution and finally described the ideal solution to this problem.

This format caught the attention of target readers, helped them understand the source of their difficulties with these projects, and proposed a solution they may never have considered: a relatively new category of software called online collaboration platforms for engineering project management. You can see this white paper at `www.thatwhitepaperguy.com/sample-white-papers.html`.

What to include and what to leave out

In a problem/solution–numbered list mash-up, you probably want to include a cover and perhaps a contents and copyright page as front matter. These items signify that the current white paper is somewhat more ambitious than a pure numbered list, where the front matter is more limited.

Also at the front, make sure to include a brief executive summary where you "tell them what you're going to tell them." Then sketch in the industry-wide problem and the drawbacks of the existing solutions as a numbered list. For example, you can build this type of mash-up around a number of pain points caused by the problem, a set of hidden dangers every buyer must avoid, a number of benefits B2B buyers can enjoy with a better solution, or a set of questions to ask every vendor. For back matter, always include some conclusions, your call to action, and the boilerplate about the company.

In this type of mash-up, leave out any specific product mentions and descriptions of particular features of your offering. These vanilla-flavored elements can make a confusing mess of this mash-up by introducing too many flavors at once.

Avoiding Two Messy Combinations

At the beginning of the chapter, I list four possible flavor mash-ups. They all sound scrumptious, but in the world of white papers, two of these mash-ups don't turn out too well. Mashing together a backgrounder (vanilla) and a problem/solution (chocolate) in one paper usually creates more problems than it solves. And when you put all three flavors together, your white paper can lose focus and confuse your reader. The following sections elaborate on the issues with each of these less-than-tasty mash-ups.

Messy mash-up #1: Backgrounder + problem/solution

This mix is really hard to get right, because each flavor has a completely different emphasis. A backgrounder focuses on one product's particular features and benefits (see Chapter 6), while a problem/solution describes a major industry problem and how to solve it (see Chapter 8). In other words, a backgrounder is like using a microscope to zoom in on some tiny details, while a problem/solution is like using a telescope to see a distant horizon.

The educational value of a problem/solution can be diluted down by the product details of a backgrounder, just like vanilla waters down the richness of chocolate. And the complex tastes of a problem/solution can easily overwhelm a backgrounder, just like chocolate can make vanilla seem awfully bland if you serve a scoop of each flavor in the same bowl.

I suppose it's natural for sales and marketing people to want to combine these two flavors to convince everyone how a specific product solves a sweeping industry problem. But this mash-up ignores a basic dilemma: Those two approaches are aimed at buyers at different points in the sales funnel. The problem/solution flavor seeks to pull fresh leads into the top of the funnel, when they're looking for a solution to a nagging problem, not shopping for a specific product. The backgrounder supports a technical evaluation by prospects near the bottom of the funnel, when they're actively seeking detailed product information, not looking for a thoughtful overview of a major industry problem.

By mixing these two opposite flavors together, you're forcing your prospects to sort through a mess of content that isn't what they ordered when they downloaded your white paper. Most of them won't bother to do it. Instead, why not take care of your prospects by giving them the content they're most interested in at the time? You'll get far better results if you separate those two purposes, two audiences, and two flavors and serve them up as two separate documents.

A simple way to avoid either mess described in this chapter is to just keep vanilla away from chocolate. Neither flavor mixes well with the other, even if some strawberry is in the mix.

Messy mash-up #2: All three flavors in one

Although Neapolitan is a popular flavor of ice cream, this three-way combo of vanilla, strawberry, and chocolate is exceedingly rare in the world of white papers. In fact, it's hard to imagine such a mishmash satisfying any B2B buyer. How can you possibly combine the product details of a backgrounder with a new, improved solution to an industry problem, and then wrap it all up in a numbered list? How can you possibly target buyers at the top, the middle, and the bottom of the sales funnel all at once? And why would you want to try?

Combining all three flavors of white papers in one seems clearly impossible. And every time I've been involved with a white paper that tried to do the impossible, it turned out to be, well, impossible. Why not do the more sensible thing and create separate marketing pieces with corresponding campaigns that can satisfy prospects at each stage of the sales cycle?

Sorting out a muddled mash-up

I was recently working on a white paper for a major software company. At the start, the requirements sounded like a straightforward backgrounder, describing the benefits of an updated product. But then my client insisted on outlining the history of this market space, the problem the product solved, and what to look for in an ideal solution. Okay, but now it was sounding more like a problem/solution. As the content came together, I pinpointed seven key factors that a successful product in that space should offer. Hmmm . . . now it was becoming a numbered list.

The content was getting muddled, but I was too close to the project to see why. As the reviewers went over the content, something felt like it didn't belong. In fact, we were mixing up all three flavors in one document. Ultimately, the fix became clear: We dropped several pages of the product-specific details, and the white paper evolved into a workable mash-up of a numbered list–problem/solution. As a side benefit, the length dropped from more than a dozen pages down to a more manageable ten. And the final white paper was well received by its target audience.

In today's self-serve era of marketing with online content, most white paper readers find and download white papers to suit their needs and interests at the moment. They know what kind of information they seek. If they sense that a white paper isn't for them, based on little besides the title or perhaps the landing page, they click away to something else that seems more appropriate to them, and the moment is lost.

Fixing a Mash-Up That Doesn't Taste Right

Clearly, some mash-ups taste better than others. So what happens when you try something that just doesn't work out? Fortunately, you can usually fix a mash-up that goes wrong. The first step is often the hardest: Take a brief pause from the project to determine what's really going on. Review your goals and the audience for your white paper. Are you trying to cover too much or target B2B buyers at different points in the sales funnel? After you recognize that you have a mash-up on your hands that doesn't work, you can set about fixing it. Doing so takes a little effort. Just as saving a recipe that isn't working can be difficult, so too can saving a mash-up that goes wrong. But I show you how in the following sections.

How to tell when you've made a mess

Did you ever bite into something that you just knew tasted funny? Where the flavors didn't blend together well but rather all pushed and pulled against each other, like a riot happening in your mouth? How about garlic ice cream; can you imagine? That's what I'm talking about: something that just doesn't taste as yummy as you expect and contains some flavor that shouldn't be in there. Maybe it's too spicy, too bitter, too salty, or even too sweet. Whatever it is, the taste is off balance and unsatisfying.

The same thing can happen with a white paper. You can mix up too many flavors, or the wrong flavors, and create a mash-up that just doesn't taste right. The main problem is that the content is going in all directions at once. Many companies, especially when they publish their first-ever white paper, try to put too much into one document. As an inevitable result, the flavors get diluted, the message gets muddled, and no one is pleased with the results. Something "tastes funny" — but it's not always easy to tell exactly why.

When a white paper just isn't working, here are the two most likely reasons:

- ✔ You're mixing up two flavors that don't mix properly, namely a backgrounder and a problem/solution.
- ✔ You never decided which flavor to create in the first place, so you're mixing all three and muddling up the flavors.

In either case, the solution is the same. You must separate the various flavors present in your draft, reconfirm your main purpose, and target an audience at one point in the sales funnel. Then pick the right flavor to achieve that purpose and use only the ingredients that belong in that flavor, either dropping or rewriting everything else.

Separating the flavors

To separate the flavors in a mash-up that isn't working, read through your draft and highlight each flavor with a different color. You could use pink for strawberry, orange or green for chocolate, and leave any product information white for vanilla. To decide which flavor any sentence, paragraph, or section belongs to, ask yourself whether it's more about your offering (vanilla) or more about an industry-wide problem and a generic description of a new, improved solution (chocolate). You likely won't have a lot of material to highlight as a numbered list (strawberry). If a sentence or paragraph could be one of two different flavors, copy it and highlight each version with a color so you can decide later.

After you highlight all the content in your original draft, quickly scan your document to see whether one flavor predominates. If so, that's a strong clue about which flavor is more vital to your draft. If all the colors are about the same proportion, it's time to go back to your original purpose as described in the next section.

Reconfirming your purpose

As explained in Chapter 5, you can work from your main purpose to pick the ideal flavor for your white paper. Here are several classic goals for a white paper and the best flavor for achieving each of them:

- ✔ To generate leads at the top of the funnel: problem/solution
- ✔ To attract attention with provocative views: numbered list
- ✔ To nurture prospects through the middle of the funnel: numbered list
- ✔ To support an evaluation and cement sales at the bottom of the funnel: backgrounder

Review what you're trying to achieve with this project. Are you seeking to accomplish two incompatible goals at once, such as addressing B2B buyers at both the top and bottom of the sales funnel? Are you trying to provide an industry overview and cover a specific product in the same document? After you start asking these questions, the goal of your white paper should pop out at you.

Using the ingredients that belong

At this point, you're ready to rework your white paper in the correct flavor. Now go back to your highlighted draft and eliminate or rewrite all the parts that belong to any other flavors except your chosen one. You can do this by either dropping the content tagged as any other flavor or restating all those parts in a more or less product-specific way — more product specific for a backgrounder or more generic for a problem/solution. If you're creating a numbered list, make sure every numbered point is expressed in parallel or similar grammatical construction. Whatever you do, you must take control of your material, selecting content that interests your intended readers at the appropriate part of the funnel.

At the end of this exercise, you should have a small pile of material that you cut or couldn't rework to fit into your revised draft, and a new draft where every section, paragraph, and sentence fits with your chosen flavor and helps to achieve your goal.

When you fix a mash-up that doesn't work and have some of your original draft left over, that content doesn't have to go to waste. You can likely use it in another white paper or repurpose it for a blog post or e-newsletter article.

Chapter 10

Special Ingredients for a White Paper

*E*veryone knows there's more to the world of ice cream than standard flavors like vanilla, strawberry, and chocolate. To whip up a truly memorable treat, you need to add some special ingredients, like multicolored sprinkles, toasted nuts, bananas, hot gooey sauce, whipped cream, and a bright red maraschino cherry to top it all off. For more adult tastes, a pinch of pepper or a splash of vodka can wake up a dish of ice cream and create a magical moment.

The same is true for a white paper: Special ingredients can help your white paper jolt your readers awake and truly step up to become more memorable than any other document they may encounter. The yummy special ingredients you can use in a white paper include a positioning blurb, an executive summary, numbered or bulleted lists, a buyer's guide, one or more case studies, and a set of conclusions with an effective call to action.

In this chapter, I provide tips and tricks on using these special ingredients, and I warn against some ingredients that can turn the sweetest white paper into a bitter concoction that no one can swallow, including hype, marketing speak, groupthink, vagueness, product mentions, and attacks on competitors.

Sprinkling on the Special Ingredients

As you become more adept at developing white papers, you'll naturally tend to look for ways to make them more persuasive. I've found that many of the tips I've picked up combine both structure and content; you must include a certain element at the proper place in the proper flavor of white paper (structure) and you must word it correctly to get the best possible results (content).

In the following sections, I describe how to use the special ingredients that can help make your white papers more memorable and persuasive. Arranged more or less in the order they occur in a white paper, these elements include a positioning blurb, a synopsis-style executive summary, numbered or bulleted lists, case studies, a buyer's guide, and conclusions that incorporate an effective call to action.

You don't have to use all these ingredients in every white paper, although in any type of problem/solution, you certainly can. I do recommend using an executive summary and a set of conclusions in pretty much every white paper, so you can "tell them what you're going to tell them" at the start and then "tell them what you told them" at the end. And every white paper should include a brief call to action that outlines exactly what your reader should do next.

Positioning blurb

A *positioning blurb* is a short sentence or two that sums up a company or an offering to help a B2B buyer understand how it fits into a broader landscape of a certain market space. A major failing of many technology companies — and the white papers they publish — is never providing an effective positioning blurb. Without it, prospects must work hard to decode the messages from those vendors and sort their way through a lot of sound-the-same jargon that does nothing to make them stand out from the crowd.

A positioning blurb is a must-have ingredient for any backgrounder. In the introduction to a backgrounder, make sure to position the offering in its market space. If the company doesn't already have an effective positioning blurb for that offering, use this simple formula to create one:

> *[Name of product or service]* is a *[down-to-earth adjective]* *[recognized niche, category, or genre]* that *[active verb, such as* provides, delivers, *or* performs*]* *[number-one benefit covered in white paper]* to *[primary target market]*.

If you want, you can add the following clause to the end of your blurb, as long as you don't resort to any hype or exaggeration:

> unlike other *[products, services, or solutions]* which *[number-one failing of number-one competitor]*

Here's a blurb written to this formula, suitable for popping into the introduction to a backgrounder (and anywhere else you need a concise, factual blurb):

> The Acme ScanOMatic 3000 is a cost-effective unattended scanning system that delivers ultra-high-resolution e-copies to office staff buried in paperwork, unlike other systems that demand frequent manual intervention.

Many CEOs spend hours wondering, "How can we make our company stand out from the competition?" The answer? To stand out, you have to do something different. You have to clearly say what your company does, who your company does it for, and why your company does it the best, and then prove it to hardheaded B2B buyers. White papers provide an excellent channel for this discussion. But if your company doesn't do much of anything different from a dozen other companies, it will be hard to stand out from your competitors and hard for any white paper to help you over this challenge.

Synopsis-style executive summary

An executive summary is essential at the beginning of any type of problem/solution white paper, either pure or a mash-up with a numbered list. These are less common in backgrounders or shorter numbered list white papers. The two types of executive summaries are a preview and a synopsis. Just like the preview for a movie, a *preview* executive summary presents selected highlights of what's to come, trying to attract readers and entice them to read the main body. A *synopsis* takes a different tactic, presenting the entire argument of the document in a nutshell. I much prefer the synopsis for the following reasons:

- ✔ You're not playing peekaboo with your content, which can irritate busy readers and waste their time. You're being transparent and helpful.

- ✔ Getting an executive to see a one-page summary of your entire argument is better than presenting just a few scattered highlights with no chance for you to connect the dots.

- ✔ If your company has any special fans on the selection committee, you're giving them a self-contained piece of content that's easy to repurpose. They can add the executive summary to their research or notes for the next meeting of the committee, which gets your key message into the hands of everyone around the boardroom table. Excellent!

Whichever approach you choose for your executive summary, the shorter the better. A full page is as long as you ever want, and if you can boil it down to a half a page, so much the better.

Numbered lists

Three types of white papers are organized around numbered points: a pure numbered list, a numbered list–backgrounder mash-up, or a numbered list–problem/solution mash-up. And you may well want to use a numbered list within the body of another flavor. Here are seven tips on using numbered points effectively, in a form that follows all these tips:

- **Tip #1: Use at least three and at most nine points.** Any less than three isn't really a list, and any more than nine can get too long and tire out your readers.

- **Tip #2: Don't use ten points.** Let's face it: David Letterman owns the Top Ten List format, after featuring one on his show every night for more than 25 years. So unless you want to sound like a David Letterman wannabe, drop your weakest point and end your list at nine.

- **Tip #3: Consider using an odd number.** Some marketing experts recommend using odd numbers like three, five, or seven, rather than even numbers like four, six, or eight. They claim that odd numbers are more believable because even numbers strike some people as too "round" or "neat." Personally, I wouldn't drop a strong point just to make an odd number of points. But I would drop every weak point and see where your list naturally ends.

- **Tip #4: Break a longer list in two.** If you have many more than ten points and they all seem worth keeping, consider breaking your list in two. You can call the first one something like, "7 Things You Must Know About . . ." and the second, "6 More Things You Must Know About . . ." An added benefit of this approach is that it gives you two pieces of content to promote, and the call to action of the first part can be to download the second.

- **Tip #5: Express all points in parallel.** Line up all your points in the same grammatical format. For example, notice how all the points in this section are in the same imperative form, like "do this" or "don't do that." (See the nearby sidebar for a detailed example.)

- **Tip #6: Don't scrimp on your research.** Just because a numbered list is supposed to carry a somewhat lighter tone, it doesn't mean you can take any shortcuts on your research. Just like in any other flavor, the more proof you can find for each of your numbered points, the more punch each point will deliver.

- **Tip #7: Organize your points for maximum impact.** Put a couple of strong points at the start, any weaker points in the middle, and another strong point at the end. This order reflects how people scan numbered lists: They tend to pay attention at the start, skip through the middle, and then focus again at the end. So make sure to end your list with a bang, not a whimper.

Lining up bullets in parallel form

You can make any list faster to scan and easier to understand if you present it in parallel construction. This means using the same grammatical form for each point. Here's an example of points not written in parallel:

✔ Red means stop; yellow means warning.

✔ To be safe, you must always cross when the light is green.

✔ If the light is yellow, someone could be turning late from oncoming traffic. It's safer to stop.

See how each item in this list is in a different format, with a different length? Can you see how this format makes your reader work much harder to decode each item? Here's one way to recast this list in parallel:

✔ Red means stop: You are not safe to cross.

✔ Green means go: You can cross safely.

✔ Yellow means caution: You should stop.

Buyer's guide

This unique ingredient occurs most often in the problem/solution flavor. The *buyer's guide* is a concise set of bullets, listing your competitive advantages as must-have features or characteristics that all buyers should look for. By serving as a checklist for buyers, this section aims to tilt the playing field in favor of your offering. A buyer's guide is usually confined to a single page or even half a page. You don't need a lot of extra verbiage around it. In fact, you can introduce a buyer's guide like this: "Here are some must-have features that any automated scanner should provide."

Remember to express each item in more or less generic fashion, not using product-specific or company-branded terms. Doing so makes the list more appropriate as a checklist. After all, it's more useful to your prospects if you describe an item in the buyer's guide as "quick, automated setup for unattended operation" instead of using company-specific terms, such as "Auto-Scan Sensor configuration for unattended operation."

A buyer's guide can also help you structure a backgrounder. In this case, instead of a set of bullets gathered together on one page, it becomes a series of sections, each one discussing another must-have feature.

Don't include items in your list that any competitor can easily claim. For example, don't use any namby-pamby phrases, such as "We are 100 percent committed to customer service." This statement is meaningless. What company would ever admit that it's only 65 percent committed to customer service? Stick to any areas where you clearly outperform your competition and can prove it convincingly.

Case studies

A *case study* is a testimonial from a happy customer who used a company's offering and was pleased with the results. This kind of third-party evidence is one of the most compelling proofs any B2B vendor can offer.

A case study works well in a problem/solution and perhaps in a backgrounder. You can format a case study as a full-page sidebar, a paragraph or two in the main body, or a small text box on the side of a page. The length is up to you; just make a case study as short as possible while still delivering an effective testimonial.

Case studies don't work so well in a numbered list because any type of sidebar tends to break the rapid flow of this format. In this flavor, sidebars are more like an interruption, distraction, or unnecessary aside, so they're seldom used.

Conclusions

A brief set of conclusions is useful in almost every flavor of white paper. Here, you "tell them what you told them" and give readers the key take-away messages from your document. The conclusions should be no more than a page and preferably shorter. In a backgrounder, you can offer a short conclusion to emphasize how all these features and benefits add up to the best offering on the market. In a problem/solution, you can sum up the problem, the drawbacks of the traditional solutions, and your new improved solution in just a few clipped sentences.

The one flavor where you can safely skip any conclusions is a pure numbered list that you want to keep as short as possible. Shaving off that final half page can make a difference. And if your main goal is to cast aspersions on the competition, you can do that within your numbered points with no need to sum it all up at the end.

Although adding conclusions may seem nonessential, they're a must-have for almost any white paper because many business readers flip to the end before they commit to reading the main body. Magazine publishers have been encouraging this behavior for many years because they want readers to look through the entire issue and notice all the ads right to the back. That's why they often include a humor piece, cartoon, or popular columnist on the very last page. For example, *Vanity Fair* places its popular Proust questionnaire filled in by a celebrity on that page. *The New Yorker* often features a full-page cartoon there. And many trade journals place their most popular columnist in that position to compel readers to flip right to the last page.

Call to action

Every effective piece of marketing material has some sort of call to action. Nothing should ever stand alone; instead, every piece should contribute toward pulling prospects into your funnel and on toward the next step in the sales cycle. That's why you should include a brief call to action at the end of your conclusions. The call to action can be a single sentence describing where to find more information or how to move to the next step in the buying process. Here's a formula for writing a call to action:

> To find out more about how *[name of offering]* can help your *[business, organization, or team]* *[number-one product benefit covered in white paper]*, *[do something]*.

Here's a call to action written to this formula:

> To find out more about how the Acme ScanOMatic 3000 can help your team clear away a blizzard of paperwork, call 1-800-SCANNER.

Of course, not every prospect is quite ready to order dozens of scanners just yet, so an intermediate step in your call to action is usually better. One neat tactic is to come up with an online survey, widget, or calculator that can make an engaging call to action that brings your prospect back to your company website for more interaction:

> To find out how much your team can save this year by using the Acme ScanOMatic 3000, visit www.acme-scanners.com/ROI-calculator.

Leaving Out the Bitter Ingredients

Four nasty ingredients can spoil even the sweetest white paper: hype, marketing speak, groupthink, and vagueness. Leave all these bitter-tasting elements out of every white paper you produce. This rule applies firmly to all backgrounders and problem/solution flavors.

In a numbered list designed to be provocative, you can ever so slightly bend these rules. Don't try this technique on the first numbered list you create. Wait until you feel more confident and then experiment a little with a light sprinkling of hyperbole. You must use a subtle hand so no one actually detects that special ingredient but instead notices only how your paper has some extra zest. If you overdo it, the entire dish can be ruined.

Two other ingredients can go only in certain flavors and must be used with much caution: product mentions and direct attacks on competitors. Using either of these two ingredients — or hype — is like using cayenne pepper: A little goes a long, long way. If you put in even a bit too much, some of your guests will turn red, clutch their throats, and gasp for air. Clearly, that's not the reaction you want your white paper to generate.

Hype

Hype is short for *hyperbole,* a rhetorical device from the ancient Greeks that means literally "excess" or "over the wall." If you think of hype as "over the top," you're on the right track. It's a big ball of wishful thinking, breathless exaggeration, and downright lying.

Don't forget that B2B buyers have three major questions on the tip of their tongue every instant: "So what?" "Says who?" and "What's in it for me?" If you try to use hype to slip some shaky claims or assertions past them, you may trigger one or all of these questions to spring up in their mind. After you trigger their doubt the first time, you may never regain their trust. And they may never finish reading your white paper. Is that really worth the risk?

Here are some examples that should have your personal "hype detector" sounding a red alert:

✔ "Our best-selling network analyzer . . ."

But what if this phrase comes from a company that sells only two different network analyzers? If one is the best seller, the other must be the failure that no one ever buys.

✔ "A vast majority of IT managers prefer commercial software over open-source code. . . ."

But where is the actual statistic, the methodology, or the name of the study's sponsor? Could this research have been paid for — and the results skewed — by some company that just happens to perceive open source as a threat?

✔ "Our most comprehensive update ever! Complete with 89 new and improved features!"

But does that number include many long-advertised features that now work properly for the first time, because the company finally got around to fixing the bugs?

Can you see how hype falls apart under the withering gaze of a skeptic? Don't think you can fool all the people some of the time and some of the people all the time; in a white paper, you can't. And by the way, multiple exclamation marks (!!) or other over-the-top punctuation (?!) are sure signs of hype.

Hype is totally inappropriate in a backgrounder, where readers are looking for precise technical details and real-world benefits. In a backgrounder, you must stick to the facts and prove your assertions with facts, like benchmarks, client testimonials, patents, specs, test results, and anything from the real world and not the misty world of make-believe. When you exaggerate with hype in a backgrounder, you risk losing your audience.

Marketing speak

Marketing speak refers to the polite, politically correct, and almost indecipherable prose that makes so much copywriting so bloated. Marketing speak encompasses all the tired clichés, buzzwords, and empty superlatives found in many press releases, web pages, and brochures. But a white paper isn't a press release, a web page, or a brochure! A white paper is supposed to help your readers understand an issue, solve a problem, or make a decision. Marketing speak won't help your readers achieve any of those goals.

One problem with marketing speak is that it's just a set of empty terms that don't explain anything or offer any value to readers. So what if you claim to have the "best-in-breed point solution for seamless integration with enterprise web 2.0 platforms"? Does all that jargon actually paint a clear picture of what you're talking about? Not to most people. If you don't already understand all those terms and somehow know what the writer means by that particular string of them, you're out of luck. This isn't white paper writing; this is just blather and bafflegab.

Another problem is that marketing speak isn't plain language; it's puffed-up mumble jumble that goes around the block instead of coming right out and saying what it means. That makes marketing speak inefficient at delivering any real content. When every customer is a "stakeholder," every problem is a "concern," and every bug is an "issue," readers have to work hard to crack through an extra layer of coding and get down to the actual message.

All in all, marketing speak only slows down readers and wastes their time. Any white paper that wastes prospects' time with marketing speak is gambling with their patience. B2B buyers from technical fields like engineering or IT have an especially low tolerance for this kind of language. If you use too much of it, they may strike your company off the shortlist of vendors to pursue. Then your marketing speak has done the exact opposite of what you wanted: Instead of nurturing prospects, it has killed their interest.

You may be under pressure from sales or marketing colleagues or your client to stick loads of marketing speak into your white paper. If so, remember the three *R*s: resist, reinterpret, and reword. Push back against these pressures, using the arguments in this section. If that doesn't work, get to the bottom of what the marketing speak is really trying to say, and then state that message in more direct and accessible terms in your text.

By all means, try to avoid using any of the following classic examples of marketing speak:

- Best-of-breed
- Best practices
- Breakthrough
- Concern
- Cloud computing
- Cutting-edge
- Disruptive
- Enterprise-class
- Evolutionary
- Global
- Granular
- Groundbreaking
- Issue
- Leader
- Leading/Leading-edge
- Next-generation
- Next step in evolution
- Outside the box
- Paradigm/paradigm shift
- Premier
- Proactive
- Revolutionary
- Right-sizing
- Robust
- Seamless integration
- Secret sauce
- Smart
- Stakeholder
- State-of-the-art
- Strategic alliance
- Transformative
- Unique
- User-friendly
- World-class

Groupthink

What do you call a group of people who all follow the leader without question? Lemmings? Zombies? Don't let your backgrounder or problem/solution white paper get spoiled by groupthink. One common form of groupthink occurs when everyone on a management team — and any new hires the team brings onboard — walks around all day telling one another, "We have the best technology. We have the best product line. We have the most responsive tech support. We have the strongest management team." But just because an executive says something doesn't make it so.

After all, this language is rather like saying, "Everybody knows that . . ." or "All right-thinking people agree that . . ." The job of any white paper writer is to turn a critical eye to these flimsy claims and say, "Oh yeah? Prove it!" If you have no proof beyond an oft-repeated management cliché, that statement has no place in a white paper. The most common form of groupthink is an unproven claim.

Instead of making an unverified assertion, you must dig for convincing proof points: awards, benchmarks, case studies, reviews, and so on. If you can't find actual numbers, use a quote from a third-party expert, such as an industry analyst, respected consultant, or leading authority in your field. Then your claim will have more credibility and more impact, and you can leave the groupthink to the walking dead.

Vagueness

If "God is in the details," then so is the compelling content for a white paper. Nebulous, fuzzy statements have no place in any flavor. Consider this: Prospects deep in the buying process download a backgrounder to get technical details they can't find anywhere else. They don't want brochure-style fluff; they're looking for precise technical details and concrete business benefits. The same applies to a problem/solution reader. If you describe an industry-wide problem by using only broad strokes, your paper is not nearly as compelling as if you fill in the fine points. And with a numbered list, if all your paper can offer is shadows, smoke, and opinion, it won't be nearly as provocative as if it's grounded in specific facts.

Vagueness isn't "sticky" like a gooey fudge sauce. It doesn't hold onto readers; instead, ambiguities invite them to get distracted and go on to something else. For example, suppose you describe an industry problem this way:

> Many companies struggle with the problem of paper burden. Reports, forms, and e-mail attachments continue to proliferate. Most companies now use off-site storage to hold a growing volume of paper files.

Ho hum! Tell me something I don't know. This lazy text has nothing to hold anyone's attention. You can make this same idea riveting by introducing some specifics:

> Despite high-speed access to the web, the typical office worker still prints 10,000 pages a year and then squirrels away 2,500 pages in files. Experts say that all that paper drains more than $50 billion a year from our nation's productivity.

Wow! This version will likely get a reader's attention and hold it. Finding some eye-popping statistics like these is one way to eliminate vagueness, but not the only one. Also look for anecdotes, dates, times, places, provocative quotes, or anything else that makes a fuzzy statement more clear and defined. Any of those ingredients can eliminate the vagueness that invites readers to drift away.

Product mentions

You can freely use this ingredient in one flavor but not the others. You can mention a product name in the title and on every page of a backgrounder because your readers expect this flavor to focus on the features and benefits of a specific offering. And you can use product mentions throughout a mash-up of a backgrounder and numbered list called something like "5 Things You Should Know about the Acme ScanOMatic 3000."

But in a pure numbered list, you can get away with mentioning a specific offering only right near the end. Otherwise, stay focused on the issue your numbered list is describing; if you don't, readers may sense that you're handing them a thinly veiled sales pitch and reject your white paper.

The same applies to a problem/solution or problem/solution–numbered list mash-up. Make sure to leave product details out of these flavors. Keep them focused on the business or technical problem and how to solve it. Your goal with these flavors is to describe a new, improved solution to an industry problem in somewhat generic terms. This content must intrigue your readers enough that they want to take the next step and seek out more details. You want to pull them into your funnel, not overload them with product information at the wrong time.

Direct attacks on competitors

You must use direct attacks on competitors carefully. Remember: A white paper of any flavor is a persuasive essay based on facts and logic. Many attacks on competitors aren't grounded in provable facts or solid logic but in emotion ("Our product is insanely great!"), ego ("We're the leader, and they're just second-rate imitators."), unverified claims ("Our product runs 500 percent faster."), or the other ingredients I warn you about in this chapter, like hype or vagueness.

A backgrounder can support a few well-founded attacks on competing offerings, if yours is clearly superior in some way. Just remember that a technical evaluator wants to find out about *your* product, not your competitor's. If you focus too much on any competitor, that can arouse your readers' suspicions and compel them to go check out that competitor. You can always say something like, "Unlike competing solutions, Acme provides . . ." and then describe one of your unique competitive advantages. But I don't advise a full frontal attack on a competitor in a backgrounder. It's not the time or the place.

A numbered list doesn't attack competitors directly. This flavor is more about sowing doubt and uncertainty and making your reader suspect "5 hidden gotchas" or find out "7 things you must know." If this flavor can accomplish that, it doesn't need to confront the competition directly.

In a problem/solution flavor, you can freely attack any competing offerings as generic categories, classes, generations, or types of solutions. You do this by describing how poor these solutions have been at solving an industry-wide problem and then showing how your new, improved solution does a far better job. As always, the more proof you can pile up, the better. Here, you're not directly attacking your competition by name but giving a thoughtful critique based on how your solution and others' fit into your market space. Approaching any competing offerings in this way helps build the educational value of your white paper and establish your credibility as a trusted advisor.

Part III

From Foggy Idea to Finished Document

12 Steps for Creating a White Paper

1. Assemble the team.
2. Hold the initial conference call.
3. Prepare the plan.
4. Gather your research.
5. Prepare an executive summary.
6. Create the first draft of the paper and graphics.
7. Get the first round of feedback.
8. Revise to create the second draft.
9. Solicit a second round of feedback.
10. Collect and check sources.
11. Prepare the final document.
12. Wrap up the project.

Find out how technology can help you generate ideas, organize your thoughts, and get your words on paper more quickly at www.dummies.com/extras/whitepapers.

In this part . . .

✔ Get an overview of a proven 12-step process for completing a white paper that can help you avoid pitfalls and prevent a lot of stress.

✔ Find out how to plan your next white paper and make sure all contributors are working toward the same goal.

✔ Get busy writing, revising, and polishing your white paper so it meets the needs of your target audience and client.

Chapter 11

A Proven Process to Complete Your White Paper

. . . .

In This Chapter

▶ Understanding the benefits of a white paper publishing process

▶ Reviewing the three main stages of publishing a white paper

▶ Improving your white paper success rate with six key factors

▶ Taming four pests that can devour your white paper

. . . .

*P*ublishing B2B white papers can be an effective way to generate leads, nurture prospects, or cement sales. But developing a white paper is a complex project with many players to coordinate and many stages to oversee. These players include a sponsor, subject matter experts, reviewers, a writer, a designer, perhaps an illustrator, plus a marketing team. These stages include planning, researching, drafting, illustrating, reviewing, designing, and promoting the final document. Not everyone understands how to pull together all these resources or manage all these stages to make developing a white paper smooth and enjoyable. That's where this chapter comes in.

In this chapter, I give an overview of the proven process I've used for many years with my own clients and show the benefits you can gain from adopting it. I sketch in the three main stages of creating an effective white paper: planning, producing, and promoting. Each stage includes a number of steps, as explained in Chapters 12, 13, and 16. I round out this chapter by discussing six critical factors that can help your white paper succeed and four pesky varmints you must guard against.

Benefitting from a White Paper Process

White papers are complex projects with many variables to control. In many cases, the publishing process is painful, and the results are less than compelling. After experiencing a few projects that didn't turn out well, I began to study what was going wrong and how I could improve the outcomes.

Eventually I saw the light: B2B vendors have publishing tools at their fingertips; many people have good skills to apply. Most marketing teams can effectively handle smaller projects such as press releases, web pages, or e-newsletters. But few know how to publish something as big and challenging as a white paper.

Gradually, I came up with a process that I've been able to field-test and fine-tune on dozens of projects. Following any organized process is better than nothing, and following my time-tested process can boost your success rate on four out of five white papers.

The following sections look at the pitfalls that can derail a white paper and explain the benefits of putting a proven process in place.

Not all white paper projects go smoothly

When I first started writing white papers in the late 1990s, not all my projects worked out as I hoped:

- ✔ A few were painfully slow, as I went through revision after revision, chasing after a moving target in my client's mind.
- ✔ Several had engaging text that was undermined by a wretched format imposed by designers inexperienced with white papers.
- ✔ One was ruined when the CEO dropped in late in the process and insisted we turn it into a sales pitch.

Any seasoned white paper writer can tell you similar stories. Writers and marketing managers can fall into many pitfalls that cause delays, misunderstandings, or even the outright cancellation of a white paper. Nobody wants that, but it happens often.

Many companies lack a publishing process

After specializing in white papers for a few years, I had a blinding flash of the obvious. I realized that the real reason so many white papers flounder isn't some lack of creativity, intelligence, or design skills. The real cause is an unpredictable or chaotic publishing process — or no process at all — so the best thinking of the client and the best practices of the industry aren't captured in the final document.

The tools of publishing are now available to anyone with a PC or tablet. But tools without experience aren't enough. Many B2B vendors lack enough knowledge about publishing to make the process go smoothly and create an effective white paper. In traditional publishing, writers, editors, and designers work with processes that have been tested, refined, and proven effective for hundreds of years. From working in traditional newspaper, magazine, and book publishing, I was well acquainted with these processes. And I realized that many B2B companies have nothing similar in place.

This insight was confirmed by a 2010 survey by MarketingSherpa, which showed that 60 percent of small companies and 47 percent of medium-sized companies with up to 1,000 employees have no formal processes they routinely follow for B2B marketing. They're all making it up as they go along. Surprisingly, more than one-third of larger enterprises with more than 1,000 employees are in the same boat. So if your company has no white paper publishing process in place, the good news is that you're probably in the same place as many of your competitors. The bad news is that with no time-tested process to guide you, developing a white paper can be a bewildering and unmanageable process.

A process you can use for your own

I determined to do something to help B2B vendors handle white papers better. I reviewed dozens of my projects to figure out what worked and what didn't, where things had gone smoothly and where things were a little rough. I set down a preliminary version of this process and started using it with my clients, refining it as I went. For the past several years, I've used this process without any significant changes. By now, the process explained in this part of the book has helped me complete dozens of white papers faster and easier than I would have believed possible. And it can do the same for you.

Consider the likely benefits if you adopt this process:

✔ You can clearly set expectations among the client, writer, reviewers, and any other parties in advance.

✔ You can head off all the most common problems and pitfalls that can bedevil any white paper project.

✔ You can avoid misunderstandings and assumptions that can blow up in your face.

✔ You can spell out what to do next, which is extremely useful when you're juggling numerous projects — and who isn't?

✔ You can streamline a complex white paper project and achieve a much better chance of success.

I find that 18 or 19 out of 20 white papers flow smoothly with this process; that's a 90 or 95 percent success rate. I expect this process to work well for at least four out of five of your white papers so that you enjoy a success rate of at least 80 percent. And studying this process will help you see why that fifth one took longer or didn't go as smoothly. When something messy and unpredictable does come along, this process can guide you as you try to get your project back on track.

Real-world factors can conspire to knock the best-planned projects off course. No tidy, step-by-step process can possibly encompass all the twists and turns the world can throw at it. So why try to impose any process on something so flaky? The truth is, every marketing team has a process — even if they've never written down any steps, drawn up any flowcharts, or done anything besides simply making it up as they go along. But making the process explicit, visible, and predictable is better than leaving it implied, invisible, and ad hoc.

Getting an Overview of the Process

The chapters in Part III give you a step-by-step process for creating a white paper, covering everything from clarifying a fuzzy idea to creating a polished PDF of your document. This process provides a time-tested template that writers and marketing managers can use to avoid all the common pitfalls in creating white papers. On the highest level, this process includes three stages: planning, producing, and promoting a white paper.

In the following sections, I give you an overview of these stages. Each stage includes several specific steps: I cover planning a white paper in Chapter 12, producing a white paper in Chapter 13, and then provide dozens of promotional possibilities in Chapter 16.

If you already have an in-house publishing process, compare it to this one to make sure you cover all the same items. Pay special attention to the planning and promoting stages, which include several best practices that may be new to you. Merging these steps with your existing procedures can create an even more robust process that gives your white papers a competitive edge.

If you already have a white paper underway, you can still benefit from this process. You can easily pinpoint what stage you're in at the moment, and then you can steer the project along by suggesting what the next steps should be. And pay attention to the recommended best practices and warnings about common pitfalls at every step. If you've skipped over any critical steps, circle back and complete them.

Stage 1: Planning a white paper

Time management experts say that every minute you spend planning saves ten minutes of doing. With white papers, that ratio is even higher, so that every minute you spend planning saves an *hour* of doing. That's why the first stage of any white paper must be devoted to planning.

In this all-important stage, the marketing manager clarifies the ideas for the white paper, outlines the project's terms of reference, and rounds up all the required subject matter experts (SMEs) and reviewers. They engage an appropriate writer and designer, either on contract or in-house, and negotiate the terms of the engagement. Then the writer begins work, doing a deep dive into the topic for research and then drafting an executive summary (outline) to circulate for review and approval.

At the end of this stage, the marketing manager has engaged all the people required for the project, put a firm budget and schedule in place, and approved an outline for the white paper. This first stage dramatically increases the odds of producing an effective white paper with a minimum of stress, miscommunication, and wasted effort. For more details and a step-by-step description of how to plan a white paper, see Chapter 12.

Stage 2: Producing a white paper

In this stage, the white paper moves from an approved outline to a finished document. This stage includes writing drafts, seeking comments, incorporating comments, creating graphics, sending the text for design, and proofing finished pages. Most writers and marketing people understand these steps.

My process also includes some recommended best practices that may be new to you. For example, the writer should compile an organized bundle of sources that the client can spot-check or file away for future reference. The marketing manager should attend to any required payments, permissions, and approvals. And the designer should insert the approved metadata and keywords into the final PDF.

Most people see Stage 2 as the "creative" stage, not realizing that planning and promotion are just as creative. Although the marketing team and reviewers may be tempted to get deeply involved in the text, graphics, or design of the document, they can make a more valuable contribution by sticking to a higher level, helping shape the ideas and refine the logic of the document. At the end of this stage, the client has a finished PDF ready to publish and all the loose ends neatly tied up. For more details and a step-by-step description of how to produce a white paper, see Chapter 13.

Stage 3: Promoting a white paper

No matter how wonderful a white paper may be, if the intended readers never find it, it won't succeed. In this stage, your marketing team swings into action to do everything possible to get the finished white paper into the hands of the target audience. For more details and more than 30 possible ways to promote a white paper, see Chapter 16.

Getting an Edge with Six Success Factors

Many white papers are started, but not all are finished, for many reasons — priorities change, new products emerge, people come and go, executives lose interest. Explaining a product in detail can turn up flaws that nobody wants to admit or conflicting opinions that can't be resolved. How can you dodge these potential problems?

A good strategy is to understand the critical factors that can make developing a white paper a smooth and agreeable process. Then try to get as many of these factors working in your favor as possible. In the following sections, I list six critical success factors for white papers.

Success factor #1: In-house sponsor

The first cornerstone of success is an effective in-house sponsor who can help the writer navigate through any company politics or difficult personalities. For example, a sponsor can help resolve comments and tell the writer which ones must be incorporated and which can be safely ignored. (See the "Taming Four Maddening Pests" section, later in this chapter, or head to Chapter 12 for more details about handling reviewers and their comments.)

A major reason behind most project failures is the lack of management support. An in-house sponsor can remind everyone of the company's commitment to the white paper. If you're the marketing manager who commissioned the white paper, you can serve as this sponsor. If you have a higher-up to champion the project, so much the better.

Success factor #2: Firm deadline

Treating a white paper as an open-ended project that you can finish whenever you get around to it isn't the best approach. To succeed, you need an immovable deadline in the real world, such as a trade show. A product release can provide a good deadline, as long as the hall is already booked and the press release already delivered so the date can't possibly slip. Some marketing teams operate with quarterly plans so that as the end of the quarter looms, everyone doubles down on their efforts to get things finished. Another term for this immovable deadline is a *time box* — a finite period after which a project absolutely, positively must be delivered. If you don't have a time box, try to create one.

Publishing any type of content takes a big push to attend to all the details, do all the necessary checking and rechecking, and get a piece finalized, approved, and out the door. A white paper is one of the most challenging pieces of content, so it takes an even bigger push to complete one. Without a firm deadline that no one can push back — a time box — your team can be distracted by other short-term activities and tempted to put off the white paper until tomorrow.

Success factor #3: Deep understanding of the topic

A white paper has a better chance of success if you can find a writer with a deep understanding of the problems being discussed; your target audience; your new, improved solution; and your company. His familiarity with the topic and the players at hand saves everyone time. After all, very few experts enjoy explaining basic concepts that the writer should already know. They're more interested in discussing advanced issues, such as design trade-offs, unexpected use cases, changes in the market space, and other nuanced topics. A writer who can engage his interview subjects on a higher level can pull out more interesting material for the white paper.

Ideally, you want to find a writer with two key qualifications. First, make sure he's well seasoned at writing white papers. If he's written any fewer than ten in recent years, he's still a beginner. Second, confirm that he has a good deal of domain knowledge about your industry so he won't waste your team's time on introductory topics.

Many people say there's no such thing as a dumb question. I disagree. Strongly. This adage may apply to the classroom but not to a white paper. When it comes to interviewing a top executive or subject matter expert, here are three types of dumb questions:

✔ Dumb Question #1: "So how does your software work?" or some other impossibly broad and unfocused query. Instead, do your homework and ask something more specific.

✔ Dumb Question #2: "When was the company founded?" or some other banal inquiry. Instead of wasting an expert's time with such trivial details, find the answer on the company's website. The web is a vast repository of knowledge; every writer should use it to prepare fully for interviews and not waste time on basic facts or irrelevant side issues.

✔ Dumb Question #3: "Here's what I think." This isn't a question but a statement intended to show off your own knowledge. Some writers talk right over their subjects, cutting them off and missing what they're saying. Avoid that type of grandstanding. You're there to listen, not to talk.

Success factor #4: Cooperative SMEs and reviewers

Speaking of experts, a successful white paper often depends on ready access to subject matter experts (SMEs) who make themselves available to the white paper writer on request. Your writer likely needs to interview them for an hour or two and e-mail them follow-up questions on the fly. The same experts often serve as reviewers, so you need them to comment on drafts in a reasonable time frame. The white paper sponsor needs to round up the right in-house experts, make sure they stay involved, and make sure they do what you need them to do — even if that takes a little tactful nagging.

Being "busy" or "on the road" aren't legitimate excuses. After all, everyone's busy, and many people travel routinely. Yet anyone traveling on business has a phone, a hotel room, and lots of time waiting in airports or sitting on trains. Insist that your SMEs use a few minutes of that time to answer e-mails or review drafts of the white paper. You don't want to leave your writer hanging for days for a quick answer to some technical question.

Success factor #5: Joint ownership

This factor can be challenging to develop. Everyone on the project — the marketing manager, product manager, engineers, SMEs, reviewers, writer, and designer — should assume joint ownership of the white paper. They must work together smoothly as a team, discuss differences openly, and settle any disagreements quickly. Of course, this collaboration isn't always within your control.

You *can* do something to help develop joint ownership of a project. As I discuss in Chapter 12, I highly recommend holding an initial kickoff call. This conference call helps get everyone on the same page and makes sure everyone buys into the project and feels some ownership for it. That camaraderie can carry a white paper through any challenges that arise during the process.

Success factor #6: Sense of urgency

The final success factor is a shared sense of urgency among everyone working on the project. People must consider the white paper significant enough to make time for it in their busy schedules and to open e-mails about it before any of the dozens of other e-mails clamoring for their attention. This factor ties in with the firm deadline and sense of ownership.

But as you know, it's one thing to set a deadline, or a series of deadlines for each step of the process; it's another to get busy executives and technical people to respect those deadlines and do what they're supposed to do in the time you've given them. Without some measure of urgency, a white paper can get shoved to the back burner, where it can languish for — well, forever.

Taming Four Maddening Pests

Four types of vermin infest the halls of many companies, ready to devour your white paper without any warning. Any one can be enough to ravage your document. This section shows you how to identify each type of varmint and how to deal with it if it threatens your white paper.

This light-hearted look at these white paper critters has a serious point. An effective content development process can help you tame these creatures and produce a white paper that gets results. You must develop a workable process that protects your white papers against these pests.

The scope-creep

This annoying little fellow refuses to stay on topic. He's always flitting about, suggesting side issues, sending you irrelevant material. He delights in urging your white paper to cover more, more, more! "Why stick to one issue," he chirps, "when you could skim the surface of six?" With a scope-creep as a reviewer, your white paper may become a never-ending story.

To tame a scope-creep, make sure to deliver an outline early. Identify your ideal audience, preferred page count, and overall scope. Get your manager and reviewers to approve this direction. Then, if a scope-creep rears his pointy head, don't say anything like, "That's a scope change," or "That will cost extra." He doesn't care. It's not his schedule or his budget. Instead, politely ask, "Does our target audience really need to know that? If so, we'll have to change the outline." If all your other reviewers feel this change is pointless, rally them to overrule the scope-creep. If this situation happens often enough, he'll soon be darting away to another project that's easier to disrupt.

The tug-o-warrior

This willful strongman is always up for a contest. He may be from sales, marketing, engineering, finance, or legal. Wherever he works, he wants everyone to see things his way. He'll argue with anyone, anywhere, and never give an inch. His call of the wild sounds like this: "I'm right, you're wrong, and this is not a democracy." With a tug-o-warrior as a reviewer, your white paper may fall into permanent limbo, because this creature will never agree with anyone on much of anything.

To tame a tug-o-warrior when you're a contractor, get half the money upfront so the company is committed to finish the project. If you're on staff, peg your white paper to a real-world event, like a trade show or a product release. That time box will give your project more urgency and help you join forces with higher management to out-muscle a tug-o-warrior. If you're locked in a push-and-pull battle where no one is budging, clearly articulate the different positions and then hold a showdown meeting or phone call to resolve them. If enough reviewers all pull together, they can topple a tug-o-warrior.

The no-see-em reviewer

You don't often see this pest in the light of day. No one knows when he'll come swooping down out of the night, clutching your white paper in his talons and shredding it to bits. Of course, he hasn't bothered to make a peep until then. Why should he waste his time giving you his views early on? He much prefers the thrill of the kill. If he sits anywhere high enough in the company to overrule your sponsor, this winged menace can be quite deadly.

To tame a no-see-em, identify all your reviewers early. Ideally, pull them all together for a kickoff call. Have everyone sign off on the outline. If a no-see-em still ambushes you, appeal to your team of reviewers and sponsor. Remind the no-see-em that everyone but him was involved from the start and agreed on the current direction. Tell him his changes are going to cost extra money and eat up more time. But sometimes, you just can't win with a no-see-em, and he'll pounce on your white paper and not let go. It's not your fault. Sometimes a white paper is just in the wrong place at the wrong time, and it gets attacked.

The dyslexic designer

This harmless-looking rodent can undermine a white paper after everyone else's work is done. A dyslexic designer loves to bury things, and he'll be happy to dig a hole for your white paper. He loves light gray letters at a tiny point size. His specialty is dropping your text into a deep gray well where no one ever sees it again.

To tame a dyslexic designer, brief him early about the unique format of a white paper. Get him thinking about how an annual report or magazine article looks. Tell him about the target audience, especially if they're executives in their 40s or 50s whose eyes have changed so they can no longer resolve tiny letters set in gray rather than black. Stress how the words must be inviting and easy to read for someone thinking about spending a lot of money with your company. Make sure the white paper sponsor gets final approval on the design. If the company has a corporate template unsuitable for a white paper, get an okay to modify it. When a dyslexic designer realizes that someone is actually looking at his work, he may stir his creative juices and produce something attractive.

Chapter 12

Planning an Effective White Paper

· ·

In This Chapter

▶ Gathering an effective team

▶ Getting everyone on the same page

▶ Drawing up a detailed plan

▶ Researching the topic in depth

▶ Outlining the white paper content

· ·

Think about other professions. Does a surgeon go into the operating room without reviewing the patient's charts and having a clear idea of the reason for the operation? Does a professional golfer tee up his first drive in a tournament without playing a preliminary round on the course to study each hole? Does a builder just start hammering without taking a long look at the blueprints for the house he's supposed to build?

If planning is important in every other field, isn't it just as important in creating a white paper? The correct answer is, yes, planning is vitally important for a white paper, too. And the more complex the project, the more important it is to have a solid plan.

Creating a white paper is certainly one of the most ambitious projects in content marketing. The final document is likely ten pages long, containing the most powerful highlights of a certain product (a backgrounder), the most provocative statements on a certain issue (a numbered list), or the best thinking on how to solve a certain problem (a problem/solution). Creating an engaging long-form document to cover that material is usually a huge challenge.

In this chapter, I describe the all-important first phase of the white paper development process: planning. In this phase, a white paper evolves from a foggy notion into a detailed outline approved by all reviewers. This chapter covers the first five steps of this process: assembling the team to work on the white paper — hiring an outside writer, illustrator, and designer if needed — and then getting everyone on the same page about the project, outlining the terms of reference for the document, doing deep research into the topic, and creating and approving a brief summary of the white paper's content. These steps include several magic bullets that can help you avoid pitfalls, prevent a lot of stress, and save many hours that could otherwise be wasted.

Step 1: Assembling the Team

A white paper team includes as few as two people — the client and the writer — and as many as a dozen, if many subject matter experts and reviewers are involved. Choosing the correct people for the team increases the chances of producing a successful white paper.

As the main players, the client and the writer must make sure the relationship works. If either person has a sense that working together may be difficult, that person should express those concerns and decline to work together. Table 12-1 outlines what happens in this step and who's responsible for each part. The following sections explain how to pull together a team and make sure the writer and client are on the same page.

Table 12-1		What Happens in Step 1
Step	**Who**	**What**
1.1	Client	Identifies need for white paper
1.2	Client	Identifies in-house subject matter experts and reviewers
1.3	Client	Picks writer, either outsourced or in-house
1.4	Client	Picks illustrator (if any), either outsourced or in-house
1.5	Client	Picks designer (if any), either outsourced or in-house
1.6	Client and writer	Negotiate project terms: scope, deadline, deliverables, fees (if outsourced)
1.7	Client and illustrator (if any)	Negotiate project terms
1.8	Client and designer (if any)	Negotiate project terms
1.9	Writer, designer, and illustrator	Sign nondisclosure agreement (if outsourced)
1.10	Client	Pays initial deposit to writer (if outsourced)

What the client does in this step

As shown in Table 12-1, in Step 1, the client assembles the whole team to work on the white paper. This team includes in-house subject matter experts, the writer, and, if required, the illustrator and designer. On some white papers, the writer fills all these roles, creating graphics and doing page design as well. On others, separate professionals handle each role. The client also identifies anyone else who should review the white paper before it's released, such as management higher-ups.

The client is responsible for putting together the white paper team in a thoughtful way, making sure not to add too many or too few people or anyone who's likely to swoop in at the last moment with disruptive views. A lack of time, focus, or clarity at the outset can lead to misunderstandings that undermine the project from start to finish.

In this step, the client also negotiates the white paper scope and deadlines with the writer, illustrator, and designer. If any of these roles are contracted from outside the company (outsourced), the client needs to negotiate fees. And any outside suppliers probably need to sign a nondisclosure agreement (NDA) to promise they won't blab about anything they learn on the project to the client's competitors or the media.

When hiring a writer (or any other outside contributors), be clear about your expectations, deadlines, and any other details that could lead to misunderstandings later in the project. You don't want either party to make unspoken assumptions about the project, deadline, scope, payment, or terms that come back to haunt you. Deciding not to work with a certain writer early on is better than finding out through painful experience that he can't deliver what you want. For tips on what to look for when hiring a writer, see the later section "How to hire a white paper writer."

Most white paper writers ask for an initial deposit before starting a project. That's only natural. These projects involve several weeks' work, and no independent writer can afford to gamble on not getting paid for all that time. (For notes on typical white paper fees and schedules, see Chapter 4.) That means if you're hiring an independent writer, you most likely need to get a PO (purchase order) or a deposit check ready for that writer. Because illustrators and designers normally put in just a few hours' work, they're most often content to submit an invoice to the client after they finish work on a white paper.

What the writer does in this step

As shown in Table 12-1, in Step 1, the writer needs to win the project from the client, perhaps against a small field of other candidates. This means that the writer needs to impress the client with his writing experience, domain knowledge, understanding of white papers, and availability to meet the deadline. Check out other characteristics clients may look for in a writer in the next section, "How to hire a white paper writer." An independent writer also needs to negotiate the fee, invoice for an initial deposit, and perhaps sign a nondisclosure agreement (NDA). (For notes on typical white paper fees and schedules, see Chapter 4.)

When you're talking to a client about a proposed white paper, make sure to get as many details as you can about the project scope, deadline, and budget. Knowing these things gives you a better idea whether the job is a good fit for you. Turning down a job at the outset is better than trying to do the impossible or working with a client you can never satisfy.

Writers, when working with a new client, ask for a 50 percent deposit upfront. Demanding a payment upfront isn't always "nice" or "convenient," but doing so effectively protects you from wasting your time on projects that don't have management support. Companies sometimes go out of business, the funding for a startup doesn't come through, or the client leaves the company with a white paper not finished. In those cases, at least you have the first half of your fee as an effective kill fee, and you can work on collecting more.

You can allow one exception to the rule about getting an initial deposit. For a huge name-brand client, such as Google, getting a PO may be enough to start work. After all, Google certainly has the money in the bank, and in my experience, the company pays like clockwork: 30 days after they get an invoice, they send out a wire transfer. So writing for a client like that isn't much of a risk.

Easing the terms of a nondisclosure agreement

I recently got an NDA from a client after receiving the initial deposit and starting on the white paper. I was startled to see an unusual non-compete clause, saying that for three years, I wouldn't work with any company that may compete with the client in an extremely broad market space defined as *internet-based publishing.* The NDA had a list of competing companies attached. But several of those companies were already my clients, and several more were prospects I was targeting in the near future!

I told the client I couldn't sign that NDA and that all my other clients for many years had trusted that I would keep the details of their technology and their company confidential. A few days later, that client sent me a new version of the NDA with the offending clause deleted.

Polishing a failed draft

Suppose you try to write a white paper in-house, but no one is satisfied by the results. You give up and realize you need a professional writer to finish the document. That's fine, but don't expect to tell any writer, "We already started the white paper, so we only need you to polish up our draft. And we'd like a discount because the work is already half done." When writers hear this, most will tell you that they don't do revisions.

Here's why. Suppose your car breaks down, and you try to fix it. You think you know the problem, but you don't have the tools or the parts to finish the repair. So you get your car towed to a garage, where you tell the mechanic, "I know what the problem is, only I don't have the right tools or spare parts. So I brought it to you, but because I got it half fixed, I want to pay only half your normal rate."

How do you think any mechanic will react? He still has to use his years of training and experience, troubleshoot the problem, use his special

tools, and find the right spare parts. When he gets your car fixed and back on the road, do you really expect him to give you a 50 percent discount? For what, exactly?

It's the same thing with a failed white paper. In my experience — and I've tried this enough times to know better — fixing someone else's unsuccessful draft takes almost as long, or longer, than starting a white paper from scratch. The writer still has to do a proper plan, pick the best flavor, dig up some more research, build a persuasive argument, and write a compelling document. When a writer does all that to get a white paper ready to go, do you really expect him to give you a discount? For what, exactly?

Let's be fair to both the mechanic and the writer. Admit it: Your failed attempt to fix your own car — or write your own white paper — doesn't entitle you to a discount from a trained professional who can get your project moving again. Do everyone a favor: Don't even ask.

How to hire a white paper writer

If you're a client looking for an outside white paper writer, how do you find the best one for you? And how do you go about hiring that person?

Before you rush off to Google "white paper writer," you can zero in on the best writer for your project by considering these four trade-offs:

- ✔ **Money versus time:** The more experienced the writer, the faster he works, but the more he tends to charge. Do you prefer to save money with a less-experienced writer who may work slower, make mistakes, and eat up more of your time? Or can you afford a seasoned pro who works efficiently, hits the bull's-eye on the first try, and creates a more polished document?

- ✔ **Writing experience versus domain knowledge:** Do you prefer a writer with a lot of experience writing white papers or someone who knows your industry inside out? Sometimes you can find both, but that combo will likely cost extra. Given the choice, most clients lean toward writing ability. After all, becoming a smooth, persuasive writer takes years, but any good researcher can learn the basics of any industry in a couple of weeks, especially with you to guide them.

- **Full-service versus text-only:** You may want to find a creative supplier who can deliver a turnkey package with text, graphics, page design, and a final PDF all ready to publish. You may also want the writer to generate related marketing materials, such as a press release, several blog posts, a couple dozen tweets, and so on, to help promote the white paper. Or you may be happy to have the writer deliver an unadorned Word file that you can send to your designer while your marketing team rolls out the promotions.

- **Project manager versus wordsmith:** If you're working on your first white paper, you may want a seasoned writer who can create a plan, take the lead during conference calls, and serve as the de facto project manager, spelling out where you are and what to do next. If you've already published many white papers, you can likely manage the project yourself, so you just need a writer to put together the content.

If you're the client looking to hire a white paper writer, figure out where you stand on each of these trade-offs and decide what services you need before you approach writers, because they'll ask. For example, here are three possible scenarios:

- **If budget is a concern and you have an in-house writer and designer**, enlist them for your white paper. If none of you have published a white paper before, use this book to help guide the process. You may have to wait to get your project on their schedule, and you should plan to promote the white paper yourself, but the price will be right: nothing beyond the same salaries everyone normally draws.

- **If budget is limited but you have no in-house resources**, look for a medium-level writer who has done at least ten white papers in your market space so he brings strong domain knowledge to the table. Plan to run his drafts through a good editor to finesse the text. Find an affordable designer-illustrator, and plan to do your own marketing.

- **If you have the budget,** hire the best suppliers you can find. Seasoned creatives will save everyone time, give you what you want the first time, and surprise you with innovative suggestions and best practices.

If you're the writer talking to a client about a project, know where you fit. Ask yourself where you come down on each of the trade-offs. Then describe your experience, services, and fees honestly to prospective clients.

For example, I tell prospects that my fees are near the top of the scale, which I can justify with my experience on close to 200 white papers. I explain that no one can touch my versatile background as a journalist, technical writer, marketing executive, and copywriter. And I assure them that my team can provide all the services they need, from planning to brainstorming promotions. If they see the value I can deliver, they hire me. If not, they move on to someone else.

Step 2: Holding a Kickoff Conference Call

Step 2 is one of the magic bullets in a successful white paper project. This step can save weeks of stress, communication breakdowns, wasted effort, scrap, and rework. Holding a kickoff conference call creates shared expectations among everyone on the project, promotes harmony on a team, and dramatically reduces one of the most common problems writers report: changes in direction partway through a white paper.

Several significant things happen during this step:

- ✔ The client confirms the availability of all reviewers; this reduces the chance of someone being absent for much of the process but emerging at the end with different views.

- ✔ The whole team reviews all the key parameters of the white paper, including the audience, purpose, call to action, scope, and title; this begins to create a shared vision of the project.

- ✔ The client and writer gather the best thinking from the whole team, not just one person. Pooling everyone's knowledge and experience can help create a more effective white paper more quickly.

- ✔ The team uncovers any differences of opinion early, when they are much easier to deal with; this reduces the chance of anyone naysaying the white paper drafts later on.

This step lays a solid direction for a successful project. Gathering everyone together to visualize the ultimate white paper follows one of the so-called seven habits of highly effective people: "Begin with the end in mind." And giving everyone a chance to have his say at the start eliminates any surprises and second-guessing that can drive a project off a cliff later.

The client and writer can schedule the kickoff call for any time that makes sense. In fact, the client often schedules the kickoff call as soon as he commits to paying the deposit. Getting a check from accounting always takes a few days, as does delivering that check to the writer. The writer must decide whether he wants to hold the call without having the deposit in his hands. Some writers are easygoing when they know a check is coming; others won't even schedule a phone call until they have the payment in their hands or see that it has cleared the bank.

Table 12-2 shows the who and what of this step, and the following sections go into detail about each of these tasks.

Table 12-2		What Happens in Step 2
Step	*Who*	*What*
2.1	Client	Starts making notes on the white paper
2.2	Client	Schedules conference call with writer and all reviewers
2.3	All	Hold conference call with all reviewers
2.4	Client and writer	Resolve any differences during conference call
2.5	Client and writer	Keep notes during call and compare notes afterward

What the client does in this step

As shown in Table 12-2, in Step 2, the client thinks about the scope of the white paper, including the purpose, audience, flavor, call to action, keywords, and so on. Then the client schedules a conference call with the writer and reviewers to discuss and confirm these details. Having all the reviewers on the line enables the client to make sure everyone is on the same page and helps develop a shared understanding of the project that every reviewer agrees with. This call generally takes about an hour.

If any differences of opinion surface during the call, the client tactfully probes to give those areas a proper airing and resolves them to everyone's satisfaction. Then the client gives everyone a final chance to raise any concerns when the white paper plan is circulated for comments during Step 3.

Both the client and the writer keep careful notes during the call. The client, the writer, or both often record the call in case they need to re-listen to any parts later.

Holding a kickoff conference call helps prevent the painful experience of having a no-see-em reviewer descend from on high to shred your white paper late in the process, without being involved any earlier. For more on the destructive capabilities of the no-see-em pest, see Chapter 11.

What the writer does in this step

As shown in Table 12-2, in Step 2, the writer participates in the conference call with all the reviewers, helping to discuss and resolve any differences (see the next section). The writer takes notes during the call and then compares those notes with the client to confirm their impressions. The writer uses these notes to complete the white paper plan in Step 3.

Resolving differences during the conference call

Either the client or the writer can lead the phone call. If any differences of opinion emerge during the conference call, the best practice is to explore these differences thoroughly to let everyone have their say. Developing a shared consensus is better than letting one person pull rank and overrule everyone else. After all, if one person is just going to make unilateral decisions, what's the point of the conference call in the first place? Instead, keep talking and try to get everyone to pick the most sensible alternative.

For example, the VP of Sales may say that the purpose of the white paper is to generate leads at the top of the sales funnel. But the product manager wants the paper to highlight the competitive advantages of the product and help cement sales at the bottom of the funnel. In other words, they're each proposing to address a target audience at a different point in the sales cycle, which are such vastly different goals that they may require two different flavors of white paper (see Part II for details on the different flavors). The team on the conference call must understand this distinction and pick one or the other flavor or else decide to do two different white papers, one for each audience.

The writer must never start writing until any serious differences uncovered during Step 2 have been resolved. Resolving these issues may take some internal discussions at the client side; or it may require another conference call to deal specifically with those differences.

In rare instances, the differences between reviewers are so fundamental that they can't be resolved; the gap is too big to be bridged. I've heard of this happening, for example, between the engineering and marketing people at a company. In such a rare case, the client and the writer must figure out what to do next. Here are some possible options:

- ✔ If only one person has a dissenting view, drop that person from the reviewing team and proceed without him, if at all possible.

- ✔ If the reviewers are split into opposing camps, escalate the issue to a higher executive who can make the decision on which way to proceed.

- ✔ If no higher executive is present, or the project is hopelessly deadlocked, simply cancel the white paper. If you hired a contract writer, you can expect him to keep the initial deposit as a 50 percent kill fee, which is standard in the industry.

Step 3: Preparing a Plan

When clients hire an advertising agency to do a campaign, the client often prepares a *creative brief,* which spells out many details to incorporate in that campaign, such as the purpose, audience, main take-aways, key competitive advantages, and any standard corporate messages, color palettes, logos, and the like. A creative brief comes closer than anything else to a white paper plan and is essentially a document that spells out the terms of reference for this kind of content marketing project.

Unfortunately, most companies never prepare any white paper plans, and their white papers suffer from this omission. Many teams are so rushed to get their white paper finished that they don't start it properly.

In this step, the writer drafts a plan for the rest of the team to review. If any reviewers have comments, the writer updates the plan to reflect those comments until the client, all the reviewers, and the writer are completely satisfied with the plan. Table 12-3 shows an outline of the tasks and people involved in this step, and the following sections provide more details on the writer's and client's responsibilities and what goes into a white paper plan.

Table 12-3		What Happens in Step 3
Step	*Who*	*What*
3.1	Writer	Creates draft white paper plan
3.2	Writer	Sends draft white paper plan to client
3.3	Client	Circulates draft white paper plan to all reviewers with deadline for comments

Step	Who	What
3.4	Reviewers	Comment on white paper plan
3.5	Client	Gathers all comments and resolves any differences
3.6	Writer	Refines white paper plan to incorporate comments
3.7	All	Repeat steps 3.2 through 3.6 until all reviewers are satisfied with white paper plan

What the writer does in this step

As shown in Table 12-3, in Step 3, the writer creates the white paper plan, which sets out the terms of reference for the project, including the purpose, audience, call to action, flavor, keywords, title, high-level outline, and any other characteristics of the document (see the "Putting together a white paper plan" section for a complete list). The client circulates the draft plan to all reviewers for their comments (see the next section), and then the writer refines it until all the reviewers are satisfied. Drawing up this blueprint in advance puts the whole project on solid ground and helps it to succeed.

What the client does in this step

As shown in Table 12-3, in Step 3, the client receives the draft white paper plan from the writer and circulates it to all the reviewers, with a fairly short deadline for getting their comments back, probably a week or less. No matter how busy people are, they can usually look at a one- or two-page plan for a few minutes. When the comments come back, the client reviews them to make sure they make sense and gives the writer some notion of how to deal with them. If some comments can be safely ignored, the client tells the writer so.

Putting together a white paper plan

An effective white paper plan should include all the following items:

- The primary goal for the document
- The target audience, including demographics, psychographics, and technographics, or a set of personas
- Where the audience sits in the sales funnel: at the top, just starting their research; in the middle, comparing different vendors; or at the bottom, close to making a purchase

✔ The call to action, or what you want the ideal readers to do after they finish reading

✔ The ideal flavor: a backgrounder, numbered list, problem/solution, or a mash-up between a numbered list and one of the others (see Part II for details about the flavors)

✔ The target keywords, or the search terms you expect the ideal readers will use to find the white paper

✔ Two or three possible titles, to be tweaked as you go

✔ An official list of reviewers

✔ A list of background material available from the client

✔ Likely sources for further research: articles, associations, blogs, forums, industry analysts, LinkedIn groups, magazines, recorded webinars, reports, reviews, slides decks, or websites

✔ A high-level overview of the recommended content

✔ The writing tool to prepare the text with, usually Microsoft Word

✔ The design tool to design the pages with, usually Adobe InDesign

✔ Recommended page design guidelines

✔ A realistic schedule for completing the project or else a real-world deadline that must be met

Step 4: Gathering Research

No effective white paper can be written without research because every white paper must be based on facts and logic, not fluff and hot air. In this step, the client assembles all the helpful background he can easily put his hands on and then passes it to the writer. The writer can expect to do some research to support the document he's writing, likely for several days. The key for the writer is to do this research effectively and to keep track of the results carefully so he can draw on it to back up the assertions he makes when writing the white paper. See Table 12-4 and the following sections for the details of this step.

Table 12-4		What Happens in Step 4
Step	*Who*	*What*
4.1	Client	Assembles background and good sources for writer
4.2	Client	Sends background to writer
4.3	Writer	Reviews background from client

Step	Who	What
4.4	Writer	Does additional online research
4.5	Writer	Interviews subject matter experts and executives
4.6	Writer	Keeps careful track of all sources

What the client does in this step

As shown in Table 12-4, in Step 4, the client assembles background material and passes it to the writer, along with a list of likely sources for further research. This material can include articles, associations, blogs, forums, industry analysts, LinkedIn groups, magazines, recorded webinars, reports, reviews, slide decks, or websites.

What the writer does in this step

As shown in Table 12-4, in Step 4, the writer reviews all the background material from the client and looks into all the proposed sources, including articles, blog posts, forums, industry analysts, LinkedIn groups, magazines, recorded webinars, reports, reviews, slide decks, or websites. The writer also interviews subject matter experts and executives from the company. Then the writer extracts the best proof points, quotes, and statistics to use in the white paper, carefully keeping track of all sources for later attribution (see Chapter 14 more information about doing research and keeping track of sources).

Step 5: Preparing an Executive Summary

After doing the research, it's time for the writer to dive in and start drafting a six- or eight-page white paper, right? Wrong. Without a direction blessed by the client, much of what the writer drafts could end up discarded. Instead, the writer should provide a short deliverable so the client and reviewers can confirm the proposed direction. This deliverable is an outline or draft executive summary, usually no more than one page long. Reading and commenting on such a brief summary takes only a few minutes.

Submitting an executive summary for the client to review benefits the project and people involved in several ways:

- ✔ The writer provides a relatively fast deliverable, showing reviewers that the project is moving along quickly.

- ✔ The writer provides a short deliverable, enabling busy reviewers to deal with a brief document that takes only a few minutes to review.

✔ The writer doesn't waste time writing a long document that may have to be scrapped in whole or in part.

✔ The reviewers don't waste time reviewing a long document that may be somewhat off target.

This step dramatically reduces the risk of any misunderstandings and rework later on. Consider this step another magic bullet that can prevent a lot of stress and strain during the white paper project. In fact, this step is so powerful that no writer or client should ever skip it. Agreeing on a one-page summary of the ultimate white paper carries the writer and client down the path toward a successful project.

Table 12-5 outlines what happens in this step and who's responsible. The following sections go into more detail, including how to put together an executive summary and what to do with comments from reviewers.

Table 12-5		What Happens in Step 5
Step	**Who**	**What**
5.1	Writer	Creates 1- or 2-page draft executive summary
5.2	Writer	Sends draft executive summary to client
5.3	Client	Circulates draft executive summary to all reviewers with deadline for comments
5.4	Reviewers	Comment on executive summary
5.5	Client	Gathers all comments and resolves any differences
5.6	Writer	Refines executive summary to incorporate comments
5.7	All	Repeat steps 5.2 through 5.6 until all reviewers are satisfied with executive summary

What the writer does in this step

As shown in Table 12-5, in Step 5, the writer boils down all the accumulated research into a one- or two-page summary with all the main points of the white paper for the client to review. After the client sends back all the reviewers' comments, the writer refines the executive summary, if needed, and this process continues until everyone is satisfied.

This step takes a lot of effort from the writer, including the hardest "thinking" part of the process. The good news is that after the writer finishes the executive summary and gets it approved by the client, the rest of the writing is relatively quick and easy, more like filling in the blanks than doing such hard thinking.

Not every writer works this way; some follow the timeless motto, "How do I know what I think until I see what I said?" In other words, some writers are used to figuring it out as they go along or doing a discovery draft. All I can say is that you're not writing a piece of fiction built from flights of fancy; you're writing a persuasive piece of nonfiction built from facts and logic. If you try to figure it out as you go along, you'll undoubtedly have to do more drafts and spend more time staring at the walls wondering where you're going than if you create a plan at the start.

What the client does in this step

As shown in Table 12-5, in Step 5, the client circulates the draft executive summary to all the reviewers and then gathers all comments by a set deadline. This deadline can be relatively short, no more than a week, because the executive summary is generally just a single page. Most people can take five minutes to read through one page, especially when they were involved in the conference call that spelled out the paper's direction. No surprises should appear in the executive summary. It should simply present a more developed skeleton based on the agreed plan.

Crafting the executive summary

When writing the executive summary, you should use fairly finished sentences. A list of bare bullet points does nothing to convey a flow of ideas or showcase your command of the material. You can think of the executive summary as a collection of topic sentences; each sentence can be expanded into a paragraph or two in the final paper. Beyond summing up the proposed direction of the white paper, you also want the draft executive summary to reassure the team that you can craft research into a persuasive story.

An executive summary can be done two different ways, as a *trailer* or a *synopsis:*

- A trailer-style executive summary includes intriguing highlights from the white paper, intended to entice prospective readers into going through the full document.

- A synopsis-style executive summary includes the whole argument of the white paper in condensed form. Have you seen those executive summaries that boil down an entire 300-page business book into just a few pages? That's what you want to do with a synopsis. You don't have to include more than two or three quotes or factoids in your summary, or maybe none at all, as long as you have all the sources you need to make your points close at hand.

How do you choose which type of executive summary to use? Personally, I prefer the synopsis, for several reasons. First, a synopsis gives a complete recap of the argument without leaving any gaps. Second, you can pop in a synopsis-style summary at the start of the final white paper, so you get to repurpose it in the finished document.

On the other hand, a trailer-style summary plays peekaboo with the content, without revealing the whole argument. This style assumes that every reviewer and reader have the time and interest to read the full document to get the entire story. This assumption is shaky. To stay on more solid ground, I highly recommend using a synopsis-style summary.

Dealing with comments on the executive summary

Whether you're a white paper client or a white paper writer, you have to deal with comments from reviewers. If you pick your reviewers carefully, most of their comments should be clear, constructive, and to the point. But what about the comments that are hopelessly unclear, destructive, or beside the point? How do you deal with those? The following sections provide a few tips.

Don't take it personally

First of all, don't take the comments personally. Even if you're dealing with someone who you suspect has a personal grudge against you — which is really quite rare — you can never be faulted for remaining calm and professional.

Second, skip past those comments and move onto another reviewer's comments. After some time has passed, go back to the upsetting comments and look at them again. Is there anything you missed the first time, some actual nugget of insight wrapped in all that negativity? If so, extract that and try to work with it.

Ignore nonsense reviewers, if you can

If you can't find anything of any merit in some reviewer's comments, think about where that person sits in the company. Is that person your boss's boss? A highly placed VP? The owner's son? Ask yourself: If we ignore this person's comments now, can he mess up the white paper later? If so, for the sake of politics, you may have to engage with him, perhaps just to let him blow off steam. The reviewer may just want someone to listen to him pontificate for a while.

Several pests can rear their heads during this step, including the scope-creep and the tug-o-warrior. For notes on how to deal with comments from these and other pests, see Chapter 11.

Give the writer some guidance

If you're the client, you owe the writer some guidance on how to deal with comments from certain reviewers. Otherwise, the writer can waste a lot of time for nothing. The writer can implement certain suggestions you don't agree with or struggle to resolve contradictory comments from different reviewers. For example, one reviewer suggests expanding a certain section, while another says to shorten it. What do you do? The more reviewers you invite into the process, the more contradictions can happen, and the more guidance you may have to give the writer. Simply take ten minutes to run through the comments on the phone with the document open on both your screens. That ten minutes can save the writer hours of frustration.

Chapter 13

Producing a Powerful White Paper

....

In This Chapter

▶ Leaving people to their proper roles

▶ Writing text and drawing graphics

▶ Getting comments on text and graphics

▶ Refining text and graphics to incorporate comments

▶ Managing sources

▶ Preparing the final white paper

▶ Finishing up the project

....

*Y*ou can think of the three phases of this white paper process as plan, produce, and promote. The middle phase is the producing part, where the white paper goes from an approved outline to a completely finished document, ready to post on the web or hand out as hard copy. (I cover the planning stage in Chapter 12 and the promoting stage in Chapter 16.)

In this chapter, I describe Steps 6 through 12 of the white paper process: creating the first-draft text and graphics; gathering comments; refining the text and graphics into a second draft and gathering any final comments; organizing all the sources referenced in the paper in good order; and attending to any payments, permissions, and postmortem to wrap up the project in a business-like way. (Check out Chapter 12 for Steps 1 through 5.) Some of these steps are standard and predictable; others are best practices I highly recommend, which may be new to many clients or writers who don't yet follow them.

Let the Writer Write!

To make a white paper happen, you need more than a writer. As Chapter 12 explains, many people can be involved in a white paper, from company executives to marketing people to creative professionals like the writer, illustrator, and designer. And here's the danger: People in other roles can be tempted to get too involved in a creative process they know little about.

For example, marketing people can rewrite every paragraph in a draft white paper to make it sound more like the advertising copy they normally see. Engineers can redraw every graphic to make it look more like the higgledy-piggledy sketches they use to explain technical issues on a white board. Salespeople can insert calls to buy the product far too early in the document, echoing their mantra of "always be closing." Although all these people have the right to make comments on the white paper content, they don't have the right to overstep their roles and hijack the creative process.

If you're the client who put together a good team with an experienced writer, illustrator, and designer, you need to defend your team's efforts from any incursions by people in other roles who may feel the need to be "creative." Ideally, a white paper isn't an exercise in creativity; it's a carefully planned business document designed to achieve a desired result from a target audience. You need to defend the white paper from anything or anyone who jeopardizes reaching that goal.

Don't let team members or reviewers waste everyone's time by trying to out-create the creators. Let the writer write, the illustrator draw, and the designer design. Let the reviewers make fair comments on those efforts, and let your creative team refine their efforts accordingly.

If you're a white paper client from a marketing team, your colleagues can make the best contribution at the start of the process with the planning and at the end with the promotions. If you need to distract them from this middle or creative stage, get them preparing the promotional campaigns now. There's plenty of room for creativity in promoting a white paper, as described in Chapter 16.

In some companies, all marketing pieces are submitted to an in-house editor to review for house style and clarity. Some freelance writers use their own editors to smooth out any wrinkles in their style. For simplicity's sake, I left the editor's role out of this chapter. If you do use an editor, any draft from the writer can go through the editor's hands before or after going to the client in Steps 6 or 8, or the final text can go through the editor before going to the designer in Step 11.

Step 6: Creating First-Draft Text and Graphics

The first step in producing a white paper is to create the first-draft text and graphics. Writers, illustrators, designers, and business people understand this step well. After planning the recipe and getting the executive summary approved, you can put together all the ingredients to create a delicious sundae.

This step groups together text and graphics instead of keeping them separate or parallel processes. The visuals in a white paper are vital; in some ways, they're the most important part. Readers will certainly remember an effective visual better than they remember any actual text from a white paper. You can see what this step is all about in Table 13-1 and the following sections.

Table 13-1		What Happens in Step 6
Step	*Who*	*What*
6.1	Writer	Expands executive summary into draft white paper
6.2	Writer	Creates all elements and inserts proof points
6.3	Writer	Polishes text, with help from editor (if any)
6.4	Writer	Sends first-draft white paper text to client
6.5	Writer	Creates raw sketches (with help from subject matter experts) and sends them to illustrator
6.6	Illustrator	Creates rough graphics and sends them to writer
6.7	Writer	Reviews rough graphics and sends comments (if any) to illustrator
6.8	Illustrator	Refines rough graphics to incorporate comments
6.9	Illustrator	Sends first-draft graphics to writer and client

What the writer does in this step

As shown in Table 13-1, the writer does most of Step 6, with some help from the illustrator (if any) and the editor (if any). The writer expands the approved executive summary into a first-draft white paper, drawing on the research he compiled in Step 4. Depending on which flavor of white paper the client chose, the writer creates all the required elements, including an introduction, the main body, a buyer's guide, a call to action, info about the company, and so on. The writer inserts enough proof points to make a convincing case and keeps track of all sources in an orderly way. The writer polishes the text through several iterations — or uses the services of an editor — to make the text smooth and persuasive before sending it to the client.

The writer (or subject matter expert, SME) is also responsible for sketching and sending raw graphics to the illustrator (if any). These sketches don't need to be polished, but they should be clear and complete enough to convey the intended message.

As the writer, you may wonder how to start any graphics or share them by e-mail. Well, you can draw raw sketches by hand and scan them into files to e-mail, or you can work in your preferred graphic program, such as PowerPoint, SmartDraw, or Visio, and e-mail those files. After you get graphics from the illustrator, you can print those out and write comments on the hard copies and then scan them back in. Or if you have the right software, you can open the graphic files from the illustrator, make comments right in them, and save them with meaningful file names (see the nearby sidebar "Coherent file names for drafts").

What the illustrator does in this step

As shown in Table 13-1, in Step 6, the illustrator creates preliminary graphics and sends them back to the writer to review. The writer may suggest some refinements so the process loops through Steps 6.6 and 6.7 once or twice before the illustrator sends the first-draft graphics to the client.

Expanding the executive summary

If you're the writer, how do you expand an executive summary into a full white paper? One quick way to get started is to paste another copy of the executive summary right after the first. Working in the second copy, think of each sentence as the topic sentence for a paragraph, and work at expanding it to a full paragraph or two. Add more thoughts to each point, drawing on what you can easily remember from your research. If you like to use mind maps, create one with the main ideas in the summary as your starting point. You can even create a separate mind map for each product feature, numbered point, or main section of your argument.

Jot down notes and sentence fragments as they come to mind. Don't even try to make complete sentences at this point, and don't censor yourself if you depart from the executive summary. You may come up with an interesting sidebar, a new numbered point to add, or another link in your argument that never occurred to anyone yet. Step 6 is the creative stage, not the judging stage. Try to work quickly and intuitively, relying on your summary for the skeleton while you flesh it out with more details.

At a certain point, you'll likely want to dip back into your research. Work back and forth between the summary, your research, your mind map, and your growing ideas any way you want. Later, you can worry about using proper grammar, adding proof points that make every point in your argument as convincing as possible, and making every section engaging and compelling to read.

Coherent file names for drafts

If the client has a file-naming scheme he always uses, the writer should find out what it is and use it. If not, here's one possible scheme for naming white paper drafts and any supporting files sent to the client:

[project name][draft][date][sender]

And here's a sample file name that uses this scheme:

Big Data in 2013 wp draft-2 May-27-2013 GG

The specifics in this file name reveal four of the five *w's*: *what's* in the file, *where* we are in the process, *when* this file was created, and *who* created it. See how easily you can scan this file name and see what it's all about?

Creating graphics without an illustrator

A professional illustrator normally charges several hundred dollars per graphic. Not every white paper team includes an illustrator, most often because the client never considered allocating any budget for graphics. In this case, the writer usually serves as the illustrator, perhaps drawing on raw input from a SME or else coming up with graphic ideas by himself.

If the budget allows absolutely no room for graphics, the writer can use one of the options I describe in the following sections.

You may think that the best way to stretch your budget for graphics is to Google some phrase and then grab the best image that pops up. Stop. Don't even entertain another thought about this option. Somebody made that image, and that person may not appreciate that you grabbed it without his permission. Or he may have grabbed it from the rightful owner and then reposted it without any credit. But any stolen goods you steal from a thief are still stolen. And getting a letter from the owner's lawyer demanding cash can be expensive — not to mention embarrassing. Using one of the next three options is far less risky.

Using Creative Commons graphics

You may come across a graphic that's been released for public use under a Creative Commons license. These are graphics that the creator has willingly shared with the world. But these licenses have different provisions, and artists may not want private companies using their art for commercial purposes. Read the provisions for that graphic carefully to make sure using it in your white paper is permissible.

Creating business-quality graphics

You can make your own white paper graphics with PowerPoint, Visio, or SmartDraw. PowerPoint and Visio are both well-known products from Microsoft, where you can drag and drop shapes or add in pieces of clip art. Most people already have PowerPoint on their PCs. The drawback of both programs is that you must start with a blank screen and build everything from scratch.

SmartDraw is less well known but well worth considering if you need business graphics for white papers, slide decks, or blogs. This cost-effective package aimed at non-artists comes bundled with scores of predrawn graphics that are supremely easy to tweak. You can search for a certain type of graphic, find one close to what you want, and then tailor it by adjusting the color, adding your own text, and adding or removing lines or boxes. In just a few minutes, anyone can create an acceptable graphic with SmartDraw.

Finding stock photos

A good stock photo can really dress up the cover of a white paper and visually suggest who the document is aimed at and what it's about. A stock photo large enough for a white paper cover generally costs less than $30 from a source like iStockphoto (www.istockphoto.com). You can either pay that amount out of your white paper fee or pass it along to the client. That small fee usually isn't a problem.

When you buy a stock photo from iStockphoto — as long as you buy the Standard license, not just Editorial — you can legally use it multiple times. One useful way to stretch a budget for graphics is to use portions of the same photo for different sections. In other words, use the full photo on the white paper cover, and then use smaller snippets sprinkled throughout the document for no extra fee.

Reviewing graphics

Graphics need reviewing, just like text does. The first set of graphics from the illustrator isn't always perfect. As the writer, your job is to give the graphics a critical viewing and ask yourself whether they're clear and complete. Would a graphic work better if it was simplified, clarified, enlarged, compressed, stretched, rotated, or flipped? Does it read from left to right and from top to bottom to match the reading conventions of our English-speaking culture? Can you remove any lines or compress any callouts?

Make sure the illustrator understands that you reserve the right to do a round or two of comments and refinements to make the graphics as effective as possible. And then like any reviewer, be precise and constructive.

If, as the writer, you create any graphics, always have the client, and ideally the appropriate SME(s), review them to make sure they're accurate. Draw the graphics up as clearly as you can and circulate them for comments before you send them to the illustrator to be professionally redrawn. Otherwise, you're gambling that the first effort from the illustrator won't need any radical revisions, which eats up time and money.

Step 7: Gathering Initial Comments

This step is a well-understood part of any publishing process. Table 13-2 and the following sections show what happens and who's involved in this step. After the writer creates a first draft and the illustrator creates the graphics, the reviewers need to look at them and comment. And the client has to manage the reviews to make sure they happen in a timely and constructive way. Of course, this whole process must be handled with patience, tact, and sometimes a dash of good-natured humor from everyone.

Table 13-2		What Happens in Step 7
Step	**Who**	**What**
7.1	Client	Circulates first-draft text and graphics to reviewers with deadline for comments
7.2	Reviewers	Comment on first-draft text and graphics
7.3	Client	Gathers all comments and resolves any differences
7.4	Client	Sends comments on text to writer
7.5	Client	Sends comments on graphics to illustrator

What the client does in this step

As shown in Table 13-2, in Step 7, the client circulates the first-draft text and graphics to all reviewers with a request to get their comments back by the appointed deadline. To set the deadline, the client checks the schedule and gives a realistic review period.

A week is about right for a first-draft white paper; never allow more than two weeks, or the project can lose momentum with team members.

Help your reviewers understand that you value their time and will consider each of their comments carefully, but they should keep the ideal reader and purpose of the document in mind rather than their personal preferences, like putting two spaces after every period or using their favorite buzzwords. As they go through a draft, every reviewer should ask, "How will the ideal reader react to this? How well will this help us achieve our purpose?" rather than "Doesn't this sentence break the rules I learned from Mrs. Thomas in fourth grade?"

As the comments come in, the client reviews them to make sure they make sense and don't contradict one another. The client clarifies any comments that are unclear, contradictory, or destructive, or else discards them outright. Finally, the client sends all useful comments on the text to the writer and all useful comments on the graphics to the illustrator.

Dealing with comments on the first draft

Very few reviewers understand the different levels of editing; many feel that their role is to work at the worm's-eye view of the text simply to check the spelling and grammar of the draft. Because Word can check spelling and grammar fairly well, tell your reviewers that you want them to focus on the bird's-eye view to make sure the white paper makes valid points and fulfills the desired purpose. Even so, you can expect most of the comments to focus on individual words, phrases, and sentences. Some reviewers mark any sentence that starts with *and* or *but* as a big no-no or suggest that you insert two spaces after each period. The good news is that these rules drummed into people's heads in grade school aren't absolute. The bad news is that these sticklers may be powerful executives in the company who insist on reviewing for this kind of banal detail.

An ideal reviewer sticks to the higher level, correcting technical details, shading the text to reflect company or product positioning, and perhaps suggesting more or less coverage of some particular area. If you find a reviewer who consistently provides this kind of useful, to-the-point comments, include him in all your future white paper projects.

You shouldn't see any sweeping comments suggesting that you make a big departure from the approved outline or include any new material that clearly doesn't belong to a white paper of the chosen flavor. If you find a reviewer who consistently suggests that you expand the content in all different directions, or go into many side issues, he may be a scope-creep. In this case, see Chapter 11 for how to deal with this pest.

Step 8: Creating the Second-Draft White Paper

When all the reviews come in — just like for a Broadway show — the writer can see whether the white paper is a hit or a miss. But unlike an expensive musical, the writer has another chance to make it good by incorporating comments from reviewers into a second draft. This step requires a little patience and tact from the writer, who must recognize that white paper reviewers aren't professional writers or editors; reviewers are business people pressed into doing an editorial task where some are far more comfortable than others.

As Table 13-3 illustrates, the bulk of this step is up to the writer. After getting all the reviews, the writer may end up with one Word file or one online Google Doc, showing everyone's comments at once. More likely, the writer gets multiple copies of the same Word file with changes tracked or comments inserted into each one. The writer and the client share the responsibility for keeping all comments organized and making wise decisions on whether to incorporate or overrule each one. The illustrator may get some comments on the graphics as well; in this case, the illustrator may need to confer with the client to see how much rework of the graphics the budget can handle. See the following sections for details.

Table 13-3		What Happens in Step 8
Step	*Who*	*What*
8.1	Writer	Queries client and reviewers on unclear comments (if any)
8.2	Writer	Refines text to incorporate comments
8.3	Illustrator	Refines graphics to incorporate comments
8.4	Illustrator	Sends second-draft graphics to writer and client
8.5	Writer	Inserts second-draft graphics into second-draft white paper
8.6	Writer	Sends second-draft white paper to client

What the writer does in this step

As shown in Table 13-3, in Step 8, the writer refines the first draft of the white paper to incorporate the reviewers' comments. If any comments are unclear or contradictory, the writer may need to go back to the client or a certain reviewer for clarification. After the illustrator finishes the next round of graphics, the writer generally inserts those graphics into the file to create a second-draft document to send to the client. Including the graphics may make the second draft easier for reviewers to visualize as the finished white paper.

If any change breaks the house style or the designated style guide for the white paper, the writer should probably reject it. If any change makes the text more clear, more precise, or more persuasive, he should probably accept it — and look for other instances in the rest of the white paper where the same comment applies.

If you (the writer) have many files with many comments on every page to deal with, consider printing out every file for reference. For a six- to eight-page white paper, that won't use a shameful amount of paper. Then arrange every printout in a separate pile on your desk and work through all the comments by looking at each page in every copy in turn. Try using a system of highlighters to mark each comment in each printout, such as green for "done," orange for "rejected," and yellow for "query for clarification."

What the illustrator does in this step

As shown in Table 13-3, in Step 8, the illustrator refines the first-draft graphics to incorporate the reviewers' comments. If any comments are unclear or contradictory, the illustrator may need to go back to the client or a certain reviewer for clarification. After the illustrator finishes the next round of graphics, he sends them to the writer to insert into the second-draft document to send to the client.

Step 9: Gathering Final Comments

This step is a repeat of Step 7. Reviewers should have noticeably fewer comments at this point than on the first draft. With a properly planned white paper, the first draft should come back with minimal comments, and the second, with next to none.

In my experience, creating a finished white paper takes no more than two drafts of text and graphics. Think about it. All the reviewers had a chance to air their views during an initial conference call. They all had a chance to review and approve the white paper plan, the executive summary for the white paper, and the first- and second-draft text and graphics. That's one conference call plus four draft documents. What more does anyone need?

As you can see in Table 13-4, this step involves only the client and reviewers. If you fit that bill, check out the following sections for details; if you're the writer, you can skip to Step 10 and work on that while you wait for the final comments.

Table 13-4		What Happens in Step 9
Step	*Who*	*What*
9.1	Client	Circulates second-draft white paper to reviewers with deadline for comments
9.2	Reviewers	Comment on second-draft text and graphics
9.3	Client	Gathers all comments and resolves any differences
9.4	Client	Sends final comments on text to writer
9.5	Client	Sends final comments on graphics to illustrator

What the client does in this step

As shown in Table 13-4, in Step 9, the client circulates the second-draft text and graphics to all reviewers with a request to receive their comments by an appointed deadline (about one week at most). As the comments come in, the client reviews them to make sure they make sense and don't undo any effective changes made to the first draft. The client sends all the useful comments on the text to the writer and all the useful comments on the graphics to the illustrator.

Dealing with comments on the second draft

No magic formula exists for dealing with comments on the second-draft text and graphics. You should have noticeably fewer comments because the writer and illustrator either incorporated all the earlier comments or ignored them on the advice of the client. If a reviewer makes the same comments all over again, he may be a tug-o-warrior, unwilling to relinquish a single point. In this case, deal with this pest as described in Chapter 11.

For simplicity's sake, this description covers a document prepared the conventional way, with drafts done in Word and e-mailed to reviewers to mark up with Track Changes. For the white papers I do online with Google Docs, things are never quite this neat and tidy. Because all reviewers can see every other reviewer's comments, often side discussions or polite disagreements among reviewers occur. But the same principles remain: Get all reviewers involved from the start, make sure the client provides some guidance to the writer, and keep everyone focused on implementing comments that matter to the target audience and help achieve the white paper's intended purpose.

Step 10: Collecting and Checking Sources

Just about every white paper needs a few references to back up its arguments and showcase the research behind it. Some have a dozen or more, and a few will top 20 footnotes in one document. For the writer, keeping all those sources straight can be challenging. But not doing so defeats the point of finding them in the first place. And if the client is queried later and can't produce any sources, it detracts from the company's credibility.

In this step, the writer bundles all the sources cited in the white paper and sends them to the client. All white paper writers should follow this step for several good reasons:

- To back up all their research for safekeeping
- To enable the client to spot-check a few references and make sure the citations are letter-perfect before the white paper is published
- To mark themselves as true professionals who do their homework and stand behind their work

Refer to Table 13-5 and the following sections for full details of Step 10.

Table 13-5		What Happens in Step 10
Step	**Who**	**What**
101.	Writer	Assembles all sources as PDFs
10.2	Writer	Keys file names of sources to footnotes
10.3	Writer	Sends sources to client
10.4	Client	Spot-checks sources (if required)
10.5	Client	Files sources with white paper project files

What happens if writers skip this step?

Most white paper writers never provide any sources to the client. This lazybones approach creates a major gap in the quality control of the document. Will no one from the client's side ever check any sources quoted by the writer? What happens six months later if a skeptical reader challenges a reference and asks to see it?

If the client has all the sources close at hand, he can quickly respond to any queries and send sources to readers as PDFs. But if the client has no sources on file, he must go back to the writer, try to rediscover that source, or else ignore those queries. Knowing how material on the web comes and goes, the original source may no longer be online at the original URL. What then?

If the client tells a prospect he can't find a source, this defeats the whole purpose of the white paper and undermines the company's credibility. Isn't it better for the writer to take a few minutes to provide all the sources to the client when the project is still fresh in their minds?

Ideally, Step 10 shouldn't require a big crunch near the end of a white paper. All writers should keep their research in good order throughout the project. Doing so can feel a little "picky" at first, but like any healthy habit, the more you do it, the more natural it becomes. And writers can attend to this step while waiting for final comments back from the client from Step 9; the worst that can happen is writers may have to rejig the order of a few sources before sending them in. For details about finding strong evidence to build a case, citing references in the text, and formatting footnotes, see Chapter 15.

A few times, long after I finished a white paper, a client came back to me asking for a source quoted in that paper. Perhaps a reader asked about it or perhaps a company executive was looking for a good factoid for a slide. By then, that sometimes meant searching for that source all over again. Since I started keeping my sources better organized and giving my clients a bundle of sources for them to file, I haven't had a single request like that.

What the writer does in this step

As shown in Table 13-5, in Step 10, the writer gathers all the sources referenced in the white paper, keys them to the same numbers as the footnotes, and sends all the sources to the client. Throughout this step, the writer uses PDF as much as possible as the universal file format:

- ✔ For a web page or blog post, the writer makes careful note of the precise URL and captures that web page as a PDF.

- ✔ For a printed report or a book, the writer scans the pages to PDF.

- ✔ For Word, Excel, or PowerPoint documents, the writer can either save those as PDFs or keep them in their native formats.

The writer can actually send the sources to the client ahead of the final text, or with the final text, as described later in "Step 12: Wrapping Up the Project."

What the client does in this step

As shown in Table 13-5, in Step 10, the client receives the bundle of sources from the writer. Then he can spot-check any references or quotes in the white paper as he wants and file away those PDFs with the rest of the project files for future reference.

Saving source material as PDFs

No client wants to get a hodge-podge of HTML, screen grabs, PDFs, and other file formats. That just complicates life. Instead, I recommend that the writer takes a few minutes to bring everything into one universal format.

If you're the writer and you're pulling white paper references from reports you found online, web pages, books, or printed documents, consider all these reasons for storing these sources as PDFs:

- Some of your research is already in PDF format.
- For web pages, you can print to a PDF, which saves the content even if that URL changes or that page is taken down (details in the following sections).
- For printed documents, you can scan to a PDF (details in the following sections).
- PDFs are easy to access with free readers from Adobe or third parties.

 PDF is an industry standard that will likely remain easy to access for the foreseeable future. To be doubly sure that you can always open your sources, archive the current version of Adobe Reader along with your sources. Or bookmark the page on the Adobe website (`http://get.adobe.com/reader/otherversions`) where you can download earlier versions of the reader.

Saving web pages as PDFs with Windows

Some of your research will likely come from web pages or blogs. Using Windows, you have several ways to save web pages as PDFs.

✔ **If you have Adobe Acrobat** — the commercial product, not the free PDF reader called Adobe Reader — you can print anything on your screen to a PDF. Here's how:

1. Navigate to the web page you want and select File and then Print from your browser.

2. In the Print dialog, select Adobe PDF for your printer and click OK.

3. In the Save PDF File As dialog, navigate to your folder of white paper sources, enter a suitable file name, and click Save.

   To find a suitable file name, follow the suggestions in the later section "Keying sources to footnotes." From the Print dialog, you can also click Properties to adjust the properties of your PDF, but the defaults should work fine.

✔ **If you don't have Adobe Acrobat,** you can create a PDF from any web page by using many free utilities and online services. Simply Google "free HTML to PDF converter" to see the range of possibilities. One of my favorite free web-page-to-PDF utilities is from Outside Software, available at `www.html-to-pdf.net/free-online-pdf-converter.aspx`. You copy the URL of the page you want to save and paste it into the converter page, and your PDF is created for free. You just need to give it a file name and save it; the whole process takes a few seconds.

Saving web pages as PDFs with Mac OS

On the Mac, this feature (like many others) is built in.

1. **Navigate to the web page you want and select File and then Print from your browser.**

2. **In the Print dialog, click PDF and select Save as PDF.**

3. **In the Save dialog, navigate to your folder of sources, give a suitable file name, and click Save.**

   To find a suitable file name, follow the suggestions in the "Keying sources to footnotes" section, later in this chapter. From the Print dialog, you can also add metadata, like Author, Subject, and Keywords, if those will help you keep your sources straight. Most people don't bother with those just for sources.

Scanning print to PDF

Do you have a printed document or book that you can't find online? You may be able to scan directly to PDFs. Check your scanner manual or online help. If your scanner can't create PDFs, use the free utility iCopy, available from `www.icopy.sourceforge.net`. iCopy gives any scanner the ability to turn out PDFs from printed pages. And it drives the scanner's document feeder so you don't have to stand over the machine like a zombie, feeding one page at a time, getting more and more tempted not to bother scanning the whole thing.

Including all the pages

E-mailing a ten-page PDF that you quoted from is easy. But sometimes you want to pluck out a single reference from the executive summary of a monster 280-page report. Even though that report is already a PDF, it can be tempting to send the client just a single page or maybe just the four-page executive summary. Think of all those megabytes no one has to deal with!

But remember the purpose of this step: to support fact-checking and answer any future queries from readers. Does sending a single page and deleting the other 279 help further these goals? Or is it a false economy that saves nothing but disk space, which is getting cheaper all the time? I believe it's better to send the whole source file. When you're providing source material, you can't really have TMI (too much information).

Scanning an entire book is illegal under U.S. copyright laws, as Google found out when authors and publishers sued it for scanning several whole university libraries. So this is the exception where I don't recommend scanning the whole document. Just scan the title, copyright page, about the author, and the chapter with the information you cited.

Keying sources to footnotes

Don't send the client a set of PDFs with random file names. To make life easier for everyone, create a table to match each source to a footnote number in the final white paper. The simplest way is to use a number in the file name of each PDF that corresponds to the associated footnote, as shown in Table 13-6. Doing so makes finding any source as easy as one-two-three. It creates an orderly workflow, too: The writer can simply work through the list of footnotes, finding or saving each PDF in turn with a matching number.

Table 13-6	How to Key Sources to Footnote Numbers	
Original File Name of Source	*Footnote*	*File Name of Source Submitted*
ACME_special_report_2012. pdf	1	1-ACME_special_report_2012.pdf
www.acme.com/blog/ may-27-2013.htm	2	2-acme.com-blog-may-27-2013.pdf
www.acme.com#benefits. html	3	3-acme.com-benefits.pdf
www.big-consulting-firm. com/big-industry-report.pdf	4 and 7	4-7-big-consulting-firm-big-industry-report.pdf

Create a folder called something like "Sources to Submit," and then save each PDF in that folder as you number it. That way, all the PDFs line up by their numbers so you can easily see whether you're missing any. Then just e-mail the client every file in that folder. They'll line up neatly on his side, too.

What if you have two or three references from the same source? That can easily happen with a long, definitive report. In that case, there's no point in sending the same source more than once. Instead, as shown in the last row of Table 13-6, just enter all the footnote numbers in order at the start of the file name. Then you can still scan down the list of file names and spot that item easily.

Spot-checking sources

If you're the client, you can simply file away the bundle of sources with the rest of the white paper project files. But why not do a little quality control and spot-check a few references to make sure they're letter-perfect? How many sources should you check? In a list of eight sources, check two or three; if they all turn up perfect, call that enough. But if you find any issues, check every source in the document.

1. **Open the white paper and find the first footnote you want to check.**

2. **Open the PDF that starts with the same footnote number.**

3. **Search for the exact text or fact given in the white paper and confirm that it's on the page given in the footnote.**

4. **Read both the source document and the reference to make sure they're exact.**

What if you can't find anything in the source to match the reference in the white paper? What if it sort of matches but seems taken out of context or distorted? First, aren't you glad you checked? Next, realize the vast range of possible explanations.

It can be a simple mix-up on file names that you can straighten out yourself. Start at the first footnote in the white paper and run through your folder of source PDFs. The writer could have easily skipped over one and got all the file names out of order from that point on. Find the spot for the missing source and check whether it's anywhere else in your list with the wrong name. If not, ask the writer to provide you a new set of sources with the missing one and all the rest of the PDF file names numbered properly.

If it's a matter of interpretation, use your common sense. Can you rewrite the sentence to create a more accurate reference and then run that by the writer as a comment? Give that a try. Or is it something more serious? Do you suspect that the writer made up a quote from thin air and claimed he found it in a certain report?

In any case, you need to get back to the writer and have a frank discussion. Tell him what you found, and ask him to explain. You don't want your white paper — and your company's credibility — to rest on shoddy sourcing. Most likely, the writer will have an innocent explanation, and it's great that you caught the slip-up before you released the white paper.

I was working on a white paper about an emerging market that one VP at the client claimed was worth $3.25 billion a year. He swore he'd read that somewhere; he just couldn't remember where. After days of digging, I turned up an analyst's report with the revenues for that market projected at $32.5 million a year. I kept quizzing him for his source, but he never produced it. I finally guessed he'd seen the report I found, misread the decimal point, and used a much higher number from then on. But he was too embarrassed to admit it. Let's face it: $3.25 billion is a lot bigger than the number I could corroborate; in fact, it's 100 times as big! White papers that exaggerate numbers that much don't stand up to much scrutiny. This issue was never resolved, and that white paper was never published — a victim, perhaps, of sloppy sourcing.

Handling unused sources

The writer may find some great sources that don't end up in the white paper but are still relevant to the topic. If you're the writer, don't just delete those sources and waste all that research! Instead, e-mail them as a separate bundle to the client with a subject line something like, "Great sources not used in this white paper." You may want to call each of those PDFs something like "not-used-big-consulting-firm-big-industry-report-2013.pdf." Then if you do another white paper for the same client, you can pull on those sources for that project.

If you're the client, check out those sources to see whether you can use them for a blog, slide deck, or any other marketing materials for your company.

Step 11: Preparing the Final Document

Like a big-name celebrity who just won an Oscar, this step needs no introduction. It's an obvious part of any publishing process. Don't hurry through it, or you may have some embarrassing mistakes to deal with later — just like a celebrity who forgets to thank his mother in his acceptance speech.

As you can see in Table 13-7, in this penultimate step, everyone gets involved — the writer, illustrator (if any), designer (if any), and client. The writer makes any final changes in the text, while the illustrator makes any last tweaks to the graphics. If a designer is onboard, he pours the text and graphics into his chosen design software and generates a PDF for the client to review. If no designer was used for the project, the writer completes the final pages in Word — or his chosen design software — and generates a PDF for the client to review.

Everyone takes another look-see to make sure no last glitches turn up, and the designer fixes any final problems. Then the designer delivers all the source files and the final PDF for the white paper to the client. At the end of Step 11, the white paper is finished and ready to be posted on the web.

The following sections explain all the nitty-gritty details of this step.

Table 13-7		What Happens in Step 11
Step	**Who**	**What**
11.1	Illustrator	Refines graphics to incorporate final comments
11.2	Illustrator	Sends final graphics to writer, designer, and client
11.3	Illustrator	Sends invoice to client (if outsourced)
11.4	Writer	Refines text to incorporate final comments
11.5	Writer	Sends final text to client and designer
11.6	Writer	Sends final invoice to client (if outsourced)
11.7	Designer	Creates draft pages with text and graphics
11.8	Designer	Generates draft PDF and sends it to client
11.9	Client	Reviews draft PDF and sends comments (if any) to designer
11.10	Designer	Refines draft pages and creates final PDF
11.11	Client	Proofreads final PDF
11.12	Designer	Puts keywords and other metadata into final PDF
11.13	Designer	Sends all source files and final PDF to client
11.14	Designer	Sends invoice to client (if outsourced)

What the illustrator does in this step

As shown in Table 13-7, in Step 11, the illustrator refines the graphics to incorporate any final comments from reviewers and sends them to the writer, the designer (if any), and the client. When the client is satisfied with the graphics, the illustrator (if outsourced) sends in an invoice.

What the writer does in this step

As shown in Table 13-7, in Step 11, the writer refines the white paper to incorporate any final comments from reviewers and sends the final text to the client and the designer. If the writer is from outside the company, he sends in his final invoice.

If the project has no designer, the writer does all the tasks assigned to the designer in Table 13-7: Prepares the final pages in Word — or his chosen design software — and creates a draft PDF for the client to approve. (See Chapter 18 for tips on designing a white paper.) If the client has any comments, the writer/designer refines the pages to incorporate these comments and then sends the client another PDF. When the client is satisfied, the writer/designer inserts the proper keywords and metadata into the PDF for SEO purposes and (if outsourced) sends in his final invoice, which may include a separate fee for page design.

What the designer does in this step

As shown in Table 13-7, in Step 11, the designer pours the final text and graphics into pages for the white paper and creates a draft PDF for the client to approve. If the client has any comments or spots any glitches in the PDF, the designer makes the required fixes and sends the client another draft PDF. The client and designer repeat this process until everyone is satisfied with the final PDF. Then the designer inserts the appropriate keywords and metadata into the PDF for SEO purposes and (if outsourced) sends in an invoice. In my experience, the first set of PDFs come back with a few formatting comments and the second with next to none. In fact, by that point the client is usually tired of looking at the thing, and he just wants to get it out and start promoting it.

What the client does in this step

As shown in Table 13-7, in Step 11, the client reviews the draft PDF of the final white paper and gives any comments to the designer. The client may repeat this process once or twice, until he's completely satisfied with the final PDF. The client may want to review the list of keywords compiled in Step 3 before the designer inserts them into the final PDF for SEO purposes.

Proofing final pages

No matter how many times you check a document, you can always miss something. Any mistakes that happen during the design steps can be especially tough to spot. When you get the final PDF of the white paper, arrange to have two or three team members who've never seen it before give it a careful proofing on hard copy. Table 13-8 lists some of the classic visual and typographical mistakes to watch for when proofing a white paper at the PDF stage.

Table 13-8	Checklist for Proofing a White Paper
Item	**What to Watch For**
Bullets	All formatted the same? All the same size? All the same shape?
Colors	All match or harmonize? All from the same corporate palette? All print out clearly in black and white?
Contents	All entries match the actual headings? Any missing entries?
E-mail addresses	All correct? Did you test to make sure they work?
Footers	Every page has a footer? All formatted the same?
Footnotes	All formatted the same? All lead to proper references?
Graphics	All figure numbers, titles, and captions correct? All formatted the same?
	All graphics print clearly in color? In black and white?
Headers	Every page has a header? All formatted the same?
Headings	All headings formatted correctly? All the proper size?
Lists	All numbers in correct order? All items formatted the same?
Logos	All used properly, not stretched or squeezed? All colors correct?
Margins	All the same on every page?
Math	All figures add up? All formulas work out correctly?
Page numbers	Every page has a number? In correct order? All formatted the same?
Phone numbers	All correct? Did you dial them to make sure they work?
Style sheet	All styles applied consistently?
Tables	All table numbers and titles correct? All formatted the same?
Text	All formatted correctly? Proper fonts? Proper sizes?
Web links	All correct? Did you test them to make sure they work?

By this point, all the text has been reviewed and approved many times, but if your proofers spot any text that they find inconsistent or hard to understand, you probably want to make some final fixes to those passages.

I was recently asked to update a white paper for a company that's a household name around the world. To my shock, the first word in the title on the cover was misspelled! That document was distributed for three years and seen by an unimaginable number of B2B prospects. How do you think such a prominent typo affected their impression of that document and that offering? The moral: Give your final PDF to someone who has never seen it before. A fresh pair of eyes can often spot mistakes that everyone else overlooked.

Putting keywords in the PDF

Not everyone knows this, but web spiders can index PDFs found on the web so that they show up in search results. That's why you should always include useful keywords right in the PDF of any white paper you post online. You already specified these keywords in Step 3, remember? In this step, the client may want to review this list. Then the writer or designer can insert all the keywords and other appropriate metadata in the final PDF.

Inserting metadata in a PDF

With the right software, the writer or designer can insert keywords and other data into the finished PDF for the white paper. You can enter metadata with Adobe Acrobat (the commercial product), InDesign, Word 2007 or 2010 for Windows, or a neat little Mac OS utility called CombinePDFs.

- ✔ **If you have Adobe Acrobat** — the commercial product, not the free Adobe Reader — you can insert metadata into your white paper PDF by following these steps:

  1. **Open the white paper PDF with Acrobat and select File then Properties.**

  2. **In the Document Properties dialog, on the Description panel, enter your preferred title, author, subject, and keywords (separated by commas) in the appropriate text boxes and click OK.**

  3. **Select File and Save.**

- ✔ **If you have InDesign,** you can insert metadata in your white paper file and then generate another PDF. If your designer doesn't know how to do this, share the following process with him:

  1. **Open the white paper file with InDesign and select File then File Info.**

  2. **In the File Info dialog box, enter your preferred document title, author, description, and keywords (separated by commas) in the appropriate text boxes and click OK.**

  3. **Select File then Save, and then select File and Export.**

  4. **In the Export dialog, select Adobe PDF with your regular PDF options and click OK.**

✔ **If you have Word 2007 or 2010 for Windows,** you can insert metadata in a less obvious way. Here's how:

1. **Open the white paper file with Word, press Alt + F, and select Prepare then Properties.**

2. **In the Document Information panel, enter your preferred title, subject, and keywords (separated by commas) in the appropriate text boxes.**

3. **Press Alt + F and select Save As and then PDF or XPS.**

4. **In the Publish as PDF or XPS dialog, navigate to the folder you want, enter a suitable file name, and click Publish.**

If you have Word 2007 and you don't see the Save As PDF or XPS option, you need to install the free Save As PDF or XPS add-in from Microsoft (`www.microsoft.com/en-us/download/details.aspx?id=7`) and then follow the preceding steps.

✔ **If you have a Mac,** you can use Adobe Acrobat or InDesign as described earlier. Or you can use a nifty piece of freeware that makes up for the limitations of Preview called Combine PDFs (`http://monkeybread software.de/Freeware/CombinePDFs.shtml`). After you have Combine PDFs running, here's what to do:

1. **Select File and Add Files.**

2. **In the Open dialog, select the white paper PDF and click Open; select Options and then Add Metadata.**

3. **In the Add Metadata dialog, enter your preferred title, author, subject, and keywords (separated by commas) and click OK.**

4. **Click Merge PDFs in the lower-right corner.**

5. **In the Save dialog, enter a file name and click Save.**

Note that CombinePDFs is shareware, so after you process 1,000 pages with it, it asks that you pay for a license. If you use it that much, you really should shell out for it.

Whatever software you use, check your keywords after you finish to make sure everything worked, as described in the next section.

Viewing metadata in a PDF

You can see — but not change — the keywords and other metadata in any PDF. What you see depends on the software you use.

✔ Under Windows with the free Adobe Reader, open the PDF, select File then Properties, and click the Description tab. You can see the existing title, author, subject, and keywords (if any).

✔ Under Mac OS with Preview, open the PDF, select Tools then Show Inspector, and click the magnifying glass button. You can see the existing keywords (if any).

Step 12: Wrapping Up the Project

Everyone knows how to wrap up a white paper, right? If you're the client, order a couple of large Hawaiian pizzas (with anchovies and hot peppers — woo hoo!) and invite your whole team to the picnic table out back. If you're a contract writer, e-mail your final invoice, order one large Hawaiian with anchovies and hot peppers, and scarf down the whole thing by yourself.

Team-building lunches are great, but there's more to wrapping up a white paper than that. Any loose ends you leave dangling can trip you up later. Step 12 describes everything you should do to close the file on your white paper before you reach for the menu for Uncle Wheezy's Cheezee Pizza.

This step includes taking care of three *P*s: payments, permissions, and perhaps a postmortem. This step ties up any loose ends about the project in a businesslike way. Table 13-9 outlines this step, and the following sections fill you in on why this step is so important.

Table 13-9		What Happens in Step 12
Step	**Who**	**What**
12.1	Client	Pays all invoices
12.2	Client	Gets permissions for sources or graphics (if required)
12.3	Creatives	Transfer all copyright to client (if outsourced)
12.4	Creatives	Request a copy of the final white paper for a sample
12.5	Creatives	Request using that client as a reference
12.6	All	Hold a postmortem to discuss project

What the client does in this step

As shown in Table 13-9, in Step 12, the client pays all invoices from the writer, the illustrator, and the designer (collectively called *creatives*), arranges for any necessary permissions for sources or graphics, and perhaps does a postmortem on the project with the writer and the reviewers to assess what went well and what could have gone better.

What the creatives do in this step

If the white paper writer, illustrator, and designer are company employees, they don't need to invoice or transfer their copyrights, because the white paper is clearly work for hire. If any of these creatives are contractors from outside the company, they already sent an invoice for their work in Step 11. As shown in Table 13-9, when that invoice is paid, they transfer all the copyrights to the white paper text, graphics, or page design to the client. They may want to get a final PDF of the document from the client as a sample and ask whether they can use the client for a reference.

Making payments — the faster, the better

Being a good client for any contractor on your white paper team comes down to a few simple things: Be reasonable, give clear direction, and most of all, pay promptly. Cutting a check in 30 days and sending it by snail mail won't thrill any freelancer, and making him wait 60 days can be downright irritating. Sending him a wire transfer the same day you get his invoice, now, that's memorable. After all, your creatives aren't in the same galaxy as a giant corporation like, say, Acme Scanners, with millions in sales and a huge cash flow. Each of them is more likely a one-person microbusiness, operating out of a home office that can handle only two or three clients at a time.

Try to finagle your finance people to pay freelancers faster than giant corporations. Find out whether you can pay by wire transfer rather than by check, which can shave off a week of postage and handling. Consider paying with your corporate credit card, or even a personal credit card, then expensing that to the company. And if one of your outsourced team members queries you about an invoice, go to bat for him; don't throw up your hands and tell him it's with your Accounts Payable. In the future, if a contractor has to choose between doing a project for you or for any other client, he'll remember who paid him faster last time, which will help him make up his mind.

I've had the odd invoice go astray. Once, my client printed out the invoice I e-mailed, but it slipped down behind her piled-high desk and was missing for two months. She was good natured during my inquiries and put through a duplicate invoice. When she finally did some housecleaning and found the lost one, we both had a good laugh. That's the kind of relationship you want to build with your creatives.

Getting permissions

Some consulting firms and publishers want vendors to ask permission before quoting from their articles or reports in any marketing material. Getting permissions is the client's responsibility, but it's certainly easier to do when you have a copy of the source document on hand that the writer provides in Step 11. And you may want to have an alternative source in mind if that third party says no.

Now suppose you have a channel partner with a good graphic you want to use in the white paper. So you call up your contact at that company and ask whether it's okay to use the graphic. Is that sufficient permission? Probably not. In this case, I recommend sending an e-mail, attaching the white paper, and asking for an acknowledgment and more formal permission back, probably from a member of the partner's legal team. You're not likely to get sued by a good channel partner, but why be sloppy? That's just another loose end to tie up.

Transferring copyrights

Although copyright rules vary by country, if a writer sends a note or e-mail permanently transferring all his copyright to a white paper, that should eliminate any possibility of any future legal hassles. A simple e-mail like the following will suffice:

> For consideration received, I, *[name of creative]*, permanently transfer all my copyright to the white paper entitled *[name of white paper]* to *[name of client's company]* as of *[date]*.

Doing a postmortem

Many larger consulting firms do a postmortem after every engagement, but a postmortem isn't a standard practice for white paper clients and writers. Perhaps it should be; nearly everyone can benefit by reviewing what went right and what could have gone better about a project.

If you do hold a postmortem, you can make it as large or small a group as possible. Get everyone together on a conference call, a teleconference, or an in-person meeting, or perhaps more informally over a coffee or lunch.

However you assemble your team, follow this number-one ground rule: Keep things constructive by focusing on processes, not personalities. Instead of saying, "Your comments on the second draft were ridiculous!" — which can only get someone's back up — say, "We need to work out how to resolve any contradictory comments that come in late in the process." Instead of pointing fingers and blaming someone else, try to identify something you can all work on solving together. The difference is amazing.

Part IV
Succeeding with White Papers

Five Must-Dos for White Paper Writers

1. Read other white papers and any nonfiction that stimulates and inspires you and keep your own file of notable idea.

2. Write every day, any type of B2B material but especially any white papers you have a chance to work on.

3. Rewrite to polish drafts, with help from your computer to read back your drafts and show objective statistics on your writing.

4. Learn from style guides, follow house style, and create your own style guide.

5. Refine your writing process with best practices and fresh ideas that can bring out your top efforts.

You may benefit from working with a researcher when it's time to gather information for a white paper. For tips on making the most of the relationship, check out the free online article at www.dummies.com/extras/whitepapers.

In this part . . .

✔ Discover how to build a strong white paper based on powerful facts, figures, opinions, and rhetoric.

✔ Get inspired to do your best writing with tips and ideas to make the process easier and faster.

✔ Pick from dozens of marketing tactics to let your audience know your white paper exists.

Chapter 14

Doing Research:
Think Like a Lawyer

. . . .

In This Chapter

▶ Building an unbeatable case for your white paper

▶ Looking for the best evidence in the best places

▶ Organizing your research

▶ Picking the most effective form of citations

. . . .

*E*very white paper needs solid evidence to make its case. After all, writing that your company is the best isn't difficult. But finding compelling evidence to prove that beyond a shadow of a doubt can be tough. Doing research to turn up the right nuggets of proof gives your white paper more authority. Strong evidence creates affinity with the reader, strengthens your claims, and proves that your white paper is more than one vendor's opinion.

Someone has to dig up all those sources, and that someone is likely the writer. Throughout your research process (as described in Chapter 12), my best advice is to think like a lawyer — and not some polite lawyer in a tailored suit in an air-conditioned office on the 99th floor. No, you have to think like a mad-dog lawyer, a street-fighting mongrel with big teeth and yellow eyes and no interest in a win-win. To research your white paper properly, you have to be the toughest dog in the neighborhood.

In this chapter, I describe how to find powerful proof to build your argument, engage your readers, and compel them to take action. This chapter shows four ways to evaluate references for maximum impact, and lists almost 20 possible sources, noting which ones are most acceptable for a white paper. And it describes how to organize your research and choose between three formats for references.

I once spent a day in the biggest library in Toronto, Ontario, Canada, trying to track down the references in several white papers from a Fortune 200 company. Even with the librarians' help, I had no success: Turns out that all the sources were vague articles not supported by any research. Clearly, the writers of those white papers never bothered to check those sources but simply parroted all the claims floating around the office. Now, I mistrust that company and will never buy anything from it again. I'm only one person. But what if I were a B2B buyer doing my due diligence, and that sloppy research cost the company a million-dollar sale? Don't let this happen! Dig up valid sources, cite them properly, and put together a case that won't fall apart under a little cross-examination.

Your Goal: Building an Open-and-Shut Case

When you think like a lawyer, you want to build a case so tight that no judge can question it and no jury can resist it. That means digging up a mountain of evidence. You need facts and figures, logic and rhetoric. You need an argument so tight it leaves the other side gasping for air. You need a flow of ideas so persuasive that your readers declare, "I've heard enough! I'm sold!" and start passing your paper around their company.

To do that takes research. It takes a lot of digging, sometimes far past the point where the other side has packed it in and gone home for the evening. It takes reading past the first screen of search results to see what else may be there. And it may take more than sitting at your desk and using Google. It may take hiking over to the nearest city or college library to consult the reference librarian, logging in to online databases to pull up journal articles, or finding a relevant association to contact for an expert witness.

That research usually includes grilling subject matter experts and executives from the company sponsoring the white paper. Most of all, this research requires you picturing the other guy trying to poke holes in your argument. If someone can ask, "Says who?" or "Oh yeah? Prove it!" you have a gap in your research that you better patch before it's too late. You certainly don't want your white paper to be tossed aside for lack of proof.

Digging Up Solid Sources and Extracting Relevant Points

Today, you can find more information faster than ever before; unfortunately, you can also get distracted and waste time very easily. Digging up strong sources and extracting the choicest nuggets from them are critical skills that every white paper writer needs. But developing those skills takes discipline and practice.

When you're looking for evidence, it helps to know where and how to look. In the following sections, I discuss four criteria to help evaluate the strength of any source: proximity, authority, timeliness, and relevance. Then I list 18 possible sources for white paper proof points, with notes and tips on each one. Finally, I describe the four most powerful types of evidence, namely facts, figures, opinions, and rhetoric. All of this should help you make the most of your research and build a mountain of evidence that no one else can topple.

Evaluating sources

So you're thinking like a lawyer and searching for another expert witness to call or another piece of evidence to introduce as People's Exhibit A. Where do you turn? If you're like most writers, you run some queries on Google and get a list of search results. But from that list, how do you choose the most effective sources for your white paper?

First things first. Just like a trial lawyer studying the jury, your first duty is to make sure you understand your target audience. Are they IT managers, HR professionals, C-level executives, or what? How old are they? What's their education? How do they feel about the issue your white paper is going to discuss? Does your client have any *personas* — descriptions of typical customers — he can share with you? Knowing your audience, you can look for evidence that will convince those readers. You'll need to know enough to evaluate each possible source on these four key factors:

- **Proximity,** or how close the source feels to the reader
- **Authority,** or how much weight the source has
- **Timeliness,** or how recent the evidence is
- **Relevance,** or how well the evidence matches your argument

An ideal source is strong on all four counts. A likely source must be strong on at least three. Any source that's strong on only two counts is probably not good enough to include in your white paper. That's when you have to keep digging.

Proximity

Proximity means "closeness" and comes mainly from being in the same industry or doing the same job as the reader. For example, a CFO in consumer electronics will relate to other executives in the same sector, to CFOs in other companies about the same size, or to others in the world of finance. On the other hand, a quote from a marketing executive for an airline won't have much proximity to a CFO in consumer electronics. When evaluating proximity, ask yourself how much your target reader has in common with the expert being quoted. If the answer is "not much," you probably need to keep searching — unless the quote scores highly on all the other three factors.

Authority

Authority means how much "weight" or "gravitas" a source has for a particular audience. In every field, only a few leading lights stand out enough to make statements that everyone else listens to. Quote this kind of authority if you can. See whether you can find which trade publications your audience reads and which websites they visit. If you can pull quotes from one of those familiar sources, those points carry far more authority. Even if you find research that completely supports your argument, if it comes from an obscure source, you may need to keep digging.

Timeliness

Everyone likes to keep up-to-date. So the more recent a source, the better. Let's face it: Quoting something from 1980 sounds ancient, even though it may be perfectly valid. If you're looking to establish a current industry trend, try to find sources from the past two or three years. For example, financial stats from before the meltdown in 2008 aren't always relevant. In fast-moving fields like software or biotech, anything more than five years old doesn't hold much water. In other sectors, you may be able to go back a decade, but always stick to the most recent sources you can find.

Relevance

You want to find powerful proof to back up your points, all the little facts or opinions that match your line of argument. So if a source only half agrees with you or if it's not exactly talking about the same topic you are, you may have to keep digging. Think about the source from an SEO view. Are the same keywords in your title right in the quote you found? If the reader looks at the article titles in your footnotes, will the connection to your white paper be obvious? Both of these tests can reveal the relevance of your sources.

Beyond these four factors, you also want your actual references from each source to be brief and punchy. Don't settle for a whole paragraph. Look for the absolutely ideal sentence or two from a report, book, or interview. If it takes a whole paragraph to introduce and explain a single source, it may not be strong enough. Keep on looking for that gem buried in all the dreck.

Finding sources for a white paper

The proximity, authority, and timeliness of a source are determined mainly by where you found it. You may think you can use any source under the sun in a white paper, but that's not strictly true. Some sources are far better than others when it comes to white papers. Table 14-1 lists all the sources you may think of drawing from for a white paper, from analysts to Wikipedia, along with my views of how acceptable I consider each source. I provide a few notes and observations on each source in the following sections.

Table 14-1	Acceptable and Unacceptable Sources	
Source	*Acceptable?*	*Notes*
Analysts	Yes	As long as they're credible
Associations	Yes	As long as they're established and credible
Blogs	Barely	Use only if you have no other sources
Books	Yes	Best to use classics in the field or titles published after 2000
Consultants	Sometimes	Make sure they're impartial
Forums	No	No credibility, usually anonymous
Go-to experts	Usually	Make sure they're impartial
Government reports	Yes	Usually have high authority
Industry reports	Usually	Make sure they're factual
Magazines	Yes	Best published in the last five years
Newspapers	Usually	Stick to recognized papers, best published in the last two to three years
Professors	Yes	Usually have high authority
Sources inside the company	Yes for background, not to quote	Good sources for background, but don't quote them directly because they're obviously biased
Trade magazines	Yes	Best published in the last five years

(continued)

Table 14-1 (continued)

Source	Acceptable?	Notes
Websites	Not usually	Be careful quoting from any website
White papers from other vendors or organizations	Yes	The more recognized the organization, the better
White papers from the same company	No	Not convincing, and could create a circular argument
Wikipedia	No	Wikipedia is a secondary source; use it to find primary sources

A question I get in almost every workshop I give is, "Is it okay to just make up your sources?" Of course not! Keep digging until you hit gold. If no evidence exists for the argument you're trying to make, don't make up fake facts to fit. White papers are nonfiction, not fantasy. Do you want to risk your credibility as a writer, and the credibility of your client, on the chance that no one will see through your fabrication?

Analysts

There are hundreds of analyst firms in the world, ranging from one- or two-person operations to companies with 1,000 and more employees. For a white paper in the B2B technology domain, stick to well-established outfits, such as Forrester, Frost & Sullivan, Gartner, IDC, McKinsey & Company, Pew Research Center, Saugatuck Technology, SMB Group, and Yankee Group. I've quoted all these firms in the past, because their names convey a lot of authority to IT readers.

You can find a list of more than 400 IT analyst firms at www.techra.com/analyst-firm-directory-mainmenu-27 and another good listing at http://analystdirectory.barbarafrench.net. Certain enterprising souls may well maintain similar directories of analysts for other sectors, but I haven't had much occasion to need them.

To find a list of analysts for a specific industry, try Googling "analyst" and the name for the industry. For example, "analyst automotive" or "analyst green tech." You'll likely get a mix of analyst sites, analyst reports, blogs, and media stories quoting a certain analyst. If analysts are credible enough for a major magazine or newspaper to quote, they're probably fine for your white paper.

Associations

Every major sector has one or more trade associations to defend its interests. Many of these associations are well established and generate solid research that can make an excellent source for a white paper. The executive directors of these associations can be good interview sources; they're usually quite knowledgeable and eager to talk.

Be careful, though; some groups are false fronts with innocent-sounding names set up by industry lobby groups to shape public opinion. Never reference a group with that cloud of suspicion over its head. If readers are informed enough to see that you're quoting from a group like that, your white paper can be permanently tainted in their eyes.

For a good list of American trade associations, try www.planningshop.com/tradeassociations.asp or www.weddles.com/associations/index.cfm. Beyond those, the *Encyclopedia of Associations* (Gale) is a book and online database of more than 150,000 nonprofits; you can access it through larger public and academic libraries.

Blogs

Anyone with a computer can start a blog. What makes any blogger's opinion worth quoting in a white paper? Unless that blogger is really a somebody, don't bother with him. You can't rely on a blog post to make a major point in a white paper; that proof is just too flimsy. At most, a blogger can confirm some assertion you've already made, when you have absolutely no other sources to offer, but even that's questionable.

Books

Quoting from a book is usually impressive, especially if it's written by a big-name author or recognized as a classic in its field. Otherwise, go for the most recent books you can find. For example, anything published before the year 2000 can sound outdated.

If you think a book could be a good source but you can't find it in your library — or you just don't have time to look — check out the "Look Inside" feature of Amazon. You can search for a phrase you're interested in, and if you find it, pick up a sentence or two for a reference, along with a page number. But you can't cut and paste from this feature, so you may want to take a screenshot for your client as proof of the citation (see Chapter 13 for details on documenting sources).

Consultants

Just like associations, some consultants are on the payroll of a certain vendor or lobby. Make sure they're impartial observers, not someone being paid on the sly to advance a certain agenda. Good independent consultants can often hit the nail on the head with an insightful quote. You may find them already published in a magazine, call them up for a quick telephone interview, or even pose a question or two by e-mail.

Forums

Some forums are well-moderated homes to civilized, thought-provoking discussion. Others are a mess of flame wars, illiterate comments, and hate. In any case, most comments are anonymous, so you can't attribute them to anyone. At best, a forum can show which way the wind blows on a certain issue, but I don't recommend using forum posts for sources in a white paper.

Go-to experts

Go-to experts have already established their credibility by being quoted in major media outlets. They're usually okay to quote in a white paper, as long as you establish that they have no axe to grind against any particular vendor, technology, or sector. Just like a consultant, you may find a quote already given, or you may request one by phone or e-mail.

Many experts are keen for publicity, so you can find them through free services like Help a Reporter Out (www.helpareporter.com) or PR Newswire's ProfNet (www.prnewswire.com/profnet). In the United Kingdom, try ExpertSources at (www.expertsources.co.uk).

Government reports

The U.S. government is one of the biggest publishers in the world. Taxpayers pay for this material, so you may as well use it. Most government reports are carefully prepared, and few people challenge the credibility of a report coming from a government department. If you can find one, use it.

The Government Printing Office is a good place to start, offering a searchable catalog of publications at http://catalog.gpo.gov/F?RN=185071156 and a bookstore where you can search by agency at http://bookstore.gpo.gov. Any college or city reference librarian can also help you find relevant government publications.

Industry reports

Every industry tends to present itself in the best possible light. Even so, industry-sponsored research can be a useful source for many white papers. Many industries have a good handle on the challenges and trade-offs facing them in the near future. Just make sure you're dealing with a fact-based report, not one yearning to turn back the clock or wishing for a better future. In fact, industry umbrella groups and associations sometimes publish their own white papers, which can be interesting to study as you work on your own. As mentioned in the "White papers from other vendors or organizations" section, quoting from a white paper from a reputable industry association is usually fine.

Magazines

A reference from a recognized magazine like *The Economist* or *Time* can help build a strong argument. Magazine writers often sum up big issues in a nutshell, so you can often find a highly relevant quote. To build timeliness, try not to cite any magazine article much older than five years. And the more recent, the better. Of course, this is simply a general rule, and some exceptions prove the rule. If you're writing about some major problem that has plagued a certain industry for 50 years and you find a perfect quote from a 1972 magazine, you can use that source to show how long this problem has been bothering people.

Newspapers

Today is the currency of newspapers, so you want to find the most recent articles you can, ideally within the past two or three years. Of course, a recognized newspaper like *The New York Times* or *The Guardian* is more respected than *USA Today* or a city tabloid. Newspaper stories are best for confirming some kind of trend you already pointed out. If some topic has already hit the popular press, it's mainstream.

Professors

A good academic maintains an overview of his field, above the hubbub of business affairs. He can weigh new ideas thoughtfully and provide a more objective view of a market space. An unknown professor probably has more authority than an unknown analyst or consultant. You can approach professors as you would any analyst, by phone or e-mail. Remember to leave lots of time, because academics don't live by the same deadlines as business people.

For most white papers, you need to interview subject matter experts or executives, and sometimes you need to speak to academics or analysts. This type of interviewing is a learned skill that gets easier with practice. For practical tips on handling interviews, check out `www.thatwhitepaperguy.com/white-paper-article-tips-on-interviewing-executives.html`. And for hints on recording your interviews, whether in person, landline, cellphone, or smartphone, see `www.thatwhitepaperguy.com/white-paper-article-how-to-record-white-paper-interviews.html`.

Sources inside the company

Few readers will be impressed with quotes from executives from the white paper's sponsor. These people may be excellent background sources and reviewers, but quoting them directly is pointless. What are they going to say? That their company has been on the wrong track for the past five years? That their products don't work? I've been somewhat appalled when executives have urged me to quote them in a white paper from their company. Nothing they say will ever be convincing, because everyone knows they're biased.

Trade magazines

Trade magazines tend to do a thorough job covering a specific industry, so if you're writing about that industry, these sources can provide excellent background. Again, look for recent pieces published within the past five years or so. The editor of a trade magazine is like the executive director of an association; if he's been there for a while, he knows the industry like the back of his hand. Many trade magazines publish an annual directory or list the top 100 firms in that industry. These lists can be great for helping you find additional sources if you need them.

Websites

Just like a blog, anyone can put up a website to say anything he feels like. So be careful if you quote from a website. If that person's views are so important, why hasn't he been published in some mainstream magazine, newspaper, or trade journal? Some vertical-market websites cover the same ground as a printed trade magazine, but anything in print tends to have more authority. Although this idea may be old-fashioned, most people realize that a printed magazine provides more checks and balances and has more invested in it than some website that can be here today and gone tomorrow. That's why I recommend keeping websites as second-tier sources; and if you can find any source with more authority, use it instead.

For a discussion on how to evaluate a website's credibility, see `http://tips.peoplesearchpro.com/sher-julian/search-tips/evaluating-web-sites.html`.

White papers from other vendors or organizations

Quoting from a white paper from another vendor or organization can be acceptable, with a few caveats to watch out for:

- ✔ Don't quote from another vendor's white paper if you compete for the same B2B sales.
- ✔ Don't copy from a competitor's white paper without any attribution.
- ✔ Don't quote from the other white paper if it's nothing more than a sales pitch.
- ✔ Don't use material from a white paper if it doesn't meet the same mantra as your own: It must provide useful, helpful information that can help readers understand an issue, solve a problem, or make a decision. If it does, feel free to quote from it.

Of course, the greater the name recognition of the other organization, the more credibility it lends to your argument.

Get permission for what you use

Many writers think that if they can find something on the web, they can use it. Be careful; it's best to quote only from web pages intended to be public, like trade magazines or press releases. A costly research report, internal company slide deck, or post on a forum are materials you need permission to share.

Suppose you want to use a market-size number from a research report that sells for $4,995, and the publisher won't give you permission to use it. What if you find a press release on the publisher's site, announcing the key fact that you wanted? Go ahead and quote it, and footnote the press release. Or search for a trade magazine that quoted that number, and then use the publication as the source.

But if you quote from pirated research or somehow manage to access private materials, you could be in for a nasty fight. You and your client don't need the headache.

Of course, the same applies to graphics and photos you find on the web. Someone created that graphic or took that photo, and she may not want you to reuse it for commercial purposes. Clicking a photo or graphic that turned up in a Google search may lead you to a legitimate site where you can buy that art. Do it. Just grabbing stuff off the web is for high-school students, not professional white paper writers.

White papers from the same company

If you use one white paper to substantiate another, you may be setting up a circular argument with no actual proof. Point to other white papers from the same company only to direct readers to further information, not for proof of your argument.

Wikipedia

Wikipedia is an amazing project driven by a great spirit of cooperation. But it's far from perfect. Articles can contain biases, uninformed views, and factual errors. Quoting Wikipedia in a white paper won't impress anyone; it only makes you look like an amateur. It's only a secondary source, anyway. Wikipedia is good for background and to help track down the original sources you should be citing, which takes only a few moments: Just look at the bottom of the article to the external websites and citations, most of which are linked back to original sources. Then check out those primary sources to get the real goods.

Understanding what makes good evidence

You know you need convincing proof to win your argument, and now you know where to look for it. But what exactly does it look like? B2B marketing can be a little more rigorous than those college English essays you wrote; after all, millions of dollars can be at stake. Proof points come in many shapes and sizes, but they fall into four main categories, in descending order of authority:

- Indisputable facts
- Rock-solid numbers (figures)
- Awards, accolades, and acknowledgments (opinions)
- Unassailable logic (rhetoric)

Indisputable facts

A fact is a concrete and provable reality, as opposed to an opinion, theory, or claim. Think of a fact as something another lawyer would stipulate (that's lawyer-talk for "shut up and agree that it's true.") For example, the sun comes up in the east and sets in the west. Who wants to argue with that? On the other hand, "that sunrise was beautiful" is just an opinion. *Beautiful* is a subjective phrase, not a fact. Know how to tell the difference. Too many business people try to pass off vague claims as facts. You have to serve as the stand-in for the opposing lawyer when you ask, "Says who?" or "Prove it!"

The simplest offering to discuss factually is a piece of hardware that you can see, touch, and measure. Software is trickier because you see only the results of running the code, which exists only as electronic bits, not as a tangible object. And a service or process is the hardest to describe factually, because it's conceptual and often varies a little every time it's delivered.

Some of the indisputable facts you can use in a white paper include the following:

- Actual size, weight, or physical characteristics of the product
- List of components or modules in the product
- Stages or steps in using the product
- Patents or trademarks granted to the company for the product
- Standards or certifications granted to the product or company, such as CE, CSA, Energy Star, ISO, NOM, UL, and so on

Rock-solid numbers

By definition, numbers seem more precise, scientific, and convincing than words, which are always a little fuzzy and interchangeable. So what kind of numbers can you use in a white paper? How can you find figures that no one can possibly argue with? To start, make sure you find the best statistics from impeccable sources. Then, for a reality check, try to confirm every stat from a second source.

For example, if one source says a market is worth $3 billion a year, but another says $3 million, you've got some work to do. Delve into how both sources sized the market, what they included and excluded, and their methods. If you can't resolve the difference or find another estimate, consider giving both as a range of opinion. Don't just pick the bigger number and drop the smaller. Can you hear someone objecting, "Says who? Your Honor, we have a number 1,000 times smaller from an equally credible source!"

In a way, the numbers you use are somewhat prescribed by which flavor of white paper you're researching. For example, in a backgrounder, you can talk about any numbers to do with the offering, such as the following:

✔ Benchmark scores or test results of the product

✔ Lines of codes in the software

✔ Miles of wiring in each system

✔ Number of features or functions provided

✔ Person-years it took to create (but don't exaggerate!)

✔ Total installed base, total number of users

✔ Years tested, years on the market

In a numbered list, you already have a set of numbers, one for each main point of your discussion. Don't clutter up that flavor with many other numbers, or you'll dull that impact. In a strange way, the power of numbers gives the points in a numbered list more gravitas, even if the whole tone of the piece is tongue-in-cheek.

In a problem/solution white paper, use numbers to show the scope of the industry-wide problem. How much money is spent fighting it every year? How much profit does it drain from the industry? Estimate the results from each existing solution, and show why that's not enough. And then give some powerful numbers to prove that your new offering attacks the problem in a bigger way than anything else. Find some credible numbers about how much better your new solution works, such as how much time and money it saves, how much more revenue and profit it generates, how much longer it lasts, or any other numbers you can justify.

Percentages are especially tricky. A percentage is nothing more than a comparison between two other numbers. So if the jobless rate falls by 10 percent, that sounds great — but it's all relative. In absolute terms, if the unemployment rate falls from a disastrous 20 percent to a still-terrible 18 percent, there's not much to cheer about.

If you can't find any benchmark tests, consider generating them yourself. When I worked in a company that sold barcode scanners for ERP systems, our customers loved the system, but we had no stats on the actual benefits. One Friday, we set up a test with an Oracle demo system. We ran a set of transactions, manually typing in every number. Then we repeated those transactions, using our scanners. That saved 88 percent of the keystrokes and 77 percent of the time. From this simple test, we got credible numbers that we used in our marketing for the next several years. By the way, we sourced those as "internal benchmarks, 12 typical transactions in Oracle Applications 11, manual keying versus automated data entry."

Awards, accolades, and acknowledgments

Notice how I moved down the list from facts to figures to opinions. But even though awards, accolades, and acknowledgments are based on opinions, at least these opinions all come from third parties, so they still boost a B2B vendor's credibility. And if your offering ever wins an industry award, appears in a magazine article or review, or gets included in an analyst report, that counts for something, too. Most of all, if you have any customers who are raving fans, you can incorporate a brief testimonial or case study in your white papers; certainly this type of an opinion would fit nicely into a backgrounder.

Any of these sources fall into this category of third-party opinions:

- Analyst reports
- Awards, best-of, editor's choice
- Customer testimonials
- Favorable comments from experts
- List of top 100 firms
- Reviews or third-party endorsements

Unassailable logic

This category isn't really evidence; it's a logical argument or rhetorical device. When you can't prove some claim one way or another with facts, figures, or even opinions, you must resort to rhetoric. You can't do this throughout your entire white paper, though, because that means you have no more powerful evidence to provide. But if the rest of your paper is backed up well, and what you say on one point or another is thoughtful and reasonable, most readers will give you the point. A little knowledge of rhetoric can really pay off here. Make sure your argument is like all the rest of your evidence: tough, solid, and free from any obvious flaws.

For example, you can ask a *rhetorical question* — especially in a numbered list — without ever answering it. This device can be useful for casting doubt or suspicion on another vendor's offering, as in, "Is it wise to pay ten times as much for a scanner that does less than the Acme ScanOMatic 3000?" A rhetorical question hangs in the air without being answered, but everyone knows the only sensible answer.

When you have enough sources at your fingertips, use the facts or figures first. When you run out of facts and figures, then use opinions or rhetoric. Don't try to build your white paper on rhetoric alone; doing so creates a brochure or a sales pitch, not a white paper.

Keeping Track of a Mountain of Research

As you build an intimidating mountain of research, you need to keep everything organized so you can find what you need when you start writing. If you haven't had to handle this amount of research since college — and you never did it well back then either — don't panic. You're an adult now, and organizing your research isn't hard. Here are four ways to keep track of your white paper research:

- ✔ Index cards
- ✔ Microsoft Word
- ✔ Microsoft Word plus index cards
- ✔ Evernote or equivalent web-based software

I don't recommend a database; in fact, I've never heard of a white paper writer using a database to compile his research. That's overkill for a ten-page white paper with six or eight sources. Just like it's overkill to use Word's built-in features for citations and sources. The most research I ever had to manage was for a set of three white papers for one client. I found more than 40 sources I stored in a giant binder and used Word to type up my notes.

In fact, the best practices I recommend in this book for tracking your research and sending your client all your sources (see Chapter 13) go way beyond what most white paper writers do today.

Writing out index cards

This tried-and-true method has been used for at least as long as anyone has been writing white papers. Many people recommend using the top-left section of the index card to write a code number, which can point to a numbered file of original documents or even the section of your paper where you can see using that reference. Then use the top right for the actual citation:

author, title, publisher, date, and page. Of course, the main body is for the actual quote. When you finish, you have a nice little stack of research in delightfully tangible form that you can shuffle and reshuffle to your heart's content.

Another take on this basic idea is to use large sticky notes, one for each source, and then arrange and rearrange them on a flat surface like a large piece of cardboard, an open file folder, or even your wall.

If you like the idea of index cards but don't fancy scribbling all your sources by hand, try using this approach with Microsoft PowerPoint. Consider each slide an index card, and type in your original research as a set of slides. Then you can use the Slide Sorter feature (from the View tab) to arrange your slides in the ideal flow. Because you're working on-screen with everything typed in, when you need any sources or citations, you already have them in electronic form.

Typing and printing out a Word file

When I use Word for my research, I first run some massive web searches, downloading and printing any articles that look interesting to me. When I've covered enough ground, I scan through the hard-copy file, highlighting the choice bits, scribbling ideas in the margins, and attaching sticky notes to pages I want to find later. This process can take a few hours. Then I go through the hard copies in front of my computer, typing all the best quotes into a Word file, one page per source, with precise citations. My selected excerpts form another, much smaller printout that I slip into the top of my research file.

When I write the executive summary (see Chapter 12), I pull out my excerpt file, knowing I can always dive back into the source material, which is right at my fingertips. What could be easier?

Okay, I'm sure some people will think that this process is hopelessly out-dated, because they like to store all their research on their iWhatevers. But I still like being able to sort and shuffle paper and to get something done even if the power goes off or the iCloud temporarily blows away.

Putting them together: Word plus index cards

You can also combine index cards with the computer. Here's one way. Type all your research in Word, and then go through a hard copy and highlight the sources you want to use in your white paper. Cut out each source and tape it to an index card. If you want, you can create one card for each main point or section of your argument, and then arrange your sources where they fit best to support each point. Then you can merrily shuffle and reshuffle your index cards until you get the perfect flow of ideas. You can even do that in a coffee shop or on the kitchen table.

Managing content with Evernote

If you want to use a cloud-based app to manage your white paper research, a good choice is Evernote. Users appreciate that it comes in numerous versions that cover Windows, Mac OS, all different mobile devices, and various web browsers. You can use Evernote to save stray ideas, web articles, scanned articles, photos, graphics, status reports, or pretty much anything else you come across in your white paper research. And you can sync all your devices so that all your notes are with you no matter which device you have at hand.

For a great introduction to using Evernote for managing content marketing ideas and drafts — which can easily include white papers — check out `http://contentmarketinginstitute.com/2012/05/evernote-for-content-marketing`.

Choosing Footnotes or Endnotes

After you gather all your evidence, how are you going to present it? Part of this decision depends on your skill as a writer, as I explain in Chapter 15. Another decision you should think about is whether to present your evidence by using footnotes, endnotes, or in-text citations. Naturally, each approach has strengths and drawbacks, as shown in Table 14-2.

Table 14-2	Pros and Cons of Citation Types	
Type	*Pros*	*Cons*
Footnotes	Give more academic look, showcase research	Interrupt reading, draw reader's eyes to bottom of page
Endnotes	Don't distract readers	Hide research at end of paper where few readers look
In-text citations	Don't distract readers, integrate sources with text	Add extra words to text, can sound clumsy or forced

The choice is yours, but here are my recommendations:

- ✔ **Use footnotes** if you have strong research from sources you want to highlight and an audience used to slightly formal white papers.
- ✔ **Use endnotes** if you have weaker sources or so many that you don't want to distract readers from the flow.
- ✔ **Use in-text citations** if you have only a few sources and don't think your readers want to look at references.
- ✔ If you can't decide, choose the least intrusive approach, **endnotes**.

The immediacy of footnotes

Footnotes provide additional information at the bottom of a page, linked with a superscript number in the text, like the one at the end of this sentence.[1] Footnotes convey a more academic or formal tone to a white paper and suggest how much research has gone into it. In a white paper, most footnotes give the source for a quote, fact, or number in the text. You seldom see any running commentary on the text, as in some textbooks or academic journals.

Footnotes are quite appropriate for the most research-based flavor of white paper, the problem/solution; they're somewhat useful for a backgrounder that includes any claims from third parties about the benefits of an offering; and they're not at all useful for a numbered list, where the emphasis is on provocative ideas, not scholarship.

If you started off using bottom-of-the-page footnotes but want to see how they'd work as end-of-the-document endnotes, you can convert them all in one fell swoop with Word. On the References tab, in the Footnotes group, click the Footnote and Endnote Dialog Box Launcher (the little arrow in the corner). When that box appears, select Endnotes and then click Convert. Then in the Convert Notes dialog box, select Convert All Footnotes to Endnotes and click OK. You can change them all back by using a similar process but clicking Convert All Endnotes to Footnotes.

The finality of endnotes

Because endnotes are gathered together at the end of a white paper, they're much less evident than bottom-of-the-page footnotes. Although endnotes are less intrusive, they also hide away the research that went into a white paper. Fewer readers will look at the last page of a white paper to check a reference.

---

1. Made you look! See how a footnote can distract you from the flow of ideas?

In some ways, this makes endnotes the least satisfactory way to handle your sources.

I recommend using endnotes when you have few sources, when you have so many sources that every page would be cluttered with footnotes, or when the offering is affordable and the audience is owners of small- to medium-sized businesses, who probably don't care how the references look. And when it's a tossup between approaches, I say go with endnotes, the least objectionable of all. You can let Word place all your endnotes on the very last page of your white paper, under a major heading like "Notes" or "References."

You don't have to live with that annoying rule that Word inserts at the top of your endnotes by default. To get rid of it, go to the View tab and select Draft. Then go to the References tab and select Show Notes. From the pull-down menu in the top border of the Endnotes pane, select Endnote Separator. Select the rule and click Delete to erase it. Then use the View tab to go back to the view you normally use. Presto! One less annoying rule getting in your way.

The tidiness of in-text citations

Magazines and newspapers don't use footnotes. Every quote and statistic is sourced with an in-text reference, something like this: "Footnotes and endnotes are soooo old-fashioned," declared copywriter Ima Writer in her March 2013 column in *White Papers Today*. "All the cool kids today are using in-text citations." See how smooth this type of citation can be? And you can pick up any magazine to see just how journalists do it.

The nice thing about in-text citations is that they're so tidy. You don't have to look anywhere else on the page or in the document: The whole reference is in one spot. The only downside is that these citations take more words, and if you're not careful, they can lead to some clunky-sounding sentences.

But in-text citations can deliver the best of both worlds: Like a footnote, the whole reference is on the same page, but like an endnote, it doesn't disrupt your reading experience. This approach may be better for a backgrounder or numbered list, where you're not trying to showcase your research but rather describe an offering or be provocative. In a problem/solution, you may prefer to use footnotes to highlight all the research that went into your white paper.

Formatting citations

The two main systems for formatting footnotes in academic papers are APA and MLA. And just for good measure, there's a third system from the *Chicago Manual of Style* (University of Chicago). Although academics may battle to the death over which system is better, it really doesn't matter which one you use in any white paper.

Most business people have forgotten everything they ever knew about footnotes since their college days. The key is to pick one format and stick to it within any white paper and ideally across all white papers from the same company. I've never had a client say a word about how I formatted a single citation in any white paper. To be honest, they were probably amazed and pleased to see any references in there!

Microsoft Word provides some built-in tools for organizing sources and formatting citations in your chosen style. These tools are clearly a big help for writing essays. But I don't know a single business writer who uses them. I didn't even know they were there until I was poking around to write this chapter. And, let's face it, for six or eight references in a white paper, you don't need power tools. If you want to explore these features — and now that I found them, I probably will — look at Citations & Bibliography under the References tab.

If you really want to understand how to follow a specific style for your footnotes, websites for college writing centers often have this kind of information. The Purdue Online Writing Lab (http://owl.english.purdue.edu) is a handy resource used by people around the world. And *Research Papers For Dummies* (Wiley) provides a good discussion of the main three citation styles.

Chapter 15

Write Like a Journalist

*A*fter you dig up a mountain of evidence to prove your case, as described in Chapter 14, the next step is to shape all that info into a clear, factual, and engaging white paper. My advice, after doing this close to 200 times, is to write like an old-fashioned journalist who's interested in "just the facts, ma'am."

Old-fashioned journalists knew their readers didn't have any patience for fancy-pants language, so they made every paragraph crystal clear. Their editors grilled them about their sources and double-checked all the particulars, so they stuck to the facts. But their readers had a lot of distractions — the boss, the spouse, the kids, the game on TV — so those journalists found a way to make every story engaging. And they had a deadline to hit, so they wrote fast.

As a white paper writer today, you need to do all of that, plus more. Your audience is even tougher, and more is at stake, namely millions of dollars in revenue for your client. So your white paper needs to be even more precise, more logical, and more compelling than anything your readers ever saw in a newspaper. That's a tall order, but this chapter can help you meet it.

In this chapter, I focus on five key tasks for any white paper writer:

✔ **Reading** many other white papers and any nonfiction that stimulates and inspires you, and keeping your own "swipe file" of notable ideas

✔ **Writing** every day, any type of B2B material but especially any white papers you have a chance to work on

- ✔ **Rewriting** to polish drafts, with help from your computer to read back your drafts and show objective statistics on your writing
- ✔ **Learning** from style guides, following house style, and creating your own style guide
- ✔ **Refining** your writing process with best practices and fresh ideas that can bring out your top efforts

This isn't a step-by-step process; you'll likely jump back and forth between these tasks and spend time on several of them during any given day. Each task supports and reinforces all the others and helps your skills and confidence grow.

Don't try to absorb everything in this chapter in one go. This chapter is so dense with tips that you may want to flip back to it for a little guidance and inspiration when you're working on your next white paper. With practice, you can do this; you can write even better than an old-time journalist.

Reading for Fun and Profit

Writers tend to read, almost compulsively. For example, if nothing else is close by, do you find yourself reading the cereal box during breakfast? That's a dead giveaway. To help you master the white paper format, you should be reading every white paper your own company or client has available, a steady stream of white papers from outside sources, and any new research or thinking related to white papers from respected researchers and bloggers.

On top of that, make time every week to read nonfiction books, magazines, and websites that inspire you. In the following sections, I explore the benefits of all this reading, and I introduce a way to keep track of all the best nuggets you find.

Reading white papers

To truly understand the white paper format and the countless possibilities of these documents, you must read lots of them. How many is enough? Well, most days of the week, I download and scan at least one white paper. That's close to 250 a year. And when I'm actively researching a white paper, I can easily look at five to ten of these documents in a day. That means I likely study more than 500 white papers a year, and I've been doing that for well over ten years. That's certainly enough to see the ongoing trends and evaluate which ones seem more effective than others and why.

As you look at a white paper that someone else prepared, ask yourself these questions:

- ✔ Who is this white paper aimed at? Where do they likely sit in the sales funnel?

- ✔ What flavor is this: a backgrounder, numbered list, or problem/solution?

- ✔ If I were a target reader, would this persuade me to take action?

- ✔ What questions do I have about this topic? Does this answer them?

- ✔ How is this white paper structured? What elements are present? Which ones are missing?

- ✔ What about the design? Graphics? Does every white paper from this company follow the same template?

- ✔ What overall impression of the company does this give me?

Whether you work in-house or you're a contract writer who just landed a new client, you must read every white paper the company has available. If the company is a major B2B vendor like Hewlett-Packard or Microsoft with hundreds of white papers, that's going to be a big challenge. The good news is that most of those white papers are likely backgrounders, so you can sample eight or ten to get a good idea what the company publishes. If the company is smaller and has only half a dozen or so white papers, take one or two hours to look at every one.

Besides being familiar with your company or client's white papers, you should look at any produced by direct competitors. Your B2B buyers are probably looking at white papers from those competitors, so you should know what they offer. Download as many as you can and go through them carefully, asking yourself the questions listed earlier in this section. Find their weak spots. Now answer this: How are you going to outdo them? How are you going to create a white paper that's more clear, more effective, and more persuasive than anything those competitors have done? If you can't, why bother publishing anything at all?

Reading related research

You should keep up with any reports that touch on white papers, especially any driven by research or significant-sized surveys of 1,000 or more people. Some likely sources include Content Marketing Institute, Eccolo Media, MarketingProfs, MarketingSherpa, and TechTarget. And you should be aware of the ongoing discussions on the handful of blogs that cover B2B content marketing in general and white papers specifically. My own site, ThatWhitePaperGuy.com, offers new articles every month, born from my hands-on experience or sparked by some question I received.

You probably don't need to set up a Google Alert or search the Twitterverse for "white paper"; doing so will turn up more white papers than you can ever look at. However, do run a Google search once a month, and look at the more interesting links to keep up-to-date in the field.

Reading for inspiration

Find some authors who inspire you. I'm not talking about Jane Austen or William Gibson; novels count as reading for pleasure. I'm talking about any nonfiction writers who deal with business, history, science, sociology, technology, or travel. For example, Malcolm Gladwell is an especially engaging writer who does both magazine articles and books about a stimulating range of topics.

Magazines certainly count as reading, but be strategic in your choices. Read material that challenges your beliefs and understanding. Science magazines are great for writers with an arts background; artsy or political magazines are useful for writers from the sciences. Also, see what kinds of things interest other people: Men, read some women's magazines, and women, read some men's magazines. If you're a Republican, read material written for liberals; if you're a Democrat, read material for conservatives. See how people with different views structure their arguments and introduce their proof points.

Websites count, too, especially those devoted to the arts, science, men, women, liberals, or conservatives, as previously noted. You may want to read websites aimed at the typical audiences you write for, such as CFOs, CIOs, security chiefs, government agency directors, small-business owners/managers, and so on. Any sizeable segment of the B2B audience has one or more associations, forums, and websites devoted to it.

Keeping a "swipe file"

A *swipe file* is a personal collection of words, phrases, ideas, and graphics that you want to remember. Keeping a swipe file is a tried-and-true practice most copywriters use to build their knowledge and get quick inspiration when they need it. To get started, you can even download a free swipe file here: www.freelancewriting.com/ebooks/ebook-copywriters-swipe-files.php. No one has yet put together a downloadable swipe file for white papers, but that could happen.

Why bother keeping a swipe file? It helps you store inspiring examples of white papers and their elements for future reference. Then you can share an example or two with a client or designer to show them some possibilities. A swipe file can be especially helpful early in your white paper writing career.

To organize your swipe file of white papers, you may want a section for each flavor plus sections for good covers, nice tables, eye-catching pull quotes, effective sidebars, excellent graphics, and anything else that may inspire you in the future. So how can you store a swipe file? Table 15-1 shows five possible methods with the pros and cons of each. I combine two methods, saving an entire PDF and printing only selected pages to file in a binder of ideas. You may prefer to keep your swipe file with the help of a software tool like Evernote that can store web links or PDFs and sync to all your devices.

Table 15-1	Five Ways to Store a Swipe File		
Saving Method	*How to Save*	*Pros*	*Cons*
Bookmarks	Bookmark landing page in browser	Quick and easy, uses little storage	Landing pages can change, needs web access to view, doesn't pinpoint element of interest
Web links	Paste link to landing page into swipe file	Can organize by topics, uses little storage	Landing pages can change, needs web access to view
Entire PDFs	Save As to swipe file folder	Quick and easy	Requires more storage, needs computer to view PDFs, doesn't pinpoint element
Individual PDF pages	Delete unneeded pages from PDF and Save As to swipe file folder	Pinpoints element, uses less storage	Needs computer to view PDFs
Individual hard copy pages	Print single page and store in file or binder	Pinpoints element, tangible so doesn't rely on computer	Relies on paper file, can be bulky

Keeping a swipe file isn't stealing; it's research. After all, you can't copyright a white paper heading or a title. This is one case where imitation is the most sincere form of flattery — as long as you don't plagiarize a whole chunk of a text from a direct competitor. That's a definite no-no. If the client ever discovered you did that, you likely wouldn't get any repeat business.

Writing Winning White Papers

Coaches are always telling their players to work on their fundamentals. Practicing the basic skills of an activity can certainly improve your performance. That's why every day, you should look for ways to practice writing any type of B2B material: e-mails, press releases, web pages, and so on. The sheer process of putting out words aimed at B2B buyers will build your experience and confidence. And try to wangle a chance to work on a white paper as often as you can.

In this section, I discuss several fundamental B2B writing skills you need to practice until you master each one. If you can do all of them, you'll have what it takes to write winning white papers:

- Getting to the point with as few words as possible
- Handling dialogue and sources gracefully
- Creating text enhancements
- Writing for translation
- Choosing one metaphor and sticking with it
- Controlling your material

Getting to the point

Brevity is highly valued in B2B writing for English-speaking audiences. Just as every event in a story must further the plot, every paragraph in your white paper must further your argument. Your goal is to deliver a compelling message in the fewest possible words. In a nutshell, get to the point.

You need to write crisp, clear, compelling text that persuades readers of your views and persuades them to take action. The best way to do that is to not waste words. Remember that old-fashioned journalist? Ernest Hemingway did some journalism in his time. Of course, he's remembered more for his acclaimed short stories and novels, and he won the Nobel prize for literature in 1954. His prose style is as lean and spare and economical as you'll ever find. To succeed in white papers, you need to write more like Hemingway than like some business people who never use one word when they can use five.

Before you write, sketch out your argument in brief; this outline can become the first draft of your executive summary (see Chapter 12 for more on creating an executive summary). To get started, set up a subhead for every major point of the white paper's argument. That framework can help you give proper emphasis to each point and make sure you don't forget anything. After that, getting to the point can be simple. Ask yourself, "What am I trying to say in this sentence? This paragraph?" Then say it, clearly and crisply.

Handling dialogue and sources

Newspaper and magazine stories are built around quotes, so journalists get a lot of practice and figure out how to handle sources gracefully. With all the skill of a dramatist, they can introduce their sources at the right time, usher them into the spotlight, give them a brief soliloquy, and then usher them gracefully off the stage. But for most business people, handling quotes from people is weird and unusual.

Quotes are best for providing opinions or for introducing a rhetorical device, particularly when you have no facts or figures to prove a point. The most common failings are using quotes that are too long and not integrated into your argument. When you did your research, you found likely sources and effective quotes, but you probably didn't trim them down to a single sentence. Remember, your prime directive (get to the point) applies to quotes, too.

For example, say you're writing about the benefits of automatic filing for Acme Scanners, and you find this lengthy quote from an executive in a trade magazine:

> "When I think about the many technical problems that still await proper solutions, my mind always goes to the fact that most corporate teams suffer tremendous paper burden. Whether or not all those incoming documents are committed to paper, we're all getting snowed under," says CIO Norman Stewachski of Worldwide Conglomerates. "The seeming magic of automated scanning, tagging, and filing of incoming e-mail attachments would save the business world untold billions of dollars."[1] (72 words)

Although the quote has good content, it sounds a little flabby. Here's one way to trim it in half but still use it as a direct quotation:

> "Most corporate teams suffer from tremendous paper burden," says CIO Norman Stewachski of Worldwide Conglomerates. "The seeming magic of automated scanning, tagging, and filing of incoming e-mail attachments would save the business world untold billions of dollars."[1] (36 words)

This revision is shorter but still not ideal. Some journalists recommend not to use quotes to give fresh information; instead, use quotes only to show reactions to facts you already stated, keeping you in control of the narrative. Otherwise, you're passing the microphone to an outside source to make your argument.

Another powerful way to use this quote is to *paraphrase* (restate without distortion) some of it and quote the key part gracefully in the same paragraph:

> Executives agree that most corporate teams suffer from paper burden. One promising solution is to automatically scan, tag, and file incoming e-mail attachments. This technology, notes CIO Norman Stewachski of Worldwide Conglomerates, "would save the business world untold billions of dollars."[1] (39 words)

Notice the footnote symbol ([1]) in each example. Even if you paraphrase a quotation, you should still include a citation to boost the authority of this proof point. If you don't want to use a footnote, you can include a few extra words to make an in-text citation:

> Executives agree that most corporate teams suffer from paper burden. One promising solution is to automatically scan, tag, and file incoming e-mail attachments. CIO Norman Stewachski of Worldwide Conglomerate noted in the May 2013 issue of *CIO World* that this technology "would save the business world untold billions of dollars." (49 words)

As you can see, you can use any one of these ways to tighten up a lengthy quote and integrate it into your argument: direct quotation, partial quotation, or paraphrasing. With practice, you can master the art of compressing a source into fewer words without distorting the meaning and gain the confidence to make sure *you're* the one making your argument, not your sources.

Creating text enhancements

Doing a white paper challenges a writer to think about more than words. You need to visualize how the finished document will look on the page or screen and how you can help it look more inviting, easier to scan, and quicker to read. Simply writing a mass of words and handing them off to a designer isn't a recipe for success. Instead, as you write and revise, look for any opportunity to save words by using a table, graphic, or any other device to break up your paragraphs.

Text enhancements include anything you can type that breaks up a solid wall of text — bullets, headings, pull quotes, sidebars, tables, or white space. These elements are all free and built into Word and any other word processor. You just have to remember to use them. The following sections provide a few notes and tips on using each type of text enhancement, from bullets to white space.

Imposing order on your bullet points

Eye-tracking research has revealed that most people scan through bullets in an unexpected way. They focus on the first point and usually the second and then skip down to the last, often failing to take in any bullets in the middle.

What does this mean for white papers? Well, most writers instinctively arrange a bulleted list by priority, with the most important point first, then the second, and so on down to the least important at the end.

But knowing how most readers scan lists, you probably want to arrange your bulleted lists like this:

- Strongest point
- Second strongest point
- Weaker point
- Weaker point
- Third strongest point

The first few times you reorder a list this way, the organization will probably feel a little strange. But if much of your audience will scan through your white paper on the screen, this approach should add more impact to your bulleted lists. (For more tips on how to use lists, see Chapter 10.)

Every page of a white paper should have at least one visual break from straight text, either a graphic or a text enhancement. But use these visual elements wisely: Having too many of them on the same page can create another problem because every element fights for attention against all the rest.

Some of these text enhancements cross over into the world of design. For hints on designing white papers, flip to Chapter 18.

Bullets and lists

Whenever you have a list of items, consider making it a bulleted list. Even two items is enough for bullets, especially if that page has no other enhancements. This book uses bulleted lists frequently, such as the following, to set text apart. Here are a couple of tips for bulleted lists:

- **Punctuate your bullet text consistently.** Most style guides recommend no punctuation unless each item forms a complete sentence.

- **Express each point in parallel structure,** using the same grammatical form. Doing so makes your bullets faster to scan and easier to understand.

The standard bullet characters are a filled-in dot (●) or a square (■) in black or the same color as the associated text. If you choose a nonstandard character for your bullets — something like ▶, ☺, or Ω — or print them in a different color from the text, that will give your reader pause. Is that really what you want? Or do you want them to scan down your list as a welcome relief for their eyes?

You can overuse bullets. For example, bullets within bullets within bullets are rarely attractive. And a full page of bullets, or a set of bullets with large chunks of text after every one, loses the main benefit of bullets: to provide a welcome change. Instead of simplifying the text, using bullets in these ways adds visual and conceptual clutter to your white paper.

Headings

Every white paper needs a set of major and minor headings. You can call them "heads" and "subheads"; Word calls them Heading 1 and Heading 2. Two levels are enough for most white papers; you want three at the most (in this case, use Word's Heading 3). Every heading doesn't have to be parallel — that is, written with a consistent structure and phrasing. And you don't want to use any cutesy puns that no one can figure out; doing so defeats the purpose of a heading — to describe what a given section covers.

Here are a few hints about writing headings for the three flavors of white papers:

- For a backgrounder, the offering's major features and benefits can provide most of your headings.

- For a numbered list, the main points of your list automatically form the major headings.

- For a problem/solution, each discrete part of the white paper can fall under a major heading, including the problem, existing solutions and drawbacks, new improved solution, buyer's guide, and conclusions. I often try to write all these headings as a continuous story, giving a reader who scans through the white paper a quick idea of the argument.

Pull quotes

A pull quote is a short phrase or sentence pulled out of the text on that page and presented in larger letters, often in a solid block of color. Not all white papers use pull quotes, but more should. With just a glance, the eyes of even the most casual reader will fall on a pull quote and absorb it. Look in any magazine to see how pull quotes are used to break up a page that's mostly text.

Keep the following in mind when using pull quotes:

- You don't have to use the text exactly as it's shown in your white paper; it's okay to drop a few words.

- You don't want to go beyond 20 words in a pull quote; fewer is better.

- You don't have to make a complete sentence or use a period at the end of a pull quote.

For example, suppose a key sentence in your white paper goes like this:

> Worse, suppressing printed statements has a hidden downside: It can damage longstanding customer relationships, generate negative PR, and even hurt revenues if annoyed customers switch suppliers.

The following would be an acceptable pull quote for that page:

> Suppressing printed statements can damage customer relationships, generate negative PR, and even hurt revenues

A shorter and punchier version would work even better:

> Suppressing printed statements can hurt revenues

You can show your designer that you want them to format a piece of text as a pull quote by typing it in a larger point size, identified as "pull quote." You may have to adjust the pull quotes or write new ones when the pages are designed, because the text should come from the page where the pull quote appears.

Sidebars

A sidebar is a separate chunk of text spun off from the main body and presented differently, perhaps in a tinted box or a different typeface. This book includes sidebars for content that's slightly more detailed or outside the main thread of a discussion. To set the text apart from the rest of the chapter, *For Dummies* sidebars are set in shaded text boxes.

Tables

Tables are an excellent way to sum up a lot of information, use fewer words, and add visual interest. A table is essentially a list with more than one dimension, yielding a two-dimensional grid with vertical columns and horizontal rows.

How do you know when you need a table? Sometimes the call for a table is obvious, like when you want to present a set of numbers, and writing several sentences to show the relationship between them would be clumsy. Another likely time for a table is to compare a set of products, choices, or alternatives. For clarity, orient the table to present the information in the most logical and accessible way. Some tables make more sense turned one way or the other. For example, the tables in Chapters 12 and 13 show the steps for creating a white paper, which seem more natural with the tasks arranged as a horizontal to-do list.

Other tables work equally well either way. For example, any table with about the same number of rows and columns often makes as much sense turned either way. Sometimes how you orient a table is a question of space on the page. Consider a table with many vertical columns but few horizontal rows, which quickly runs off the width of a page. In that case, either turn the whole page on its side — which is always a bit awkward — or redo the table with the rows turned into columns and see how it fits that way.

To format tables, check with your designer for ideas, look for good models in your swipe file, or try the formats built into Word. After you insert a table into Word, check out the Design tab under Table Tools.

White space

I'm always amazed when I see a white paper where the text runs 100 or 120 characters wide. This makes it so hard on the reader's eyes that no one will ever get through that document. A recommended measure for easy white paper reading is 60 characters at most. Three-column magazines have text lines around 40 characters wide, and newspaper columns are even narrower.

For a white paper, I recommend setting your page margins to at least 1.25 inches all around. And I like to leave a wider margin on the left, like 2.0 or 2.5 inches for white space where a designer can place pull quotes and graphics.

Another simple way to get more white space is to create another paragraph every few lines. Whoever said that you could have only one or two paragraphs per page in a white paper? Of all the text enhancements you can use, breaking the text into more paragraphs is the simplest of all.

Writing for translation

Will your white paper be circulated in different languages? Here are a few tips to make your text easier for a translator to work with and cut the risk of any international incidents.

- **Avoid vague adjectives.** Adjectives such as _long, quick, large,_ or _expensive_ are vague and may have different meanings for people in different places. For example, a _long-term project_ can mean anything from a 6-month project to a 30-year project. In any language, it's better to get down to specifics by using numbers rather than adjectives.

- **Avoid local references.** Local references are allusions to anything unknown in other countries, including people, places, activities, food, and holidays. Don't assume a global audience knows what you mean when you touch on any of these references. For example, most people in the world have no idea how to play baseball. Any references inspired by the sport, such as _ballpark figure_ or _swinging for the bleachers,_ will just confuse people. For Canadians, hockey phrases like _power play_ or *breakaway* are similar no-nos. And for anyone from a Commonwealth country, cricket phrases like *carry your bat* or *grubber* are meaningless to people from most other countries.

✔ **Avoid idioms.** By the same token, avoid colorful idioms or metaphors that people take for granted in North America. Phrases like *The Big Apple* or *Marketing 101* won't mean much to a reader from another culture. If you include phrases like these and a translator renders them directly into another language, they'll likely be meaningless. And if a translator looks for another idiom to replace yours, he may miss the bull's eye or upset the apple cart. And then your carefully written white paper may be up the creek on thin ice, er, without a paddle.

✔ **Avoid contractions.** In English, contractions like *don't* and *we'll* help sentences sound more conversational. But they're nothing but trouble for translators because they hide letters, mask tenses, and create uncertainty. It's better to avoid contractions altogether when writing for translation.

✔ **Use short sentences.** Use shorter, simpler sentences than you would if you were writing for native speakers. Shorter sentences are easier for everyone to handle anyway, including native readers. If you write the opposite way, creating long, complex, roundabout, run-on sentences with multiple phrases all piled up on top of one another like some sort of train wreck; well, you can see how they can be harder to understand and tougher to translate, can't you?

Choosing one metaphor and sticking with it

Rich imagery helps writing come alive. A *metaphor* is a rhetorical device that links two different things together, such as an abstract concept and a physical object, or two items from different domains with one similar quality. This link can paint a vivid word picture in a reader's mind. But you must control your imagery, or your argument can sound scatterbrained. Consider this ill-formed sentence:

He has a lot of black sheep in his closet.

Ridiculous, right? That mixed metaphor starts off with one image but ends with another. That's a sign of an inexperienced or lazy writer. It's jarring, doesn't hang together, and sounds like a first draft nobody bothered to fix.

A classic mixed metaphor occurs within a single sentence. These statements blast off like a rocket to Mars, lose their way in the dark woods, and end up at the corner of Non and Sense. And you can have mixed-up, muddled-up, shook-up metaphors within the same paragraph, section, or document. What's the alternative? You can deliberately choose and use one unified set of images throughout a white paper to create a more powerful impression of a thoughtful, well-considered document.

Hitting a home run with a unified metaphor

I once wrote a white paper on how e-commerce websites need to meet three main challenges: security, availability, and scalability. I came up with the image of a triple-threat baseball player, that rare talent who's equally good at hitting, running, and fielding. Then I jotted down all the baseball terms I could think of in a couple minutes: home run, strikeout, bottom of the ninth, World Series, foul ball, pennant, in the strike zone, umpire, pop fly, bleachers, and more. That created a word list to draw on for my first draft.

I introduced the metaphor in the first two sentences of the white paper:

> To be effective, your e-commerce website must meet three critical requirements — security, availability, and scalability — just like a baseball player who can run, hit, and

field. And it's not enough to do one or two well; a star performer has to be a triple-threat who excels at all three.

Then whenever I wanted a metaphor for the body of the paper, I looked back at my baseball word list; that always gave me a term or sparked another idea. I never had to search for an image or pull it together during the rewrite. In the conclusions section, I went back to that imagery and mentioned winning the World Series. That white paper hit it out of the park!

(Please note that this image worked well for the target audience: 90 percent men, all in the United States. For a mixed audience of men and women around the world, I wouldn't choose that kind of sports image.)

My best advice here is to *ring the bell* — touch on the same image — three times: once at the start, once at the end, and at least once in the middle. To apply this rule, introduce a metaphor in the first sentence or two of your white paper. Return to the same image at the end, giving it a twist that adds a sense of completion. And touch on it at least once more in the main body of the paper instead of flying off in some other direction. Handling your metaphors this well takes practice and effort. But why use random imagery when you can pull it all together as a unified message?

You can even make these metaphors the first things you write. Try this tip at the start of your writing session: Come up with a "master metaphor" to tie everything together, and then jot down all the terms you can think of from the same domain. From then on, whenever you need a metaphor, draw it from your word list. This step doesn't eat up time; in fact, I believe it actually saves time, both in writing and rewriting.

Controlling your material

The single most important thing you must do as a white paper writer is to control your material. Otherwise, it will control you. Here are two quick questions to check who's in charge:

- ✔ **When you start to write a white paper, do you wonder what the heck to do first?** If so, you probably realize that you're no pro at writing white papers and you should get more familiar with them. Knowing what to include and what to leave out, how to find and trim down a quotation, and how to build a persuasive argument seems almost impossible. In other words, it's probably difficult for you to control your material. Don't worry. This book can help, and more practice will build your knowledge and confidence. You'll likely make mistakes, but you'll benefit from them.

- ✔ **Do you feel like it takes all your effort just to get a white paper drafted, let alone thinking about anything like ringing the bell (see previous section)?** If so, you can control your material but just barely. Again, more practice will help you write these documents with less strain and master more advanced techniques until you're firmly in control.

Only a handful of writers ever reach the pinnacle of white paper writing, where the process comes easily, almost without any conscious thinking or planning. These folks are considered professional white paper writers; they can control their material, ring the bell, handle sources smoothly, and build a persuasive argument from a mix of facts, figures, opinions, and rhetoric. For example, only 8 percent of nearly 600 respondents from a survey of white papers writers were rated "highly experienced" because they'd written more than 40 white papers. I personally worked on 30 white papers before one turned out so well that I still use it as a sample. Controlling your material is partly a matter of learning but mainly a matter of practice.

How will you know when you've mastered the art of writing white papers? Well, writing always takes effort. But after you reach mastery, you no longer have to struggle just to get your ideas down; you do that much faster and give them more shape and form with more decisiveness. You know some things intuitively, like where to insert a quote or factoid or when to move on to your next point.

A big part of controlling your material is knowing what *not* to do, how to avoid the mistakes you made in the past. Gradually, you discover how to rewrite so that each draft gets stronger, more concise, and more persuasive. And if your client asks you to tweak the tone to make it "more businesslike" or the opposite ("more conversational"), you can do that in one confident pass through your draft instead of dissolving into a quivering mass of jelly.

Rewriting Before You Submit

Get me rewrite! Old-time journalists knew the value of a rewrite. That was when the copy desk editors tightened, checked, and cleaned up their drafts to get them ready to print. Sometimes they even bounced a draft back to the reporter for a rewrite.

That still happens often on glossy magazines. And that's not a bad thing. Personally, I believe that writing *is* rewriting. And so do many other seasoned writers. A first draft is only a starting point. If you know what to do, you can improve any draft with some careful rewriting. You can base a rewrite on comments from reviewers, statistical analysis of your text, or your own growing judgment about what can be improved.

With all that going for it, who wouldn't rewrite? Well, beginning writers — those who aren't in control of their material (see the preceding section) — can be so exhausted simply typing up a first draft that they just want to get it off their desk. Sometimes they don't even reread their draft before they send it off to their client. I'm not sure what they expect will happen. Will the client magically know how to find and fix all the deficiencies? Not likely. Clients aren't professional editors with years of experience detecting flaws in a text, articulating the problems, and suggesting ways to fix them. Instead, reviewers will more likely give comments like "needs more details" or "too wordy" that leave inexperienced writers shaking their head in bewilderment, not sure what to do next. But you can avoid all of this by doing a proper rewrite or two before you show anything to your client.

In the following sections, I discuss these best practices that can make your rewrites more effective:

- Avoiding throat-clearing
- Having your computer read back your draft to you
- Getting readability statistics on your text
- Changing passive voice to active voice

More white paper writers should follow these practices. They work, they're free, and they help create a superior white paper for your client.

Avoiding throat-clearing

One common failing to look for is a rambling introduction that takes up a couple of paragraphs without saying anything much. Called *authorial throat-clearing,* this is a remnant of you warming up during your first writing session. In the old days, it was the start of a business letter saying, "It has come to my attention that . . ." In a white paper, it's likely a few sentences like the following:

> In today's uncertain economy, companies must try to stretch their resources as far as possible. Doing more with less is today's mantra at all levels of the enterprise. That's why more and more companies are now considering moving part of their IT to the cloud. . . .

Often these sentiments are so obvious that you can easily cut them. What company doesn't want to stretch its resources? But some writers dearly love to retain this deadwood, feeling it makes an effective introduction. It doesn't. Cut it on your rewrite, and tell readers something they haven't heard before.

Having your computer read your draft

Hearing a draft of your white paper read out loud shows you all the rough edges that could use a polish. It also enables you to concentrate on the flow of the words and the power of the rhetoric. Whenever I do this, I'm alerted to little fix-ups that can make the phrasing smoother, the sentences crisper, and the effect more persuasive. Text-to-speech is already built into your PC or Mac with alternate apps available as free downloads. Sure, the voices sound a little robotic, but it's still a quick and easy way to help polish up a draft.

I had my Windows PC read me back most of this book, one paragraph at a time, so I could hear where I needed to polish it. Windows has the Narrator utility built in, but I find it clunky; it's really designed as a screen reader for the visually impaired. Instead, I used NaturalReader, a free download from www.naturalreaders.com. You can set up NaturalReader as a floating toolbar in Word, so all you do is select text and click Play to read it back.

Like many things on the Mac, a text reader is already built in, and it works very smoothly. You can select a different voice or adjust the narrator's speed by opening System Preferences and clicking Speech and the Text-To-Speech panel. Using this utility is dirt simple: Open your white paper file on your screen, highlight the text you want to read, and press Ctrl + T. You can also try the NaturalReader Mac download from www.naturalreaders.com, which gives you a floating toolbar with voice controls you can access from any application without having to go into System Preferences.

Getting readability statistics on your text

Writing is subjective, so who's to say whether something is really clear or well written? It's all a judgment call, right? Well, yes and no. Several formulas have been developed to give people some sense of the readability of a passage. These formulas can't evaluate whether your sentences make sense or your tone is appropriate for your current white paper, but they can give you an idea about how easy it is to read your draft. And the good news is, the most popular ones are already built into Word ready for you to use.

Two simple techniques can improve your writing's readability scores: Use shorter words, and use shorter sentences. Using more paragraphs helps, too. In other words, you can make your white paper text easier to read by using three keys: Backspace to delete long words, period (.) to break up long sentences, and Enter to break up long paragraphs.

Readability stats built into Word

Did you know that a perfectly good readability checker is built into Word? It's turned off by default because not everyone wants to bother with it, but you can easily turn it on and use it to help you measure your writing. This readability check runs quickly right after any spell-check and gives you numerous statistics about your current file.

To turn on readability statistics, follow these steps:

1. **Select File (Word 2010) or the Office button (Word 2007) and choose Word Options and then Proofing.**

2. **Select Check Grammar With Spelling and Show Readability Statistics.**

To see readability stats, select Spelling & Grammar on the Review tab.

The readability statistics appear in a small window after the spelling and grammar check runs. Figure 15-1 shows two sample windows with the actual results from two drafts of the same white paper.

Readability Statistics		Readability Statistics	
Counts		**Counts**	
Words	2728	Words	2692
Characters	13975	Characters	13771
Paragraphs	46	Paragraphs	93
Sentences	95	Sentences	138
Averages		**Averages**	
Sentences per Paragraph	2.9	Sentences per Paragraph	2.6
Words per Sentence	27.2	Words per Sentence	17.3
Characters per Word	5.0	Characters per Word	4.9
Readability		**Readability**	
Passive Sentences	20%	Passive Sentences	14%
Flesch Reading Ease	35.4	Flesch Reading Ease	49.6
Flesch-Kincaid Grade Level	14.8	Flesch-Kincaid Grade Level	10.5

Figure 15-1: White paper readability, before (left) and after revision (right).

Illustration courtesy of Gordon Graham

White paper readability, before and after revision

A client came to me with a draft white paper that most reviewers thought was too hard for their target audience to read. So I revised it, capturing Word's readability stats from before and after. As shown in Figure 15-1, the original scores are on the left and my revision's scores on the right.

Under *Counts,* notice that the total word count didn't change much: down by less than 2 percent. But the number of paragraphs and sentences shot up as I radically shortened them. Under *Averages,* note how the average number of words per sentence fell dramatically from 27.2 to 17.3. And under *Readability,* see how that paid off: the *Flesch Reading Ease* improved by more than a third (the higher the number here, the better), and the *Flesch-Kincaid Grade Level* was lowered from college to high-school reading level (the lower the number here, the better). The reviewers said my revision was perfect for their audience.

Statistics are one thing, but looking at some actual sentences shows how I boosted the readability. Here's some original text:

> Acme's experience indicates that higher-priced RTB impressions, where our models indicate a higher expected influence in driving advertisers' goals, were up to 100 times more effective in influencing consumer behavior than lower-priced ones, a pattern that persists across industries, customers and campaigns. This implies that counter to conventional wisdom, in an RTB world, rather than creating value for the advertiser, a media buyer focused too intently on CPM may actually erode it. (71 words in 2 sentences)

And here's how I revised that:

> Acme has found that paying more for a higher-quality impression through RTB can be up to 100 times more effective at influencing consumer behavior. This pattern applies across industries, customers, and campaigns. This means that in today's real-time advertising world, focusing too much on CPM can actually limit an advertiser's results. (50 words in 3 sentences)

You can figure out how to do this, too, if you focus some energy on rewriting.

Changing passive voice to active voice

Notice something else in the readability stats from Figure 15-1: a measure for Passive Sentences (the lower the score here, the better). In the rewrite I describe in the previous section, I squeezed that number down by one-third, from 20 percent to 14 percent, about the same as most magazines and newspapers. You've probably heard of the *passive voice,* but not every writer knows exactly what it is, why it's considered poor style, or what to do about it. This section answers those three questions.

Passive voice is a sentence that uses some form of "to be" or "to get" plus another verb and usually drops the object of the action. This sounds complicated, but it really isn't. A few examples prove that everyone who speaks English uses passive voice every day:

Any attached file is scanned automatically.

The package got delivered late.

That white paper was not promoted properly by the agency.

Passive constructions are considered weak because they waste words. A passive sentence in English is roughly 15 percent longer and usually conveys less information. Passive voice creates roundabout sentences that often describe an action without naming any actor. My favorite example is from Ronald Reagan, when he sort of admitted that his administration had done wrong in the Iran-Contra affair: "Mistakes were made." Notice what's missing? The active way to phrase this sentiment would be, "We made mistakes" or even "I made mistakes."

To change the passive voice into the *active voice* (a sentence that states who is performing the action), figure out who's doing what to whom and then use the basic verb without any form of "to be" or "to get." This saves words and improves the readability of your sentences, as in these examples:

Billions of dollars' worth of sales are driven by white papers.
(passive voice, 11 words)

White papers drive billions of dollars' worth of sales.
(active voice, 9 words or 18 percent shorter)

That white paper was not promoted properly by the agency.
(passive voice, 10 words)

The agency did not promote that white paper properly.
(active voice, 9 words or 10 percent shorter)

Of course, you can't completely eliminate the passive voice, and every writer uses it every few sentences. Passive voice is useful when the object of an action is more important than the actor or when you're not sure who the actor really is, as in:

The Acme ScanOMatic 3000 was named "Product of the Year."

The scanner got unplugged over the holidays.

If you ever see a high score on the order of 30 percent or 40 percent for *Passive Sentences* in the readability statistics, you should recast at least half of them. When you recheck your readability, notice how many words you shaved off and how much better your scores come out. Eventually, writing in a more active voice will become second nature to you.

Writing with Style

Some people think style is a side dish, something you just dip words into at the table, like dipping fries into ketchup. Or mustard. Or mayonnaise. Each different dipping sauce gives a different taste sensation, and that's what style is all about. That's a fun image, but I don't agree. I think style starts back in the kitchen when you choose which potatoes to use, how to chop them up, which parts to keep and which to toss in the compost, and how long to leave them in the fryer — not to mention what kind of oil to use and how often to change it. In other words, writing style covers everything: the words you use, the way you assemble them into sentences, and the way you arrange your sentences to build your point of view.

"Style is knowing who you are, what you want to say, and not giving a damn," said Orson Welles, the history-making actor and director. Without boldness, you have no style. Without passion, you have no style. Without a point of view, you have no style. Writing effective white papers takes boldness, passion, and a distinct point of view. Without those things, you may as well write a memo on the cost of potatoes.

Good style can mean choosing words with skill, following the guidelines laid down as an organization's "house" style, always treating terms consistently, or all three at once. And besides years of practice, a great way to gain insight and get better at all three of these elements of style is to use style guides.

Learning from style guides

If you're fortunate enough to work in a team with other writers, you can compare notes on how to solve different writing challenges. But even if you're the only writer in your company or the only contract writer in your town, you can still learn from dozens of writers and editors working in other organizations. Their best thinking and recommendations are captured in some excellent style guides.

This section points to my own favorite style guides, arranged in alphabetical order. You can find more style guides aimed at technology and longer reviews on my website at www.thatwhitepaperguy.com/white-paper-articles.html#book-reviews.

How many style guides should white paper writers have on their desks? I recommend *The Elements of Style* (Longman) plus one or two more. I have all the books mentioned here plus more. But having one or two that you actually use is better than a whole shelf full of style guides you never look at.

The Associated Press Stylebook

Designed for quick reference by busy newspaper reporters and editors, *The Associated Press Stylebook* (www.APstylebook.com) is arranged alphabetically, with further chapters on sports, business, punctuation, and media law. Opening my copy to a random page, I find entries for dot-com, double-click, Down syndrome, and Drambuie: All of which I'd likely wonder how to spell or hyphenate. *The Associated Press Stylebook* isn't the hippest reference around, but if you use it for your house style, you'll be safely in the mainstream of American journalism, and your white paper style shouldn't offend anyone.

The Elements of Style

If you don't have a copy of *The Elements of Style* (Longman) on your desk, you're not a real writer. If you've never encountered this little book, you're in for a pleasant surprise. It's short, simple, costs less than $10, and you don't even have to read it. Yes, you heard me, you can just flip through this book for guidance and inspiration when you need it. Like millions of other writers before you, you'll find it instructive.

The Elements of Style has been criticized as old-fashioned, too prescriptive, and just plain wrong on some fine points of grammar. But after reviews from hundreds of people, it's still rated 4.7 out of 5 on Amazon.com. Maybe you can skip the first part with its rules of usage, which may be outdated in places, but don't miss the 11 elementary rules of composition and the 21 approaches to style. Here's a tiny sampling:

✔ Avoid fancy words.

✔ Use the active voice.

✔ Use definite, specific, concrete language.

✔ Work from a suitable design.

✔ Place the emphatic words of a sentence at the end.

With each guideline comes a short, often delightful explanation. For example, here's a classic sentence under the timeless advice to "omit needless words":

> A sentence should contain no unnecessary words, a paragraph no unnecessary sentences, for the same reason that a drawing should have no unnecessary lines and a machine no unnecessary parts.

Buy a copy of this book, highlight it, and open it frequently, especially if you feel discouraged about your writing. To me, flipping through *The Elements of Style* is like a bracing shot of good coffee — maybe fortified by something stronger — that always gets me reinspired and back to writing my best.

Wikipedia Manual of Style

In Chapter 14, I warn against using Wikipedia as a source in a white paper. But that doesn't mean this crowd-sourced encyclopedia has nothing to offer. In particular, the online *Wikipedia Manual of Style* is quite well done. I especially like the section called "Words to watch" available here: `http://en.wikipedia.org/wiki/Wikipedia:Manual_of_Style/Words_to_watch`.

This section lists the typical problems that can afflict Wikipedia entries, including bias, vagueness, euphemisms, and unsupported claims. All the same problems crop up in white papers, and avoiding them is a matter of good style. For example, here's a list of words that Wikipedia calls "puffery":

> . . . brilliant, celebrated, cutting-edge, eminent, extraordinary, famous, great, leading, legendary, notable, outstanding, prestigious, remarkable, renowned, respected, virtuoso, visionary, world-class . . .

I've seen just about every one of those terms used in marketing materials from B2B companies. These words, and all their relations, are ineffective because they give rise to a simple question: Says who? If you find yourself using such puffed-up language in a white paper, you've fallen into marketing speak. Delete it, and then go back and prove the claim you're trying to make.

The Wikipedia style manual also calls out unsupported attributions:

> . . . experts declare, it is believed, it is often reported, it is widely thought, many are of the opinion, many scholars state, most feel, research has shown, science says, some people say . . .

These phrases are called *weasel words* because they claim to report an established consensus without providing any actual evidence. What's the alternative? If you have proof, show the best few pieces in your white paper. But if you have only one source, or none at all, don't try to snow people with this type of expression. It won't persuade anyone.

The Yahoo! Style Guide

No matter what you may think of Yahoo!, it remains one of the most popular destinations on the web. Its writers and editors have a ton of experience preparing content for websites, and much of their advice can be applied directly to white papers. This style guide (`http://styleguide.yahoo.com`) includes examples to illustrate each point, before-and-after rewrites of many passages, and a 40-page list of bothersome words that you can download and tweak for your own house style. This book is much more than a style guide; any white paper writer can use it as a lively training course in how to write more effectively.

Following house style

Some companies have an internal style guide that captures their views on certain issues, like where to put commas or hyphens in a phrase like *the red green and black and white wires*. When you plan a white paper for a new client, ask whether the company has a house style guide; if so, get a copy and check it out. If you have the luxury of working with an editor, you can focus on your message and rely on the editor to bring your text into line with the house style.

If your client lacks both a house style guide and an in-house editor, the style you use is up to you. Remember to specify in your proposal which style guide(s) you plan to follow. Doing so can help solve any well-meaning but silly comments from reviewers who think there's a "right way" to spell or hyphenate some phrase.

If you're writing for a European company, ask whether it uses British or American spelling for words like *color/colour* and *labor/labour*. Don't automatically use the British spelling; many European companies sell mainly to the United States. Maybe it's a hangover from the American Revolution, but that *u* seems to irritate Americans much more than the lack of it bothers Europeans.

A style guide isn't just about spelling. It can also include how to format the elements of a page, such as various levels of headings, figure titles, footnotes, headers and footers, pull quotes, tables, and so on. Many companies have guidelines on how to use their logos and product names. You can attach templates, if any, for various types of documents, and you can point to the external references you want everyone to follow.

A style guide can boost consistency, settle arguments, and save time by capturing many little decisions all in one place. Although many writers are self-admitted "word nerds," keep your eye on the ball: The goal of your white paper is to help your company or client generate leads, nurture prospects, and cement sales. No style guide adds anything to the bottom line compared to a truly effective white paper.

In the next sections, I walk you through using a house style guide and even how to create your own in a matter of minutes.

Tweaking a style guide as needed

There's no absolute "right" or "wrong" about house style; there's only what works and what doesn't. So if you come across something in the house style that interferes with your ability to create an effective white paper, speak up. A style guide wasn't carved in stone and handed down by the Almighty from some mountaintop. People created it, and it should evolve over time. If people don't make suggestions, how will it ever improve?

Make your point calmly and clearly, show an example, and send your input to someone in a position to make a decision. If it doesn't go your way, accept the decision. Weightier issues are debated all the way to the Supreme Court, and one side always loses. And if you happen to be the custodian of the style guide, don't be too defensive and unwilling to bend. You probably don't want to let your writers say "ain't" or "dude" in your white papers — but if they occasionally mix up *that* and *which,* it ain't the end of the world, dude.

Creating your own style guide

Most B2B buyers can't tell whether you use *fewer* or *less than* correctly, but almost anyone can spot a typo or an inconsistency, like when you write *smart phone* one place and then *smartphone* a few lines later. Those little things can have a big impact: They can distract a reader from your argument and undermine the company's professional image. One survey showed that mistakes like those make B2B buyers wonder about the quality of a company's products and even the intelligence of its people.

If you're working without an editor or house style to guide you, you can protect yourself against these slip-ups by creating your own style guide. And you don't need to sink days into developing one. Here are two quick methods I learned from a seasoned editor who worked for many book publishers in Toronto. She had the same issue as any independent white paper writer: How do you keep styles straight when you're working for several different clients?

✔ **Method #1: Style on the fly:** While drafting or revising a white paper, start a new file, and as you work, record any term that you can handle in more than one way, such as *email/e-mail.* Decide which way you prefer, and note that in your style file. Then use Word to find all occurrences in the form you don't want to use (say *email*) and replace them with your preferred usage (*e-mail*) to make your whole document consistent. Then use your preferred style from then on.

At the end of your work session, make sure your whole word list is in alphabetical order for quick reference, and add notes under general headings, like "Punctuation." And presto! You have a good start on a style guide plus a white paper that follows it. For a smaller company, this list may be all you ever need. And to show how thorough you are, you can even send your draft style guide to your client as a separate deliverable.

✔ **Method #2: Style in 60 minutes:** Using existing materials from your company or client, you can follow these steps to generate a house style guide in the shortest possible time. Even in 60 minutes, you can get a lot done.

1. Gather a good selection of documents from the company, such as press releases, marketing materials, manuals, and any previous white papers, either PDFs or hard copies.

2. Create a new file and type in an initial heading, something like "Style Guide for *[Company]* as of *[date]*."

3. Start scanning through the first document for words you can handle in more than one way, such as *GB* or *gigabytes*. Type in all the alternatives in alphabetical order. If you're looking at PDFs on your screen, search for both alternatives and note how often each one occurs. Add up those occurrences to see which version is more popular within the company.

4. Scan for the next term. On the first few pages, you'll find lots. This number will taper off as you capture all the most common terms used in the company's materials.

5. Continue eyeballing and entering each new term in alphabetical order. You may want to stop after you've scanned for 50 minutes or worked your way through most of the documents.

6. Take the next ten minutes to decide how to handle each term in your list.

   To use the whole web to help you decide, go to www.google fight.com and type in both versions, such as "back up" and "backup." You'll see how many times each alternative occurs on the web, like a popularity contest.

7. If you need to call a meeting to review and confirm your decisions, circulate your file in advance as the agenda.

Refining Your Writing Process

No one can tell you how to write. No one else can dictate when, where, or how you should get started, do a rewrite, or find out more about the craft. But you don't need to suffer through some clunky, ungainly process whenever you sit down to write a white paper. Part III of this book suggests a step-by-step process for completing a white paper so you always know where you are and what to do next. But how do you actually accomplish any of these steps? How do you create and refine a writing process that really works for you?

This section encourages you to think about your writing process with an open mind and consider ways to make your process faster and easier. Among these ideas are figuring out the ideal time to write, switching hats between writer and editor properly, and allowing enough time for your ideas to gel. This section also touches on how to get yourself going, use a mind map, and write in short bursts of time. Last but not least, I recommend using positive visualizations that can bring you more confidence, courage, and peace of mind as a writer.

Figuring out your best time to write

Everyone has a daily energy pattern. Some writers are like vampires: They come out only at night, tapping on their keyboards as the winds howl outside. I'm a bit of a night owl myself, but I also like getting up early to get writing at 6 a.m. or so. As for that in-between time, from mid to late afternoon, I never get much written then. The best things for me to do at that time of day are answer e-mails, return phone calls, do some research, or go for a walk. I know from experience that's my downtime.

How about you? Do you have a handle on the peaks and valleys of your day? I'm not talking about those temporary surges of energy from drinking coffee or eating power bars. I'm talking about your natural rhythm, the daily energy pattern that recurs even on weekends when you have no job duties. If you don't understand your own pattern, keep a log for a month or two. Note when you feel energized and can produce creative work and when you're at low ebb and barely awake. If you work as an independent writer where you can organize your own workday, this is critical. If you work in-house and must pretend to be alert all day long, this can be challenging. In either case, when you know your pattern, make sure to spend your peak times writing.

Wearing the right hat at the right time

Every writer has a split personality. (Finally, an accurate diagnosis for your condition!) It's true, although I prefer to express this with a different image — having two hats to wear. One hat is the writer's, probably a black beret or blood-red fascinator perched jauntily on your head, with huge bright feathers blooming out to convey your carefree, creative side. The other hat is the editor's, perhaps a banker's black bowler, a card-dealer's green shade, or even an orange hard hat (especially if you're planning a lot of discussion with the writer) — anything to convey a sensible, practical, worldly outlook.

When you wear the writer's hat, your job is to put out a torrent of words without looking back, with no judgment and no critique; it's time to create, connect, and expand. When you switch to the editor's hat, your job is to look at that creative output with a keen eye, making a slew of judgment calls; it's time to analyze, make distinctions, and trim. After the writer gets out a draft, the editor takes over to shape and polish that into a finished document.

This arrangement works perfectly well, as long as you don't plunk your hard hat on top of your fascinator. When both sides struggle for control, it can feel like the editor is sitting in judgment over every word the writer puts down or like the writer is still spewing out words far past any reasonable cutoff point. In other words, trouble starts when neither side will yield control at the appropriate time. Your challenge as the "hat-check manager" is to put on the proper hat at the right time and make the other one wait its proper turn.

Allowing ideas to ferment

One California vineyard used to claim, "We will sell no wine before its time." This statement presumably meant that every bottle was properly aged to reach a drinkable state. I advise you to make the same rule for your white papers. "Not selling any white paper before its time" means having enough patience to do your research, digest it, plan, draft, polish, sleep on it, and then polish your draft at least once more before submitting it to any reviewers. You can't do all that in two days; there's just too much information involved to process it that fast.

Personally, I need two fermentation periods for every white paper:

- ✔ After a conference call, before I make up a white paper plan
- ✔ After doing a few days of research, before I write an executive summary

Each fermentation period is at least a day or two. If that sounds like a leisurely pace, it's not; I routinely have five or six white papers on the go, at various stages of completion. But I always try to carve out a little time at those critical points in each project to let the latest input bubble and percolate. I'm not saying every writer needs the same amount of time, but if you study the "creative process," you'll find that many researchers confirm the need for a certain incubation period during which raw input is processed into insights.

If you're really pressed for time, review your notes on a project just before bed. I do this when I'm juggling way too many projects, and when I wake up the next morning, it's as though part of my mind was reviewing that material all night long. I can usually start writing immediately, as though I'd allowed a whole day to mull over those notes.

Tricking yourself to get started

Did you know the most common time of the week to commit suicide is 9 a.m. on Monday morning? Some people really hate their jobs! Even those of us who enjoy our work sometimes take a while to get back into the swing of things after a vacation, or even just a great weekend. The same can apply to getting back into a white paper after a fermentation period.

At times like that, I've discovered how to trick myself into getting started. For example, I may say to myself, "I'm not going to do any writing; I'm just going to review the plan." Soon enough, I'm making notes on what to do next, on where I found some great research, and so on. Or I tell myself, "I'm not going to actually write anything; I'm just jotting down some thoughts." Pretty soon I'm writing longer and longer notes, and those notes are turning into complete sentences and eventually into paragraphs of a draft.

Those tricks may work for you, or you may need to develop some of your own. Either way, find a technique for getting back in the saddle after a break from a white paper.

Using a mind map

You've probably heard of mind mapping. It's essentially a visual form of out-lining, where you draw a spiderweb or fishbone diagram of the central points of your white paper. You can use different colors, shapes, sizes, or anything else that helps map out your subject visually. Many copywriters swear by this technique, saying it saves them time and helps them solve problems. I can see how mind mapping can help build a complex argument and make sure it all hangs together. I don't often use it; but the few times I've been stuck and tried a mind map, it's helped me break the jam.

You don't need anything but paper and pencil to make a mind map; just put down one big idea from your white paper, draw in another idea that grows out of it, and you're off and mind mapping. Or you can try out different mind-mapping software, including free or low-cost apps for your Android or iOS devices.

Writing in short bursts

Writing is hard work; there's no doubt about that. So instead of expecting to write for an entire afternoon, why not break up your writing into short, doable bursts? The Pomodoro Technique is one proven way to do that. Basically, this technique involves getting a kitchen timer, setting it to 25 minutes, and working diligently on your white paper without tolerating any interruptions until the timer goes off. You'll be amazed at how much you get written in that burst: maybe a whole page, maybe a couple of pages.

Then you can take a break for five minutes to do anything else you want: Check Facebook, get a drink of water, stare out the window, whatever. After your break, turn on your timer and get back to work for another 25 minutes. After four Pomodoros (25-minute bursts of work), you can take a longer break of up to half an hour. Check out www.pomodorotechnique.com/goodies for more about this technique plus some free downloads.

The unexpected benefit of using this technique is that, like many people, you may actually write better when you write faster. You don't have the luxury for procrastinating, throat-clearing, or negative thinking about how much stress you're under. You simply have to produce, just like an old-time jour-nalist on deadline.

Using positive affirmations

Why are bad habits so hard to break? Why do some people fail at everything they put their hand to? I'm no psychologist, but I believe this has a lot to do with negative influences. Even friends and families can hold people back with self-limiting beliefs.

The simplest way I've found to get more positive is with affirmations. An *affirmation* is a short statement that expresses a desired goal as if it already happened, reinforcing how great you feel to have achieved it. And it's a long stretch from wishful thinking. For example, "I'm going to quit smoking on New Year's Day" is just a wish, placed far in the future, and not anchored with any emotion. To create an effective affirmation, turn that desire into something more specific and powerful, such as, "I really love having so much energy now that I'm living without cigarettes." Notice the difference? This affirmation confirms that you've already quit smoking, is set in the present, and focuses on a strong benefit you enjoy in place of smoking.

This technique works for many people. I think it's something like self-hypnosis; but instead of letting other people and your own negative thinking hypnotize you, you take charge of the process and turn it in a new, more positive direction. You can Google terms like "positive affirmation" to find out more about this.

 If you practice any other forms of self-centering, such as exercise, meditation, or prayer, remember to use them when you're in the thick of a white paper project. Especially at the start of your white paper career, these are big, challenging projects that can feel like slogging up an impossibly steep mountain. Use whatever works for you to calm down, be positive, and believe that you will get there.

Challenging the myth of writer's block

Did you ever hear of any old-fashioned journalists complaining about "writer's block"? They didn't have time — they had a deadline to meet!

Most writers who claim to have "writer's block" are really suffering from something else. For example, they could have a poor process for writing, or maybe they're trying to work at the wrong time of day. They may be wearing the wrong hat, letting the editor come out and pass critical judgments on their first efforts, while they should be writing rough drafts. They may have lost the capacity to trick themselves into getting started or have skipped doing a mind map. They may be trying to write for an entire day when a few short bursts would get them through the slump. They may be indulging in negative self-talk, telling themselves, "I'm not a writer! I'm no good! I will never write anything good!"

Turning negative thoughts into positive attitudes

Long after I became a professional writer, my writing process was still painful. I used to start every project with cringing self-doubt, like I was a complete imposter who couldn't possibly pull off what my client wanted. Every project was agony to start, not bad in the middle after I got going, and then acutely painful at the end when I wondered whether my client would like what I delivered.

One day, I heard a talk about creative visualization or the process of "acting as if." A light bulb went off. I realized I'd spent years imagining writing as an excruciating process. That night, I came up with a new mantra, "Writing is easy and fun for me!" Then I repeated that out loud dozens of times a day for weeks. It worked! All my hesitation and insecurity dropped away. Ever since I turned around my visualizations, I get a big kick out of digging into every project, and I don't ever want to stop writing.

Having a poor process for writing can feel like a giant hand pushing back against all your efforts. If this ever happens to you, instead of labeling it "writer's block," go through this section again and try some of these ideas:

- ✔ See how you can change your working conditions.
- ✔ Try some mind mapping.
- ✔ Trick yourself to get started again.
- ✔ Try to do a short Pomodoro for 15 or 20 minutes; if that works, take a break and then do another and another.
- ✔ Ease off on the expectations and judgments.
- ✔ Try some positive affirmations.

Then get back to work. You can do this!

Chapter 16

Promote Like a Madman

You can create the most compelling and persuasive white paper in history, but if the prospects in your target audience never encounter it, all your efforts go to waste. Promoting your white paper is the all-important final phase in publishing an effective white paper. Your goal is to get your document in front of as many target readers as you possibly can.

In this chapter, I discuss why you must recognize this need for promoting your white paper, ideally treating it like a mini product launch. I explain that you get the best results when you measure your results, keep on doing whatever works best for you, and continue your promotions for months. And to help you decide how to promote your white paper, this chapter lists 40 tactics to choose from — everything from creating a landing page to setting up an online advertising campaign.

No company has the resources to use every tactic for every white paper. Try the most likely ones, measure your results to discover which tactics work best for which flavor of white paper, and then make sure to do everything that pays off for you.

Recognizing the Need for Promotion

Sad to say, some companies create a white paper, stick it in the online library buried deep in their website, and hope that their prospects notice. When these companies see disappointing results, they often conclude that "white papers don't work." But no tool works right if you don't use it properly. This approach misses the point of *publishing* a white paper — *to publish* means to make something public. You need to make your white paper public to all the target readers you can possibly reach.

Your marketing team needs to work hard and smart during three critical periods:

- ✔ **Before the white paper is finished,** when they need to make promotional plans and get the campaigns ready

- ✔ **As soon as the white paper is released,** when they need to swing into action, implement those plans, and promote the white paper everywhere

- ✔ **For weeks or months after the white paper is released,** when they need to track the results and continue using whatever tactics get the best results

Without doing all of that, you likely won't generate the volume of leads, engage the number of prospects, or cement the number of sales you need to justify the cost of creating the white paper. In fact, more investment in more white papers is frittered away through weak promotions than through any other pitfall.

You must promote your white paper long enough and well enough to generate the results you need to make your white paper a success. Without adequate promotions, your white paper can sink like a stone and make getting the budget to do the next one even harder. With effective promotions, your marketing team can look like the heroes and geniuses they really are.

Promoting a white paper like a product launch

Some marketers wonder how to promote a white paper. After all, it's just a document, not a real product or service in its own right. Yet you already know how to do it. The best practice is to promote a white paper like a product launch. Do most of the same things you do when your company has a new product or service to bring to market.

Obviously, you won't have the same budget to play with, but the promotions you do for a product launch make an excellent starting place. Some items are simply too costly, like throwing a free cocktail party at an industry event. Eliminate any item that's too expensive or time-consuming to consider for a white paper. But don't chuck out entire categories of promotions, like social media or advertising, just because you think they won't work. Try everything and see what happens. Until you try each tactic at least a couple of times, you won't know whether it works for your particular audience in your own niche.

Measuring your results

As you know, different audiences have different preferences. Some prefer one channel or another and respond to one tactic or another. No one can tell you in advance which tactics are going to work for your audience and which are going to flop. Some marketers just try a few things here and there and then move on to their next project. But that leaves a lot to chance, with a big gap where your marketing dollars can leak out.

You can close that gap by measuring your results from each promotional tactic. Then you can calculate the ROI of different tactics and compare them to see which ones are most effective. Depending on the size of your company and scope of your marketing budget, you may need different metrics to measure your results for different white paper promotions.

Table 16-1 defines the most common metrics used to track white papers and notes the key purpose of each metric. As you can see, many of the metrics listed here may be interesting but not especially useful, like the ones related to blogs, Twitter, and Facebook. Others — such as downloads, leads, sales, and revenues — are vital for calculating the specific ROI on a white paper campaign.

If your marketing team can track these metrics, you can use them to make a convincing case for the effectiveness of white papers. After all, if you can say, "We can attribute $3.2 million in revenues directly to our Q2 white paper campaign . . ." no one's going to argue when you suggest publishing a few follow-up documents.

Table 16-1	Common Marketing Metrics for White Papers	
Term	*Definition*	*Purpose*
Clicks	The number of times anyone clicked on an ad for a white paper	An alternate way to measure interest in a white paper; a raw number used to calculate CTR (see next)
Click-through rate (CTR)	The total number of clicks divided by the total number of impressions for an ad	To measure the effectiveness of a web banner or pay-per-click ad
Comments	The number of comments posted after a blog entry about a white paper	To measure the reach of the white paper content in the blogosphere

(continued)

Table 16-1 *(continued)*

Term	*Definition*	*Purpose*
Cost-per-lead	The total cost of a campaign divided by the number of leads generated by that campaign	To compare the cost-effectiveness of various campaigns and tactics
Downloads	The number of times a PDF white paper was downloaded from a web page	A key metric to track the reach of a white paper
E-mail bounce rate	The number of undeliverable e-mails divided by the total number of e-mails sent	To measure the quality of an e-mail list; a *hard bounce* is a permanent problem, such as an e-mail address that no longer works, while a *soft bounce* is a temporary problem, such as a full inbox
Landing page bounce rate	The ratio of visitors who leave a landing page quickly, as though they weren't interested in it	To measure roughly how engaging a landing page is to visitors; a high bounce rate means the wrong visitors are seeing that web page
Leads	The number of leads generated by a white paper, qualified by marketing, and passed on to sales	A key metric to track the marketing ROI on a white paper campaign
Likes	The number of times something was "liked" on Facebook or YouTube	To measure the reach of a white paper on Facebook; may not be relevant to sales
Media pickups or mentions	The number of times the white paper was mentioned or quoted in offline media (newspapers, magazines, radio, or TV)	To measure the offline PR impact of a white paper

Term	*Definition*	*Purpose*
Opens	The number of people who opened an e-mail for a white paper	To calculate the open rate (see next)
Open rate	The total number of opens divided by the total number of e-mails sent	To measure the effectiveness of an e-mail campaign for a white paper
Page views	The number of times a web page with an HTML white paper was visited	To measure the reach of a white paper formatted as HTML, not PDF
Permalinks	The number of times the white paper was linked to by other blogs	To measure roughly the reach of a white paper in the blogosphere
Registrations	The number of visitors who filled in a registration form so they could view or download a white paper	To count how many prospects a white paper generated; note that the more questions you ask, the fewer registrations you get
Reposts	The number of times a white paper was reposted or quoted in other blogs	To measure the reach of the white paper content in the blogosphere
Retweets	The number of times a white paper was retweeted on Twitter	To measure the reach of a white paper on Twitter; may not be relevant to sales
Revenues	The amount of revenue resulting from sales to qualified leads generated by a white paper	Probably the most important metric of all, and very persuasive if you can track it
Sales	The number of sales resulting from qualified leads generated by a white paper	A key metric to track the results generated by a white paper campaign

Digging up sales and revenue numbers

You may be frustrated trying to unearth any numbers for the sales and revenues driven by any particular white paper. Here are four possible ways to find these metrics, assuming your finance, IT, and sales teams give you their total cooperation. Some combination of these four approaches should yield you numbers you can use.

✔ **Use your CRM.** If someone in your company routinely enters "source of lead" into your customer relationship management (CRM) system, use that field to find how many sales came from leads generated from each specific white paper. Train whoever maintains the CRM system to enter a partial title or part number so you can tell one white paper from another. Otherwise, all your white papers may get lumped in together and you won't have any numbers to tell you whether some were more effective than others.

✔ **Cross-reference registrations.** Compare the names, companies, and locations of the people who registered to download the white paper with the names, companies, and locations of people who bought since the white paper was released. Any hit could be another sale generated by the white paper.

✔ **Calculate revenues from deal size.** After you have the likely number of sales attributed to a white paper, multiply the number of sales by the average deal size for that product or service to find the revenues that white paper drove.

✔ **Total up actual revenues.** Knowing the name of each customer who bought because of the white paper, you can look up the actual revenues from each sale, and any related follow-up sales, then total them all up.

Repeating the most effective promotions

After you start measuring the results from your white paper, look for patterns and trends. Some metrics, such as downloads, registrations, or retweets, are faster to measure. Others, such as sales or revenues, can take months or even years to measure, especially if your company has a longer sales cycle. At the start, you probably want to focus on a few short-term metrics and track them carefully, day by day or even hour by hour.

Whenever you see one tactic creating an uptick in downloads, for example, do it again to check whether it works the second time. If so and it's something you can repeat — like publishing a blog post or e-mailing to your house list — keep on repeating that tactic as long as it keeps on generating results.

Many marketers forget that you can boost your results by sending the same message to the same people more than once. This tactic uses the age-old marketing concept of *repetition* — which explains why you keep on seeing the very same TV ad for toilet paper over and over again. Eventually, you may see that brand in the supermarket and reach for it, even though you're not sure why.

Don't give leads to sales too soon

Just because someone downloaded a white paper doesn't mean that person is ready to talk to a salesperson. In fact, it's pretty irritating to get a phone call like this, "I noticed you just downloaded a white paper from our site, and I wanted to follow up and see whether you have any questions. . . ." Egad, give the person a day to read the thing! This kind of overeager sales process can destroy any goodwill your white paper creates.

If you're on a marketing team responsible for generating leads for your sales force, you need to sit down with your VP of Sales and define what makes a "sales-ready lead." Then your team can score all the leads you generate and pass them on to sales only after they're properly qualified and considered worth pursuing.

Here are some things to consider when scoring leads:

✔ **Job title:** Do they fit your target audience? Are they at a level with enough authority to make or at least recommend a purchase? Or are they from some unlikely department, or are they students or journalists doing research but unlikely to buy?

✔ **Budget:** Do they have an actual budget for their project? Or are they just "seeing what's out there" with no real intention of ever buying?

✔ **Time frame:** Are they ready to buy now? If not, when will they be? Or are they just wondering whether your offering can help their business?

✔ **Buying process:** Do they have a selection committee? Who else is on it? How often do they meet?

You can't often know these things without interacting more with each lead. Perhaps you can design a brief survey or ask a few more questions on your next registration form as you nurture leads and continue to feed them useful content. Perhaps a marketing person will need to contact them by phone to find out where they stand; that's more acceptable to a B2B buyer than having a pushy salesperson call too early.

Tip: Be sure to build your white paper into the sales process your company uses so it can help generate leads at the top of the funnel, nurture prospects through the middle of the funnel, or cement sales at the bottom of the funnel.

In B2B marketing, this tactic means that you can send the same piece of direct mail to the same list, and additional people will open it the second, third, and fourth times. Or you can send the same e-mail announcing a white paper to anyone who didn't open it the first time, perhaps tweaking the subject line as a test. Anyone who opens the second e-mail is a free bonus who took very little effort to reach. Another example: You can tweet exactly the same message once a week, or every two weeks, to keep on pounding the drums about an evergreen white paper that still works for you. This approach is a standard content marketing procedure with Twitter, so none of your followers will likely complain.

To use a little repetition of my own, remember these three tactics that you can safely repeat: sending a piece of direct mail to anyone who didn't already respond, sending a repeat e-mail to anyone who didn't open the earlier one, or tweeting exactly the same message once a week or so.

Continuing your promotions

To squeeze every last drop of juice out of a white paper, don't just push it for a week or two and then think your work is done. You can usually wring more results out of an effective white paper for months. The ideal promotional period varies with the flavor of white paper.

For example, a backgrounder has the shortest life span; as soon as the product changes, or the excitement of the product launch dies down, that white paper may lose its appeal. A numbered list sits in the middle of the pack; a provocative take on an issue that's still topical can keep on generating buzz for many months. And, of course, the long-distance champion is the problem/solution, which can keep on generating results for a year or more. As long as prospects are still downloading it, you can keep up some modest promotions for it. At least, you can tell new prospects, new channel partners, and new employees about it. And as long as the industry is still suffering from the problem that white paper dealt with — even years later — you can often give it a refresh, update any research, and republish virtually the same white paper with a whole new promotional campaign.

In 2006, I wrote a problem/solution white paper for a client in New England who helps local retailers and mom-and-pop shops promote their services to new arrivals in their neighborhoods. Seven years later, it's still up on the client's website, attracting a consistent trickle of interest. Over the years, it's been downloaded close to 2,000 times.

Choosing the Right Promotional Tactics for Your White Paper

The rest of this chapter presents 40 promotional tactics you can use for any white paper. Clearly not every one works for every audience. Be aware of these options, try as many as you can afford, and focus on the ones that generate measurable results. Table 16-2 lists all the promotions I consider must-do's along with a rough guide to how much effort and money each one takes to implement. All these items are listed in chronological order, so I recommend that you work through this table from top to bottom. For example, everything leads to the landing page for your white paper. Without that, where are you going to point the B2B prospects interested in that document?

So creating an effective landing page is the very first must-do tactic, the "square one," for any white paper promotion.

Table 16-3 lists the promotions I consider optional.

Table 16-2	Must-Do White Paper Promotional Tactics	
Tactic	*Difficulty*	*Cost*
Create a landing page with an abstract.	Medium	Low
Feature it prominently on your website.	Medium	Low
Mention it in company newsletters.	Easy	Low
E-mail your sales force (if any).	Easy	Low
E-mail your channel partners (if any).	Easy	Low
E-mail your house opt-in list.	Easy	Low
Tweet it on Twitter.	Easy	Low
Blog about it.	Easy	Low
Announce it to LinkedIn groups.	Easy	Low
Publish a press release.	Medium	Medium
Send it to relevant journalists.	Easy	Low
Send it to relevant bloggers.	Easy	Low
Get it mentioned in channel partner newsletters.	Easy	Low
Post it on free white paper sites.	Easy	Low
Create a slide deck.	Medium	Low
Send your slide deck to your sales force (if any).	Easy	Low
Send your slide deck to your channel partners (if any).	Easy	Low

Of course, delving into the details on any one of these topics — like e-mail marketing, LinkedIn, or Twitter — could easily fill another book or two. Check out www.dummies.com for titles on all the promotions touched on in this chapter and more.

This list can hit only a few highlights and remind you about some possible tactics you may have forgotten or never considered. You can always flip through this chapter whenever you launch any new white paper to remind yourself of some other possibilities that you haven't tried yet.

 A marketer's job is never finished. No matter how much you do, you can always do more. Don't let these lists overwhelm you. Perhaps plan to accomplish all the must-do's, and then pick a number of the most promising options from Table 16-3, and ignore all the rest.

Table 16-3   Optional White Paper Promotional Tactics

Tactic	Difficulty	Cost
Mention it in your e-mail sig line.	Easy	Low
Mention it on your LinkedIn page.	Easy	Low
Mention it on your Google+ page.	Easy	Low
Sponsor a podcast.	Medium	Medium
Sponsor a video chat.	Medium	Medium
Send it to relevant analysts.	Easy	Low
Submit a guest post to relevant blogs.	Medium	Low
Post it on channel partner websites.	Easy	Low
Get it mentioned in industry association newsletters.	Hard	Low
Post it on industry association websites, portals, or forums.	Medium	Low
Submit it to trade magazines.	Medium	Low
Syndicate it through a content network.	Easy	High
Create a self-running presentation.	Medium	Low
Post your slide deck online.	Easy	Low
Use your slide deck for a webinar.	Hard	Medium
Give a presentation at an industry conference.	Hard	High
Give out hard copies at trade shows and events.	Easy	Medium
Give out soft copies on flash drives at events.	Easy	High
Use it as a conversation starter.	Hard	High
Use it as a leave-behind.	Hard	High
Set up a Google AdWords pay-per-click campaign.	Medium	Medium
Make an online display ad campaign.	Hard	High
Advertise in trade magazines.	Medium	High

Beginning your promotion at home

The first step in publishing a white paper is to post it on your website where people can find it. You must immediately create an effective landing page for the white paper, make as big a splash as you can on your company's home page, and tell all your closest subscribers and prospects about it. This section provides a few tips on each of these tactics.

Create a landing page with an abstract (must do)

You need a web page to be the go-to page where interested readers can find the white paper. Don't clutter the page with a lot of extra text, side offers, or the company boilerplate. Focus on one thing: Getting visitors to download the white paper. On this page, nothing else matters.

Here are the basic elements of an effective landing page:

- **Short, fixed URL:** Keep the URL of the landing page short so people can type it in if they see it offline. Make the URL fixed so it won't change in the future. And include this URL in the action step for every other promotion.

- **Thumbnail and abstract or executive summary:** To show prospects what they'll get, include a thumbnail of the cover. Provide a brief abstract of the white paper contents, focused on the benefits an ideal reader will derive from it. Or include the entire executive summary to give visitors a good preview of the contents.

- **Registration form:** If you want visitors to register before they can download the white paper, include a registration form right on the landing page. Don't ask for too much info; name, company name, e-mail, and zip code are plenty to start. Research shows that the more fields you ask for, the fewer people register. Just because your CRM system has many fields for every prospect, don't expect someone looking for a white paper to type all those in for you.

Feature it prominently on your website (must do)

Show your white paper on your company's home page; the bigger and bolder, the better. Of course, the larger the company, the harder it can be to command space on the corporate site. If you can do it, feature the cover of the white paper to build more appeal. Direct interested visitors from your home page to your landing page with a single click on the thumbnail.

Mention it in company newsletters (must do)

If you have an e-newsletter you send to a house list of subscribers, mention the white paper in it. Perhaps highlight some intriguing factoid to get people's attention. You can safely mention the same white paper in a couple of issues in a row; any more and it can start to sound stale.

Using cost-effective e-mail

E-mail is a wonderfully low-cost way to get your message out — if you use it carefully. You can mention the white paper in your e-mail signature, and e-mail a compelling message about it to your sales force, channel partners, and house list of opt-in friends and prospects. In every e-mail, point to the landing page so your recipients can always find the document and also forward your e-mail to others. This section provides a few tips on each of these tactics.

E-mail your sales force and channel partners (must do)

You must let your sales force know about the white paper and how their prospects can benefit from reading it. Then let them continue to spread the word and distribute the white paper to their contacts.

By the same token, you must let all your channel partners know about the white paper. Even if a few of your partners are "frenemies" who sometimes compete and sometimes cooperate with your company, let them know about the white paper.

E-mail your house opt-in list (must do)

Maybe you already e-mailed your house opt-in list with your e-newsletter. If you have a separate house list for friends, clients, prospects, former employees, or other stakeholders, you should tell them all about the white paper.

Sending one e-mail isn't enough. Not everyone opens every e-mail that you send. Many people, even though they're interested, may be on the road, distracted, or just too busy to get around to it the day it pops up in their inbox. So resend the same e-mail to everyone who didn't open it the first time. Presto! You'll likely double the open rate for your message.

Mention it in your e-mail sig line (optional)

Insert a few words in your signature line about the white paper, including a link to the landing page, and use it for the next month or so. This tactic is extremely low effort and low cost. If everyone on your marketing team adds a line in his signature, you can reach thousands of stakeholders and prospects. I call this tactic optional only because you may already be using your sig line for other purposes, your company may have a standard format you can't deviate from, or your sig line may already be long enough.

Talking it up through social media

Social media provides a powerful medium for promoting your content, engaging an audience, and developing prospects. To use social media to promote your white paper, write several blog posts about it, tweet it on Twitter for weeks, mention it on your company LinkedIn and Google+ pages (if any), and tactfully announce it to any relevant LinkedIn groups. You can also use it as the basis for creating a talk radio podcast and a talk show video. This section provides a few tips on each of these tactics.

Tweet it on Twitter (must do)

No matter what you think of Twitter, this tactic is a must-do because it's so quick and low cost. In a series of tweets, stress the title, the benefits of reading the white paper, and any unique factoids or provocative statements that it contains. With a free service like HootSuite (www.hootsuite.com), you can write a month's worth of tweets in an hour or two. And not every tweet has to be unique; many Twitter users repeat the same tweets every week or so without losing their followers.

Blog about it (must do)

You can turn any white paper into several blog posts. For example, every key feature and benefit in a backgrounder can become a separate blog post. A numbered list can be stripped down for a post that directs readers to the full white paper for details on each point. And a problem/solution can be broken into four blog posts: the industry-wide problem, the drawbacks of traditional solutions, the new and improved solution, and what to look for in an ideal solution. If you stir up any debate so that people start to comment and argue, you can fan the flames to carry on the discussion, always pointing back to the landing page for the white paper that started all the fuss.

Announce it to LinkedIn Groups (must do)

If you're not already following certain LinkedIn Groups that deal with your market space, you should be. After you follow any group for a while, you get to know its culture. Then you can tactfully announce the white paper in a way that fits each group. This tactic is a must-do for a problem/solution white paper that contains truly educational content.

Mention it on your LinkedIn and Google+ pages (optional)

If your business has a company LinkedIn or Google+ page, announce the white paper there. If not, think about whether these pages would make sense for your business.

Most B2B marketers don't bother with Facebook for one simple reason: Most people use Facebook to keep in touch with other people. Few people use it to research B2B products and services. Instead, they use Google+, LinkedIn, professional forums, trade magazines, and journals. Unless you have compelling evidence that your target B2B audience is on Facebook, actively comparing notes about their B2B purchases, don't waste your time with it. Don't listen to stories about what companies like Coca-Cola (B2C) and Intel ($$$) are doing on Facebook, and why you should be there, too. Keep your eye on the prize: B2B sales, not Facebook "likes."

Sponsor a podcast (optional)

Do you have any subject matter experts or executives who can present the ideas in the white paper in an especially interesting way? Think about interviewing them in a talk radio format and recording your conversation as a podcast. You can distribute this podcast on your website as a streaming and downloadable MP3. A little music at the start and end and a lead-in like a radio announcer make it sound more professional. And a podcast doesn't have to be long; 10 or 15 minutes should do nicely. At the end, give the URL of the full white paper several times, like how radio ads repeat the phone number of a local business so you can remember it or jot it down.

Sponsor a video chat or vlog (optional)

If you can do an audio, why not try a video? Find some willing guests and a good host from your team, and you can create a pseudo-talk show segment about the ideas in the white paper. Of course, creating the talk show set, arranging good lighting, and even doing some makeup so your guests don't look like they're sweating under an interrogation lamp all takes effort. But doing these things is less costly than it was a few years ago, and seasoned videographers are available to help in most cities, if you need one.

This video should be lighter in tone than a podcast, so try to generate some laughs. And it should likely run only five or ten minutes max. You can edit out any slow bits to keep up the pace. Run the URL of the landing page across the screen several times throughout the show, like an infomercial showing a 1-800-BUY-NOW number. And then post your video to your website and YouTube channel (if any).

Getting it to the influencers

Some people are influencers who can reach a wide circle of readers or followers. To help reach these people, you need to publish a press release and send it along with the white paper to any analysts, bloggers, or journalists who cover your space. You can also submit guest posts to any blogs that accept them. This section provides a few tips on each of these tactics.

Publish a press release (must do)

Every white paper deserves a press release, which can be as simple as a one-page announcement that a white paper on such-and-such a topic is now available from such-and-such URL. Emphasize the intriguing elements of the content and the benefits to the target reader. Give the release itself a snappy headline, maybe some spinoff from the white paper's title. Then spend a few hundred dollars to send it out through an online press release syndication service; that's worth it.

Send a package to relevant journalists (must do)

You do maintain a list of all the journalists who cover your market space, right? If not, start building one now. That exercise may take a day or more, but having such a list (and keeping it up-to-date) is worth it. When you have this list, send your press release and white paper to each journalist and editor through the appropriate channel:

✔ Use **courier** for major journalists and columnists working for leading business publications or websites.

✔ Use **express post** for medium-level journalists working for medium-level trade magazines and websites.

✔ Use **e-mail** for everyone else on your list, including any journalists who are minor, over-the-hill, or actively hostile to your company. Don't expect them to look at it.

Then continue to engage with the most promising and receptive journalists, patiently. Don't phone them up and ask whether they got your white paper and are going to write about it. They hate that! Pestering most journalists makes them less likely to write about your company. Ideally, your white paper is so intriguing and thought-provoking that they'll mention it, or at least keep your company in mind for a mention in the near future.

Having worked as a journalist for many years, I can tell you that e-mail is a terrible way to distribute anything to the media. When I was editing a software industry newsletter, I was swamped with e-mails from morning to night, at least 200 a day, and often more. No white paper ever stands out in that kind of tsunami. But when someone sent me a package by courier or express post, I sat up and took notice. And when a handful of companies actually sent me a bottle of wine at Christmas, I remembered them — heck, I'm only human. That's not to say you can bribe your way to better coverage. But at least you can rise above the thousands of other companies whose marketing teams do nothing more imaginative than click Send.

Send your white paper to relevant bloggers (must do)

If you don't already maintain a list of all the top bloggers who cover your market space, start building one now. That exercise will take time, especially if you get lost in reading their past posts and seeing who else they link to. When you have this list, send your press release and white paper to the relevant bloggers by e-mail. First, you may want to have someone on your team start following their blog and posting relevant comments so they recognize your company name. Then follow up with bloggers who show the most interest.

Some blogs accept guest posts that would interest their audience. If you think a post based on your white paper matches the interests of any blogger in particular, query him about submitting a guest blog. He may jump at the chance to have someone else provide some professionally written content that's on topic for his audience.

Send a package to relevant analysts (optional)

Another list you, and every B2B marketing team, should build is for all the analysts who cover your market space. You have no guarantee that any analyst actually follows your niche, so locate the closest or most interested ones, even if that takes calling them up one by one. When you have this list, send your press release and white paper to the relevant analysts by snail mail. To them, this material will likely be "deep background," so speed isn't critical. Then stay in touch with the most receptive analysts.

Promoting it through third parties

Another fabulous way to get any white paper out there is to promote it through third parties with whom you have some natural connection. You can arrange to post the white paper on the websites of your channel partners and get it mentioned in their newsletters. Similarly, try to get it posted on the websites of any related industry associations, portals, or forums, and mentioned in their newsletters. You can also submit it to relevant trade magazines as an opinion piece or guest column. And, of course, post it on any white paper sites that aggregate content for no fee. This section provides a few tips on each of these tactics.

Get it mentioned in channel partner newsletters (must do)

If any of your channel partners publish a regular e-newsletter, they may be willing to publish a notice about your white paper with a link to your landing page. They always need relevant content and announcements for their subscribers, so they may welcome your request to mention or link to your white paper. You should probably write up an item for them so it takes absolutely no effort for them to publish, and all the details are accurate.

Post it on free white paper sites (must do)

A certain number of websites aggregate content aimed at particular markets, where you can post the white paper for no charge. And all the commercial syndication services like KnowledgeStorm (www.knowledgestorm.com), TechTarget (www.techtarget.com), and Ziff Davis (www.ziffdavis.com) have free services where you can submit a white paper. Posting on these sites is worth doing; you never know who may find your white paper on one of those sites.

Post it on channel partner websites (optional)

If any of your channel partners have a website with a place for content like white papers — or even if they don't — that can be a likely place to announce your white paper and attract good prospects.

Some partners may be okay with using your landing page, while others want any prospects to register with their site to get your content. You don't necessarily want to help another company, even a channel partner, build up their list by using your content. Try to negotiate some way to access the list of people who download your white paper, or create a special version of that white paper with a call to action that brings readers back only to your site for the next step.

Get it mentioned in industry association newsletters (optional)

Most industry associations publish some form of newsletter or e-newsletter, and they always need news and relevant content for their subscribers. Ask whether you can get your white paper mentioned in their newsletter. You should probably write up a draft announcement so it's even less effort for them, and all the details are letter-perfect.

Post it on industry association websites, portals, or forums (optional)

Many websites devoted to a certain market niche publish white papers that interest their visitors. Most of these sites likely want to post your content themselves, and you have less bargaining strength than with one of your own channel partners. After all, they're doing you a favor by putting your content in front of their audience of likely prospects. You may be able to negotiate a free mention in their e-newsletter or something similar in return for your content. And you may want to create a special version of that white paper with a call to action that brings readers back to your site only for the next step.

Submit it to trade magazines (optional)

Do you follow any trade magazines that you believe would be interested in publishing the white paper, or portions of it, as an opinion piece or guest column? Familiarize yourself with the publication before you approach it. You can read through six months' worth of back issues or check out the media kit, which describes the mission and audience of the publication. For more discussion on how to approach a trade magazine editor about repurposing a white paper, see Chapter 8.

Syndicate it through a content network (optional)

If you have the budget and you really want major exposure, you can arrange to syndicate the white paper through a content network like KnowledgeStorm, TechTarget, or Ziff Davis. You may have to pay a setup fee, and you'll certainly pay for every lead you receive. These fees can quickly add up to thousands of dollars. Larger companies use these services all the time to generate leads to qualify and nurture through the sales funnel. A certain number of these leads must eventually turn into sales, because these companies continue to use these services. But let the buyer beware: You need deep pockets to use this tactic.

Using a slide deck

Any flavor of white paper can be readily transformed into a slide deck, giving you another piece of content to promote. When your deck is complete, you can share it with your sales force and channel partners and post it online on several slide-sharing sites. You can even use your slides to create a webinar or a presentation at an industry conference or event. This section provides a few tips on each of these tactics.

Create a slide deck (must do)

A slide deck makes a natural complement to a white paper: If the white paper is the ice cream, the slide deck is the cone that supports and presents it. For a backgrounder, each significant feature or benefit can fill one slide. For a numbered list, each point can inspire one or two slides. For a problem/solution, you can devote one or two slides to each section of the classic structure: a widespread problem, each traditional solution and its drawbacks, the new improved solution, and the buyer's guide. When the visuals are done, add speaker's notes to each slide so other users can provide more details about the content.

Send your slide deck to your sales force and channel partners (must do)

When your slide deck is complete with speaker's notes, send it to your sales force so they can use it to boost their own sales efforts. They'll likely study your presentation and even use some of the same phrasing. And they may well present your slide deck or some part of it to their prospects. This is a practical sales tool that you can distribute as a spinoff of your white paper.

Also send your slide deck with speaker's notes to all your channel partners. Doing so serves three purposes that should help motivate and retain your partners: reminds them about your company, helps train them on the problem your offering solves and its powerful features and benefits, and puts a good selling tool in their hands.

Create a self-running presentation (optional)

Think about recording the speaker's notes as voice-over narration so you can create a self-running presentation. You just need a good presenter with a pleasant voice who understands the content and a decent microphone. The final results can run off your website, from your YouTube channel, or from an unattended kiosk in your trade show booth.

Post your slide deck online (optional)

With or without narration, you can post your slide deck online on one of several slide-sharing sites. Although these sites are a long shot for attracting ideal leads, you never know. And the price is right — free. Four to get you started are Scribd (`www.scribd.com`), SlideShare (`www.slideshare.com`), SlideBoom (`www.slideboom.com`), and myBrainshark (`www.mybrain shark.com`).

Use your slide deck for a webinar (optional)

This tactic is ambitious, but it's a great way to repurpose a white paper and squeeze even more ROI out of it. You can use your slide deck with speaker's notes for an online webinar for prospects. This tactic does require certain infrastructure, some way to take online registrations, and webinar software to enable participants to see the slides, hear the audio, use chat to post questions during the show, and so on. You'll need to promote the webinar strongly for a few weeks.

And be prepared to follow up with those who registered but didn't attend. They're still interested; they just expect you to send them the recorded version to view in their own time. Make a recording of the webinar and give all the participants access to it. And, of course, put up that video on your YouTube channel.

Give a presentation at an industry conference (optional)

If your white paper is truly fresh and informative, ask to get on the agenda at an industry conference. You do keep a list of all the relevant conferences and events for your market space, right? If your proposal gets accepted, ask your company's best presenter to make the trip, and bring along a box of the white paper printed in color for handouts to those who come to the presentation. You can also write up this presentation in a trade journal or website devoted to your market space, generating even more PR.

Talking about it face to face

Be ready to give out hard copies of the white paper at any trade show or industry event that anyone from your sales or marketing team attends. And if these tactics make sense, your sales force can use the white paper as a conversation starter or leave-behind on sales calls. This section provides a few tips on each of these tactics.

Note that I label three of these four tactics as "high cost" in Table 16-3 because of the vast expense to exhibit at a trade show or get face time with an executive at a B2B prospect company. These expenses include flying across the country, renting a car, staying in a hotel, eating in restaurants, and all the other high costs of traveling. These costs can really drive up your cost-per-lead to an unsustainable level.

Give out hard copies at trade shows and events (optional)

Be armed and ready at any trade show or industry event that you or your team members plan to attend. Bring a box of white papers printed in color to put in your literature stands and give out to likely prospects. That expense is a minimal add-on to the many costs of exhibiting at a show.

Give out soft copies on flash drives at events (optional)

Another way to distribute a white paper at an event is to load it on a flash drive emblazoned with your logo. You can purchase flash drives in bulk for only a few dollars each, and the provider can copy your content onto each drive. Then you can give those out, the same way exhibitors used to give out CDs. But the typical caveat applies: Many casual passersby will grab a flash drive and then go home and give it to their kids without once looking at the contents. So you may want to hand them out sparingly and reserve them for serious prospects only.

Use it as a conversation starter (optional)

Your sales force can use the white paper to start conversations with likely prospects. In fact, a white paper gives a salesperson a perfect reason to reach out to the contacts they're trying to develop, to offer them some useful or educational content. This tactic is most useful for salespeople who work trade shows, make cold calls, network, or otherwise develop their own in-person appointments with prospects.

Use it as a leave-behind (optional)

A white paper can be left behind with prospects after a sales call, especially if it reinforces some of the topics discussed during that meeting. To really work well in this situation, it helps to have a whole library of white papers so that the salesperson can select precisely the one that fits the occasion best. Again, this tactic is useful only for salespeople who meet with prospects in person.

Advertising, online and offline

No doubt about it, advertising can be pricy. Not every company can afford it, and not every white paper deserves it. But if you're selling B2B systems worth millions of dollars and you routinely spend several hundred dollars for a qualified lead, advertise away! It still works for many businesses, especially those selling horizontally across many sectors, where the audience is harder to find than in a vertical market, which is easier to target.

Of course, you can advertise a white paper in many places, and this brief mention can't possibly deal with them all. Two main distinctions to remember: online versus offline advertising, and direct-response versus image advertising (or branding).

- ✔ *Online advertising* covers electronic media like the web, mobile devices, and e-mail, while *offline advertising* includes everything else: newspapers, magazines, radio, TV, the Yellow Pages, and so on. Online advertising is generally more targeted and instant, so you can see the ROI of your campaigns and adjust them within minutes. Offline advertising is generally more scattershot and slower, so you may be committed to running ads and paying for them long after you realize they're not generating any business.

- ✔ *Direct-response advertising* aims to generate a specific result, such as taking the next step in the sales cycle toward buying a product. *Image advertising* aims to promote a brand, without triggering any specific action. You want to use direct-response ads with a twist: Instead of encouraging viewers to buy, you want them to download your white paper. In this context, always advertise the content of the white paper, not the product, the brand, or the company.

From time to time, an ad salesperson may approach you with a "great opportunity" to buy space in some magazine, directory, or website at a big discount. This scenario is an opportunity only if you already decided that you want and need to advertise in that outlet. Otherwise, it's an opportunity to throw away some marketing dollars. Make a marketing plan and stick to it; don't get blown off course by every random deal that comes your way.

Set up a Google AdWords PPC campaign (optional)

If you believe good prospects will search for certain terms that exactly match your white paper, you can set up a pay-per-click (PPC) campaign through AdWords and start buying clicks.

AdWords isn't something you can master in an afternoon. A whole industry has grown up to advise companies how to design these campaigns. If someone on your team understands PPC and you have the budget to spare, by all means give it a try. Just don't forget to cap your monthly budget so you don't get stuck with any runaway costs. But if you've never tried PPC before, you should probably leave it alone until you've exhausted nearly every other option in this list.

Make an online display ad campaign (optional)

If you think PPC is out of this world, online display ads are out of this galaxy. In fact, I've never heard of any company taking out online display ads for a white paper. Maybe some do, and maybe this tactic will become the norm in the future. A cute little ad that pops up on a relevant web page, showing the cover of a white paper your prospect would be interested in — who wouldn't click on that? You may need to enlist the help of an interactive agency to get started and bring in some positive results. Again, if you have some expertise and a budget to experiment with, go ahead. But I would put this tactic near the bottom of the list.

Advertise in trade magazines (optional)

If your white paper speaks to a certain defined vertical market with its own trade magazines, you may want to consider advertising it in those magazines. You don't need a full page; you can buy one-quarter or one-eighth of a page and probably do just as well. You can run the same ad for several issues running, or maybe every issue for a whole year, if you're confident it will generate the kind of leads you're looking for at a cost-per-lead you can stomach. Again, use your ad to show the cover of the white paper, stress the benefits of reading it in a few short snippets of text, and emphasize the URL of the landing page.

Part V
The Part of Tens

Enjoy an additional *White Papers For Dummies* Part of Tens chapter for free at www.dummies.com/extras/whitepapers.

In this part . . .

- ✔ Get tips for avoiding ten common problems that can creep into your white papers.

- ✔ Discover best practices for designing an eye-catching white paper.

- ✔ Find suggestions for improving a white paper title.

Chapter 17

Ten White Paper Problems and How to Solve Them

*M*ost people like ice cream, but not everyone can whip up a tasty batch on his own. The same applies to white papers: Even though a marketing team may know what a white paper looks like, they can easily create a mess if they don't have a good recipe to follow and some experience developing effective content. Many white papers don't turn out well, often because they're missing some key ingredients or they weren't planned properly from the start.

In this chapter, I look at ten common problems that afflict many white papers today and how you can solve them. Fortunately, if you identify these issues in time, you can save your white paper from being passed over and pushed to the back of the freezer, never to be taken out and savored by any prospects.

Boring, Nondescript Title

Many potential B2B buyers first encounter your white paper as a short snippet in a list of search results with only its title to go by. How can a white paper with a boring title ever get noticed? You have to keep the title lively by doing one (or more) of the following:

- ✔ Use active verbs and numbers.
- ✔ Include the benefits to the reader.
- ✔ Pitch it to a specific job title.

✔ Suggest that it offers inside information, tips, or gotchas that readers need to know.

✔ Add urgency with time-specific words, like *now* or *today*.

You can even combine all these tips to create a winning title, such as "7 Things Every IT Director Must Do to Protect Your Network Today."

But don't just slap an intriguing title on a tired, worn-out document. That's as bad as calling a tub of freezer-burned, well-past-its-best-before-date vanilla a fresh batch of chocolate walnut-crunch. You can even call that false advertising. Instead, use the freshest research and the perfect recipe to whip up a white paper of the ideal flavor, and make sure it delivers on the promise of its title. For more tips on how to pump up a white paper title, see Chapter 19.

No Summary at the Start

Just about every executive today has too much to read, too much to remember, too much to do, and too much to think about. A white paper that doesn't ease into the content is like a pushy waiter who starts serving up ice-cream sundaes before even showing you the dessert menu.

Be polite. Help your readers decide in advance whether your white paper is what they want by providing an introduction, abstract, overview, or executive summary at the very start. In other words, "tell them what you're going to tell them." Give them a one-page summary with a brief recap of the key points covered in your white paper. They'll likely scan that much and then decide whether to go on. And even if they don't, at least you get your argument in front of them in a nutshell.

Some people say a summary is useless repetition, asking, "Why not just get on with your story?" But any teacher can tell you that a little repetition is a good thing that helps your message sink in. And any waiter knows you offer the dessert menu before you start dishing out banana splits.

No Conclusions at the End

Echoing your summary at the start, every white paper should include some brief conclusions at the end. But why? Isn't this just more useless repetition? No, providing an introduction at the start and conclusions at the end are well-established conventions in many forms of communication. These elements apply perfectly well to white papers, too. In the executive summary, you tell your readers what you're going to tell them; in the main body, you tell them; and in the conclusions, you tell them what you told them.

The conclusions are especially useful for busy executives who flip to the back of your document to see "the bottom line." If you repeat your key take-away messages in a few short sentences at the end, that doubles the chances that those messages will get through. You work hard to get the right B2B prospects to download and review your white paper, so don't let them go without a suitable wrap-up. In fact, the conclusions to a white paper are like the cherry on top of an ice-cream sundae: a small touch that gives the whole dish a well-rounded sense of completeness.

No Call to Action

The final sentence of your conclusions should be your call to action, where you outline what you want your readers to do after they finish reading. You may suggest that they find out more about what they read, continue to engage with your company, or take the next step in the buying process. Here's an easy formula for creating a call to action:

> To find out more about how *[name of offering or company]* can help your *[business, organization, or team]* *[#1 benefit covered in white paper]*, *[do something]*.

The more specific the action you want your readers to take, the better results you get and the easier it is to track the outcome. This may mean that you set up a landing page, design a webinar, create an ROI calculator, or do something else to keep your readers interested. One white paper can't do it all. Ideally, a B2B vendor builds a multistep marketing campaign with all the appropriate content to draw prospects into the top of your sales funnel, nurture them through the middle, and pull them toward a sale at the bottom. The call to action in each of your white papers should urge readers to take the next step along that path.

Not the Right Length

Your white paper should make an impression in the first two or three pages. But that doesn't mean a two-page flyer can serve as an effective white paper. Such a short document just doesn't have enough room to deliver the kind of depth called for in a backgrounder or problem/solution. And if you do a short numbered list of just a page or two, it's more realistic to call it an "article" or "blog post," not a white paper.

For most business people, five to six pages (or 2,500 to 3,500 words) in the main body is about the right length for a backgrounder or numbered list. This length is enough to deliver your message, especially if you format it to be easy to scan. Use white space, bullets, tables — anything to break up the solid wall of gray text. For a backgrounder, technical people can often tolerate a longer white paper that offers more detail, even up to 25 or 30 pages. But in a problem/solution, if you run on much longer than 10 or 12 pages, you can lose a lot of your audience.

You can sidestep this problem by breaking up longer documents into separate white papers of five or six pages apiece, each on a more focused topic. Doing so gives you an added benefit: You get two or more chances to reach your target audience, instead of taking an "all or nothing" approach with a single document stuffed with too much information.

Sales Pitch in Disguise

Publishing a thinly veiled sales pitch labeled as a white paper is the worst practice in white papers today. Some lame-brained marketers even reformat glossy brochures with a less attractive look and call them "white papers." But this tactic is guaranteed to backfire. Every survey ever taken of B2B buyers says the same thing: White paper readers hate sales pitches. They hate any bait-and-switch games that a vendor plays. They hate wasting their time. If you advertise "triple-rich chocolate" but actually dish up skim-milk vanilla, your B2B prospects will quickly realize it, chuck aside your white paper, and think very poorly of your company.

An effective white paper helps a business reader understand an issue, solve a problem, or make a decision. Readers expect a white paper to provide useful information that helps them on the job. Jumping into a sales pitch irritates anyone looking for helpful, objective information. It can even kill your chance of staying on that prospect's list of possible vendors. So if you're writing a sales letter, call it a sales letter. If you're writing a brochure, call it a brochure, not a white paper. Don't let sales-y copywriting contaminate your white paper and turn it into a sales pitch that turns bitter on the tongues of all your prospects.

Not Enough Proof to Back Up Claims

Just because your CEO says something doesn't mean anyone else will believe it. Do you believe everything you hear? Just because your website makes some claim doesn't mean every visitor will accept it. Do you believe everything you find on the web? This problem is where many white papers fall down: Without enough solid facts to support their claims, they have no power to engage or persuade anyone about anything.

A white paper needs a good structure of supporting evidence: facts, figures, names, dates, places, statistics from impeccable sources, quotes from industry experts, and stories from happy clients. Think of this proof as the cone that gives the ice cream its support so it can stand tall. Without well-researched and convincing proof, a white paper is about as interesting as a puddle of ice cream melting on the sidewalk.

For more on finding and using convincing proof points, see Chapter 15.

Not Enough, or Not Good Enough, Graphics

Any white paper gains more flavor when you include at least one concept graphic to sum up its key points. You can be sure that almost every reader looks at the graphics as he scans through your document. And nearly everyone can grasp a picture faster and remember it better than text. But for many marketing people and writers, coming up with effective graphics can be tough. Fortunately, you have options.

You may be able to find some appropriate graphics in-house and tweak them for your purposes. Make sure to simplify lines and boxes flying off in all directions, the way most engineers sketch. And redo any tired PowerPoints. Draw all the colors from the same palette, perhaps one that harmonizes well with your company logo. If you can't find what you need and you have a few dollars in your budget, you can sketch out your ideas and then give your rough sketches to a professional artist to create more finished versions.

If budget is an issue, you can find affordable photos on a site like iStockphoto (www.istockphoto.com), which is well indexed and overflowing with possibilities. Or try SmartDraw (www.smartdraw.com), the easy-to-use graphic software intended for business professionals. For more about SmartDraw, see Chapter 15. One final suggestion: Test out each graphic on a few people from your target audience. If they don't understand it, go back to the drawing board for another revision.

No Logical Flow of Ideas

To help a problem/solution white paper linger in the mind like chocolate lingers on the taste buds, you need an effective flow of ideas. If your white paper has no overall design to hold it together, few readers will find it compelling or memorable, especially if they "read" with a typical skim-scan-and-skip approach.

Try one of the following tried-and-true methods for building a logical argument, dating back to the ancient Greeks.

- ✔ Start with the known, and then delve into the unknown.
- ✔ Start with the past, describe the present, and project into the future.
- ✔ Start with an overview and drill down to the details.
- ✔ Start with the most important and move to the least important.
- ✔ Start at the beginning of a process and follow it step by step to the end.

For more specifics on how to structure a problem/solution white paper, see Chapter 8. A backgrounder or a numbered list can be more modular, with less need for a tight logical argument connecting A to B. But even so, you can't afford to skip all over randomly. You need to use the same level of detail throughout. Your readers can absorb your points better when you express each section or numbered point with a parallel structure (using the same grammatical form). Whatever you do, find an appropriate logical structure and stick to it.

Not Written by the Right Person

Many white papers are written by people who never asked for the job and don't feel comfortable doing it. Sure, most product managers, developers, or salespeople can jot down a few notes for a white paper. But with no prior knowledge of what to include and what to leave out, their work will likely be incomplete and not very tasty for your B2B prospects — as though you let an inexperienced chef into the kitchen to whip up a batch of ice cream with no idea how to do it.

Instead, find a professional writer or editor who specializes in white papers, if possible, to write, or at least review, your white paper. This person can be from your own company or from an outside firm. As I discuss in Part III of this book, your marketing team should be involved in the planning and promotion of your white paper, but not necessarily in the production.

You're likely better served by hiring a white paper expert from outside to complete that stage, in close consultation with you. This approach can save time, money, and frustration. Sure, you may already have full-time engineers or product managers on the payroll, but surveys show that they work much slower than experienced writers, with more false starts, hesitation, and scrap. All the salary and overhead an employee sinks into struggling to do a white paper can easily cost more than the fee for an outside writer who gets down to work and finishes up quickly.

Before you publish your white paper, have a professional writer or editor review it to make sure your draft isn't suffering from any of the problems identified in this chapter. Doing so is like inviting a real chef into the kitchen to taste and perfect your concoction before you inflict it on any of your patrons.

Chapter 18

Ten Tips on Designing a White Paper

*N*othing undermines a good white paper faster than poor design. No matter how compelling and persuasive the text may be, if people can't read it because of a poor design, they'll quickly move on. Then all your effort and expense are for nothing.

In this chapter, I provide ten down-to-earth tips for anyone designing a white paper. If you're not sure how to design a white paper or you've never done one before, read on. If you're a marketing manager who needs to direct a designer to format your white paper, this is for you. If you're a white paper writer stuck trying to use Word to turn out respectable-looking pages, you've just hit pay dirt.

Design to Enhance the Content

A white paper is somewhere between a marketing piece and a scholarly essay, so it's quite different from anything you've ever designed before. A white paper isn't a brochure, so it shouldn't be as slick and colorful as one. But it needs to be more appealing than your father's business report. Think of a page from a magazine, like *Scientific American* or *Vanity Fair,* or the front part of an annual report, before all the numbers. That kind of crisp, elegant editorial design is what to shoot for with your white paper.

As you know, the texture of your typography and the look and feel of your pages have a powerful subliminal effect on your readers. Type too small to read easily, awkward page breaks, and even useless hyphens (all of which I discuss later in this chapter) give a poor impression of the skill and attention that went into the document. If readers think your white paper has a sloppy design, they may not even finish reading it, and they're much less likely to take any action based on its recommendations.

Effective design enhances the content of the white paper instead of drawing attention to itself. Your design must add value and clarity to that content instead of adding distractions or hurdles to legibility. Let the white paper's message shine out from your pages, the same way a fine wine glows inside a crystal goblet. The goblet doesn't exist to aggrandize itself; its prime purpose is to contain and showcase the wine.

Consider Your Readers' Eyesight

Most people's eyes begin to change in their 40s, and they start to need larger type to read comfortably. By coincidence, most B2B white papers are aimed at business decision makers, most of whom are in their 40s and older. And many people this age prefer to read on paper, so they likely print out a white paper rather than read it on-screen. Younger designers, take note: You're not designing white papers for yourself and your peers; you're designing for older people.

That means forget gray text and color backgrounds. Black text on a white background has been the standard for legibility for hundreds of years; why change it? Forget 9-point type. Bump up the body size type to 10 or 11 points; it's free. So what if your text spills to another page or two? Forget page-long paragraphs, with every line crammed into the next. Respect the paragraph breaks the writer used and don't eliminate them. Then leave a few points of white space after each paragraph to let it breathe. And if you see a paragraph running half a page long, ask the writer to break it into several shorter paragraphs. Give your older readers' eyes some relief, even if you think that makes the text look almost comically too large.

Realize That Text Isn't a Graphic

One crazy thing I've noticed about many designers — and this is certainly crazy from a writer's point of view — is that they treat text like a graphic, like a photo, diagram, or block of color. They never read it, so they don't realize that in a white paper, the text *is* the content.

Don't just pour in the text around everything else, like it's gray goo that's supposed to ooze into all the spaces between the headings and pictures. Don't look at a page like an industrial design, where all the chunks need to more or less balance each other. Look at your pages as text-driven content, where your challenge is to make the text as inviting and easy to read or scan as in any magazine you pick up — any magazine, mind you, aimed at people in their 40s and older.

 As a white paper designer, your goal is to do effective editorial design, not display design. Display is for advertising, packaging, Web splash pages, and retail store windows. Editorial design is for pages to be read, like in magazines and books. Here's a tip: Try actually reading your pages after you design them. If that's so hard that you want to stop reading, take a hint and redo that page to make the text easier to read.

Make Every Page Count

I once downloaded a white paper from a major software firm that was almost two-thirds overhead. Seven out of 11 pages were front and back matter, the "wrapper" around the content! Sure, every white paper needs a little front and back matter, just like a sandwich needs two slices of bread to hold it together, but when the front and back matter add up to nearly two-thirds of a white paper, something is terribly wrong. It's like a sandwich with three pieces of bread piled on both the top and the bottom. That makes it hard to find the actual filling, hard to chew, and hard to digest.

One of my pet peeves is leaving a page completely blank, or even worse, inserting a blank page covered in nothing but some theme color. Some misguided software templates lay out a white paper like a two-sided book, with a blank page on the back of the front cover and a back cover to tie it all together. Forget it! Most B2B buyers either look at your white paper on-screen or print it out single sided. Those other pages are just a waste of time and money.

Imagine all the people printing your white paper with those extra pages. You've just wasted hundreds or thousands of pieces of paper covered with very expensive ink or toner. Even if people view your document on-screen, you've still given them an empty expanse to scroll through. And for what? Absolutely nothing of any value. So be sure to compress the front and back matter, cut the worthless blank pages, and make every page count.

Control Page Breaks

Another one of my pet peeves in white paper design is awkward page breaks, such as the one in Figure 18-1. It's as though no one was paying any attention to the flow of the content and just dumped it mindlessly onto the pages. Why would anyone start a major section at the very bottom of a page, with only a line or two of text after it?

In this case, the new section is also smack up against a footnote, which is crammed up against the footer. Isn't all that rather jarring and unnecessary? There's nothing wrong with leaving a little white space at the end of a major section. Just start the new section on a new page. After all, your readers know how to flip a page or scroll down the screen. They've been doing it for many years.

cost of handling, downloading, reading, and filing all this paperwork is astronomical. Over the years, this cost has been calculated by various studies from $21 to $49 per printed page.[3] Certainly, this adds up to a huge expense yet contributes questionable value to the business results of the enterprise.

"Worst Practices" in Paper Handling

Consultants confirm that most enterprises continue to implement many proven "worst practices" in handling

3: Sue Stinsen, "The High Costs of Handling Paper," Harvard Business Journal, March 2012, pp 41-45

Slaying the Paper-Burden Dragon   www.acmescanomatic.com   *page 2*

Figure 18-1:
An awkward
page break.

Illustration courtesy of Gordon Graham

Adding more white space and pushing the new section to the next page, shown in Figure 18-2, makes this page look much better. That little fix costs nothing but a few seconds of thought. But that white space gives readers a momentary visual and mental break and helps them understand the structure of the document.

cost of handling, downloading, reading, and filing all this paperwork is astronomical. Over the years, this cost has been calculated by various studies from $21 to $49 per printed page.[3] Certainly, this adds up to a huge expense yet contributes questionable value to the business results of the enterprise.

3: Sue Stinsen, "The High Costs of Handling Paper," Harvard Business Journal, March 2012, pp 41-45

Slaying the Paper-Burden Dragon   www.acmescanomatic.com   *page 2*

Figure 18-2:
An improved
page break.

Illustration courtesy of Gordon Graham

Avoid a Wall of Gray

Some designers have the idea that a white paper is supposed to be serious, and by that, they think "a wall of gray." They think all they have to do is just pour the text into the pages and be done with it. Any white paper with text formatted as a wall of gray may look serious, but it won't invite anyone to read it.

 You can break up a wall of gray in many ways. Use the free text enhancements — boxes, bullets, callouts, headings, lines, shading, sidebars, tables, and so on. Look through your white paper and make sure that nearly every page has a major visual break, such as a callout, a graphic, a sidebar in a tinted box, or a table. And make sure that every single page has several smaller enhancements, such as bullets or headings. These visual breaks provide welcome eye relief for your readers and help highlight the key messages of each page.

Leave Lots of White Space

Another symptom of the wall-of-gray approach is teensy-tiny, itsy-bitsy, little margins around the text. It's as though someone told the designer that if he lets the document run any longer than six pages, he'll be taken out for electroshock. So the designer crams in all the text with next to no white space at the top, bottom, or edges — breaking all the rules of editorial design.

For example, the classic advice is to limit any horizontal line of type to about 12 words or 66 characters max. That applies both on-screen and on paper. Then why do some white paper designers run a line of type all the way from one edge of the page to the other? Why do they try to squeeze 100 or more characters into every line? Long horizontal lines of type are hard for readers' eyes to scan and tough for their brains to process. If you format a white paper with minimal white space, you'll lose most of your readers. Again, white space is free. So what if your final document is eight or ten pages long? If the content is compelling and the design is inviting, your readers won't mind.

Avoid Smug Shots

So you're looking for a stock shot for a white paper. That's a fine way to break up the wall of gray. But by all means, skip the shots of the beautiful people wearing impeccable suits hunched over a pristine PC or shaking hands in some foyer drenched in sunlight. Everyone knows those are fake, posed shots. Where was the last office you saw where everyone looked like a model and dressed like royalty? Pick photos that show average-looking people wearing typical clothes, doing something a little more interesting than shaking hands or peering at computer screens.

For example, does your product ever get used outside? If so, try to work in a nature shot. Does your service ever touch on transportation, manufacturing, or healthcare? Find a photo of a giant earthmover, or sparks flying in a factory, or a nurse tending to someone in a hospital bed. Those settings are far more interesting than your typical "smug shot" of beautiful people in a sunny office.

Control Hyphenation

Most software does a terrible job of hyphenating English. If you let it, it will break words like *sy-stem, Or-acle,* and *Ac-me.* If any old-school typographers saw those monstrosities, they'd turn over in their graves. Traditional typography called for at least four letters before any hyphen and at least three letters carried to the second line. Most typographers wouldn't hyphenate a word with fewer than six letters. So don't rely on automated hyphenation, and leave your text ragged right. Then scan your right margins, and if you see a major white space that you absolutely must eliminate, take two seconds to insert a manual hyphen.

You can split a word by its sounds, syllables, or root words. I like to use some combination of all three, and, if possible, create recognizable root words by inserting optional hyphens. For example, in the word *thankfully,* the most sensible places to put a hyphen are *thank-fully* or *thankful-ly.* This simple tactic builds readability instead of tearing it down with meaningless breaks like *than-kfully* or *thankf-ully.*

Never break the name of your company or any of your products with a hyphen. That leads to horrors such as *Ac-me* or *ScanO-Matic.* That's just not done. Most software has a way for you to include those words on a list of terms that are never hyphenated.

Refine a Corporate Template

Some companies have a corporate template that they expect all designers to follow. These layouts may be perfect for a press release, an internal business report, or a data sheet, but they're not always ideal for a white paper. Some of the guidelines I dispense in this chapter may conflict directly with the official company template. Then what? Well, standards do evolve, and they can be changed.

If you feel strongly that the corporate template detracts from the readability and undermines the white paper content, make your views known. If you have the scope, make up two versions of the white paper: one following the existing template and another with your recommended changes. Circulate both versions to your team, your customer advisory board, and your manager. Look into the research on readability. Get a second opinion from an experienced designer or a white paper expert. Ask me; I'll be happy to give you my two cents' worth. I hope good sense and good taste prevail and your corporate template is refined to present your white paper in the best possible format.

Chapter 19

More Than Ten Ways to Spice Up a White Paper Title

. . . .

. . . .

Your white paper title can make or break it. Think of your title as the menu listing for an ice-cream sundae. Which item would you likely order: "chocolate sundae with fudge sauce" or "Chocolate Mountain Volcano with Hot Fudge Lava"? Me, I'm climbing that mountain!

In the same way, you must add a little flair to your white paper title. As you know, B2B buyers routinely do their own research and scan pages of search results to find useful information. Your white paper title is often all that prospects have to go on to make their decision about whether to download or read your white paper. If your title falls flat, they'll skip right past it, meaning that all the effort you put into creating that document was a waste. Anything you can do to make your title more compelling to your target audience can have a dramatic effect on your white paper's success.

Consider this extremely ho-hum title for a white paper:

> "Roundup of Advanced Capabilities of Late-Model Scanners: A White Paper from Acme Software"

Would you download that? Not likely. In this chapter, I show you ten (or so) possible ways to strengthen such a weak title and help your white paper succeed.

Stressing the Benefits to Readers

Almost anyone who sees your white paper title in a list of search results asks, "Why should I spend my valuable time reading this? What's in it for me?" Why not tell your readers explicitly what they'll gain from reading your white paper, right in your title? That's probably the single best way to strengthen a weak white paper title. If you don't, do you expect them to read between the lines or use their psychic powers to intuit your intentions?

The classic business benefits that interest most executives include

- Making money
- Saving money
- Saving labor
- Cutting waste
- Streamlining processes
- Eliminating processes
- Any other way to "run lean and mean" or "do more with less"

The classic technical benefits that interest executives include

- Automating processes
- Controlling IT costs
- Avoiding mistakes or rework
- Overcoming constraints or trade-offs
- Linking smoothly with existing systems
- Any other way to contribute to the company's strategic objectives instead of just "keeping the lights on"

Here are two possible new titles, one highlighting business benefits and the other a key technical benefit:

"Save Time and Money with Today's New Generation of Scanners"

"Automate Your Filing with Today's New Generation of Scanners"

Using Active Verbs, Not Passive Labels

Our boring title is a passive label, full of bland nouns and ho-hum adjectives that just sit there like a frozen lump of fat, sugar, and chemicals. You need to add some heat and deliciousness with active verbs that propel your title up the list of search engine results. Here are two possible improvements, using more active verbs:

> "Saving Time and Money with Unattended Scanning"

> "Slaying the Paper-Burden Monster with Automated Filing"

 Notice how both examples start with a verb gerund that ends in *-ing*. This tried-and-true format suggests taking action in the present. Don't project your readers into the future or drag them back to the past with your verb endings. After all, there's no time like the present: Carpe diem!

Identifying Your Target Reader

Naming your target audience by a specific job title helps B2B buyers see whether your white paper is truly aimed at them. The simplest way to add a job title is to use a subtitle, as in "A Special Report for CFOs." You can even work in two job titles if you're careful, as in "A Special Report for IT and Finance Executives." In this case, always list your primary audience first and your secondary one last.

 Never try to address more than two different roles, or your title starts to sound pretty clumsy. If you have three distinct audience segments, you may be better off creating three separate "clones" of the same basic content, tweaked to include suitable jargon for each role. Then show the appropriate job title for each version of your document, as in the following examples:

> "A Special Report for IT Executives"

> "A Special Report for Finance Executive"

> "A Special Report for HR Executives"

Converting a Weak Title to a Subtitle

What if your boss or some high-powered reviewer wants to use a title that you think isn't effective? Will all your hard work come to naught because of a few ill-chosen words on the white paper cover? Thankfully, a simple solution exists: Knock down the weaker title to a subtitle, and insert your more powerful wording as the main title. That way, everyone ends up more or less happy.

Consider the weak title "The Scans Have It." This title provides no benefit to the reader, no active verbs, no target job title, no connection to much of anything at all. But suppose your VP loves that title, and there's no talking him out of it. Simply knock that title down to the subtitle and put something far more effective in front of it, perhaps something like this:

"Saving Time and Money with Today's New Generation of Scanners: The Scans Have It"

If you're lucky, your target readers will click on your title before they even notice those final words.

Why Not Try a Question?

Don't you love a good question in a white paper title? Isn't that an intriguing way to challenge readers? Can you ever go wrong with a question for a title? I could go on, right? But you get the point, eh? Turning a weak title into a question can give it an engaging twist:

"Is Your Firm Getting Crushed by Paper Burden?"

"Today's New Generation of Scanners: Are They Up to Snuff?"

"Are Competitors Eating Your Lunch with Automated Scanning?"

Recasting Your Paper As a Numbered List

Any number sounds more precise than any qualifier. "I had a temperature of 103" sounds more scientific than "I was burning up from a really bad fever." See if you can think of some way to work a number into your title.

Of course, if you plan all along to write a numbered list, the title will simply fall into your lap like a gift. If, instead, you find yourself with a boring title and a ho-hum document done in another flavor, you may be able to recast it as a numbered list mash-up. Think about all the commonplace patterns that occur in everyday life as well as pop culture: three coins in the fountain, four strong winds, five easy pieces, six feet under, seven deadly sins. Even if you didn't plan it that way, you may be able to reorganize your white paper around a set of numbers that give it new vigor. Doing so can involve some rewriting, but it can pay off with a much more compelling document. Consider titles like these:

"4 Little-Known Ways to Save Time with Automated Scanning"

"5 Benefits of Today's Fifth-Generation Scanners"

"6 Tips on Unattended Scanning and Automated Filing"

Using "How to" Phrasing

Western civilization, and especially America, is a can-do society that values know-how. Just try Googling the phrase *how to* to see the popularity of this little phrase; I got more than 3.5 billion hits! You can insert "how to" in front of almost any phrase and see that it works just fine. After all, your white paper is supposed to help readers learn *how to* understand an issue, solve a problem, or make a decision. Here are a couple examples:

"How to Save Time and Money with Today's New Generation of Scanners"

"How to Gain from Unattended Scanning and Automated Filing"

Leaving Out Product Names

Unless you're writing a backgrounder to explain the features and benefits of a particular offering, never use a product name in the title of your white paper. Including a product name in a white paper title will cut downloads by 50 percent or more. Why? Because a product name in the title makes your white paper sound like a sales piece that won't give B2B buyers the useful information they're seeking. They're not ready to evaluate your product; first they want to understand the issue. For a problem/solution flavor, name the problem with the promise of overcoming it, as in the following:

"Slaying the Profit-Sucking Monster of Paper Burden"

What if your VP of Sales insists on including a product name, in the misguided belief that anyone out there cares? If you fight this battle and lose, the best approach is to knock down the product name to a subtitle. Make sure to give the product name right at the end of the subtitle to de-emphasize it to the max:

"Slaying the Profit-Sucking Monster of Paper Burden: A Special Report on the Acme ScanOMatic 3000"

Cutting Out Jargon and Buzzwords

Many sales and marketing people love jargon, but you know better, right? Although some B2B buyers no doubt Google an occasional buzzword, many more are searching for helpful content about an actual problem they're facing. Loading up your title with say-nothing buzzwords won't help your white paper stand out from the crowd. I highly recommend that you drop the jargon and find a fresher approach, using any of the other tips in this chapter. For example, suppose you find yourself dealing with a white paper title that sounds something like this:

> "Best-of-Breed Enterprise-Class Automated Filing with Seamless Integration of Fifth-Generation Scanning"

You know you have some tinkering to do. When you cut out the buzzwords, you're left with these remains:

> "Automated Filing with Fifth-Generation Scanning"

That's actually an okay start for a title. Pump it up with some benefits, the job title you're aiming at, and an industry problem, and you can transform it into a reasonably effective title:

> "Automate Your Filing with Today's New Generation of Scanners: A Special Report for Insurance Brokers Drowning in Paper"

Using Selected Keywords

In your title, try to work in the keywords that you think your target readers are searching for. If you believe they're going to look for *unattended scanning* or *automated filing,* make sure to include those terms in your title. Doing so will propel your white paper into their search engine results, higher up in the list. On the other hand, if those terms aren't yet popular, use whatever synonyms your ideal readers are most likely to use. Choose the most popular terms that you can but always craft your title to sound as natural as possible.

Not sure what people are searching for? Check the popularity of various search terms with Google's free AdWords Keyword Tool; just Google that tool name to get the current location. You don't need to be an AdWords customer to use this tool. In just a few seconds, you can test out any keywords, get many suggestions for related keywords and synonyms, and check the popularity of all your possibilities.

Testing Titles in Advance

Whatever you think of a white paper title, the ultimate test is up to your target audience. To improve your odds, try out some proposed titles on your ideal readers in advance. Where do you find them? Does your company have a Customer Advisory Board or user group? If so, this group is an ideal forum for generating white paper ideas and testing titles. Is there an industry event coming up that lots of your customers plan to attend? That's a great time to gather some of them together over coffee or lunch. Are you in touch with any customers on a regular basis? Why not e-mail a select group of them a short-list of possible white paper names, and ask them which one would attract their attention best?

Even better, create a set of multiple covers with the same look but a different title for each. Then ask which one they'd most likely download. If one emerges as the clear favorite from this testing, use it. If not, consider going back to the drawing board and tweaking your suggestions some more.

Your title is one of the most important parts of your white paper. It's worth spending time on some variations, testing it out on sample readers, and using these tips to help make it as strong as possible. If great numbers of your ideal readers find, download, and read your white paper, your title is clearly doing its job. If not, try again. There's no law against tweaking a title and republishing the very same white paper again.

Index

Q

• *V* •